DIVINE REVELATION

SUSAN G. SHUMSKY

A FIRESIDE BOOK
PUBLISHED BY SIMON & SCHUSTER
New York London Toronto Sydney Tokyo Singapore

FIRESIDE
Rockefeller Center
1230 Avenue of the Americas
New York, NY 10020

FIRESIDE and colophon are registered trademarks
of Simon & Schuster Inc.

Designed by Kathryn Parise

Manufactured in the United States of America

10   9   8   7   6   5   4   3   2   1

LIBRARY OF CONGRESS CATALOGING-IN-PUBLICATION DATA

Shumsky, Susan G.
    Divine Revelation / Susan G. Shumsky.
          p.   cm.
    Includes bibliographical references and index.
    1. Divine Revelation (Organization) 2. Spiritual life.
    I. Title.
    BP605.D59S58   1996
    299'.93—dc20   96-3787
                                                                    CIP

ISBN 0-684-80162-0

    Divine Revelation is a service mark registered with the United States Patent Office.
    The following parties have kindly given permission to reprint excerpts:
    From *Being a Christ!*, Ann P. Meyer and Peter V. Meyer (Lemon Grove, California: Dawning Publications, 1975), by permission of Peter V. Meyer. From *The Satan Trap* by Martin Ebon, ed.; copyright 1976 by Lombard Associates, Inc.; used by permission of Doubleday, a division of Bantam Doubleday Dell Publishing Group, Inc. From Keshavadas, Sadguru Sant, *Sadguru Dattatreya* (Oakland, California: Vishwa Dharma Publications, 1988), by permission of the publisher. From Paramahansa Yogananda, *How You Can Talk with God* (Los Angeles: 1985), by permission of the publisher. From Leslie Brown, "Ramtha's New Age Shrouded in Doom." *The Morning News Tribune* (Tacoma, Washington, May 24, 1992), A1, 20, by permission of the publisher. From Ernest Holmes, *The Science of Mind* (New York: Putnam Publishing Group, 1989), by permission of the publisher.
    All of the testimonials in this book are real, but some names, occupations, or places of residence have been changed.
    Divine Revelation can familiarize you with this highly specialized, complex subject but in no way claims to fully teach the techniques described. Therefore, personal instruction and verification of experiences by a qualified teacher are recommended. *Divine Revelation* is not to be interpreted as an independent guide for self-healing. Susan Shumsky is not a medical doctor and does not diagnose diseases or prescribe treatments. Exercises or suggestions from this book should be followed only under the guidance and supervision of a medical doctor or psychiatrist. Susan Shumsky, her agents, assigns, licensees and authorized representatives, as well as Divine Revelation, Teaching of Intuitional Metaphysics, and Simon & Schuster, make no claim or obligation and take no legal responsibility for the effectiveness, results, or benefits of reading this book, of using the methods described in this book, or of contacting anyone listed in this book; deny all liability for any injuries or damages that you may incur; and are to be held harmless against any claim, liability, loss or damage caused by or arising from following any suggestions made in this book or from contacting anyone listed in this book.

I AM
That Perfect, Eternal
Divine Presence.

I AM
That Love, That Light, That Power
That Dwells within You.

I AM
The Joyful Expression
of the Divine on This Earth.

Come with Me, Take My Hand.
I AM Always with You.

I Love You. Be at Peace.

—The "Still Small Voice"
of God Within

This book is written with great love as a gift to each and every one of you who desires to know God fully and to meet God personally. It is especially dedicated to those of you who feel within your hearts that you will never be satisfied until you are blessed with direct contact with that Holy of Holies whom you seek with such longing.

CONTENTS

FOREWORD

How can we make a quantum leap?—to change our critical, judgmental observations of ourselves or others and allow ourselves just to Be?

From the usual viewpoint a person may think of himself or herself as ordinary, unimportant, or relatively insignificant compared to the extremely talented, brilliant, or famous. Numerically, compared to the billions all over the world, each person is just a minuscule fraction of the whole. It is no wonder that one of the greatest causes for emotional pain stems from a lack of self-acceptance. People may wear a bravado image and attempt to act out a personality they would like to be. Or to pose sheepishly to impress others in order to gain an advantage. As Shakespeare wrote, "All the world's a stage, and all the men and women merely players." Yes, the persona is a very convenient mask, but it is a barrier to REAL expression. You can BE just by BEING yourself, not acting the part of another!

I remember the time I was working as an engineering manager for a firm scheduled to launch some of the early space vehicles. Scheduled performance for manufacture and test was imperative to make the launch date on time. Job pressure pervaded the entire organization. Competition ran high. Fear of failure was evident by the fact that many managers had suffered with stomach ulcers. Reputation was at stake.

One day shortly after my daily "lunch hour meditation" in my parked van, I awakened to the fact that I was untrue to myself—99 percent of the time! That I was caught in the maze of posing to impress my superiors. That I was saying things I wanted them to hear so they would have a good opinion of me. From that day forward, I made a resolution to be true to myself. I prayed for the courage to be self-honest.

What a revolution this was for me. Rather than worrying about how I would adjust the facts so I could please the boss, I looked to the real facts and stated them as such. This brought me greater success.

"The mind of man is the mouth of God" (Neville). It is in the reaching for our God within, the Greater Aspect of our Being, when we stop being analytical worrywarts. We cease being critical observers. We stop our sanctimonious condemning judgments and allow ourselves just to BE!

"Here I AM!" is the beginning of self-revelation and listening to that "still small voice" within.

Dr. Susan Shumsky has a varied background for seeking many paths to enlightenment. From her pursuits in seeking God in the Far East to right here in America—finding the Greater Aspect of her Being. She demonstrates, powerfully, her magnificent touch with the infinite, thus receiving the vision to write her clearly communicated and insightful book.

This book will guide you to just simply and authentically BE yourself and to hear the "still small voice" within yourself. I know you shall enjoy, as I have, her text, *Divine Revelation*.

Peter V. Meyer, D.D., Founder/President
Teaching of Intuitional Metaphysics, Inc.

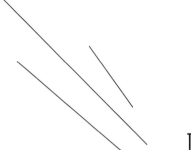

A NOTE TO THE READER

Y ou have picked up this book because you are ready to hear its message. Nothing in this universe happens by chance. In the words of Albert Einstein, "God does not play dice." Therefore you have been led by a deep inner prompting to read this message and understand its meaning.

You are about to embark on a marvelous journey of self-discovery. Be open to what you are about to receive. The wisdom contained in these pages has been inspired by a divine connection with that one presence that governs the universe. Be not afraid to hear its message and digest its meaning. You may be ready to take a new step in your life, a step that can bring new meaning and purpose, a step that can lead you to a life of greater glory than you could ever imagine. Be open to this possibility.

I am not asking you to leave your intellect and skepticism behind, for it is the questioning mind that seeks to know the truth. It is better to question than to believe gullibly without hesitation. I am here to offer you something that humanity has always longed for—a glimpse of the divine. I wrote this book to help you find your way home again, home to the source of all life, all truth, and all joy. Reading it will help you open to the divine presence, in whatever form you believe it to be. That which you have longed for is not far away. It is within your grasp.

Be prepared for a journey of ultimate questions and ultimate answers. Be ready to awaken to a new universe within you, a universe of wisdom, power, and happiness.

—*Susan Shumsky*

INTRODUCTION

As a child I often wondered about the universe and where I belonged in it. I questioned whether God existed, and if so, who God was and where God lived. I was puzzled by the experience of prayer and the emotions it evoked within myself and others. It seemed strange that people could find solace in a God whom they had never met, for whose existence there was no evidence whatsoever.

My own childhood concept of God was a wise old man with a long white beard who lived far away in the sky. After praying to God a few times and getting no response, I concluded that He did not hear my requests or that I was unworthy to receive a reply.

As long as I can remember I had a deep desire to communicate with God directly. I admired the prophets like Abraham and Elijah, who could hear God's voice. "And the Lord spake unto Moses face to face, as a man speaketh unto his friend."[1]

I often tried to ask God questions myself, expecting to hear a booming voice answer from a cloud. No voice came. Yet this idea of hearing God's voice never left me.

Seeking Spiritual Knowledge

I embarked on a spiritual quest while attending art college in California, where I began to study Eastern philosophies. After reading about *nirvana* in the Buddhist texts, I knew that I wanted to attain it. Upon reading Alan Watts's book *The Way of Zen,* I had a burning desire to find a "meditation guide."

One night a friend suggested that I try to meditate myself. So I lay on my bed and prayed for an experience of meditation. To my surprise I was propelled into an ecstatic state! I remember feeling a big cord of energy running through my body from my feet to my head. This intense rush of energy felt like I had been plugged into an electric socket! Much to my dismay I was unable to repeat the experience.

My first exposure to East Indian philosophy was Paramahansa Yogananda's book *Autobiography of a Yogi.* I felt a connection to Indian teachings and desired to follow a spiritual path. A friend invited me to visit a meditation center, and I felt an immediate affinity with the founder of the teaching. There I learned to achieve *samadhi,* a state of profound inner peace and happiness greater than anything I had ever imagined.

Soon I found myself on the banks of the Ganges River in the Himalayas with the founder of the teaching, an Indian spiritual master, learning to become a meditation teacher. This experience led to seven years' studying and traveling with this great saint in India and Europe. During this time I enjoyed a reclusive life, meditating up to twenty hours per day for weeks or months at a time. Occasionally I closed the door to my room and stayed in deep meditation, not emerging for several weeks. At other times I was in silence for months at a stretch.

I was completely absorbed in my guru's presence and perceived him as larger than life. Regarding him as the source of my power, I eventually became so reliant on him that I was blinded to the real source of spiritual power, which is *within.* I was seeking God in a personality rather than within myself.

My guru was wise, because he wanted me to discover where God dwells and where my true source of power lies. Therefore, after seven years, he sent me back to the United States, declaring that I was too dependent on him. I was, of course, completely devastated.

I continued to live in my guru's *ashrams* for another fourteen years. However, as years went by, I became disappointed with my spiritual progress. I noticed that I was not displaying what I would call "spiritual qualities" in my life. After all the years of meditation, I felt that I was still not manifesting unconditional love, humility, compassion, nonjudgment, or self-acceptance. In fact I perceived myself as thoughtless, selfish, sarcastic, pessimistic, bad-tempered, domineering, and downright bitchy.

Something was missing. I experienced a state of deep inner silence, yet my inner enlightenment lay dormant, with few crops growing on the fertile ground that I had achieved. During meditation I experienced bliss and happiness, but when I came out, my life did not change. I just wanted to go back into meditation again.

A Spiritual Awakening

A great personal transformation resulted from my learning a technique of meditation taught by Dr. Peter Meyer and Dr. Ann Meyer Makeever of San Diego, whose seminal work, *Being a Christ!*, embodied that teaching. The Meyers learned this teaching from a saint called Babaji. Babaji, also named the "Yogi-Christ"* by Paramahansa Yogananda in *Autobiography of a Yogi*, lives in the Himalayas and is believed to be immortal. Years of deep silence had prepared my consciousness for this profound teaching, which enabled me to hear the divine voice that I had sought since childhood. Yet this was not a booming, loud voice for me. It was a quiet, loving, tender, "still small voice" of comfort and serenity within my heart.

I remember my initial "breakthrough" experience facilitated by my teacher, Rich Bell. He guided me into deep meditation and then led me to a gate through which I passed into another world, the realm of Spirit. I began to see a tremendous light, first white and then a beautiful pale blue. I felt I was entering a state of awareness that I had not previously traversed. The inner feeling of happiness was indescribable. I wept with joy when I met my "I AM" self, who gave me a name and an inner "signal" and then spoke words of comfort and peace through me.

This experience of direct revelation from Spirit and the subsequent changes in my life were such a great comfort and blessing to me! I felt I had at last found something that I had been seeking for lifetimes, a solace in times of trouble, a place of peace that I could turn to for help, guidance, healing, and love. Never was I alone again.

My experiences deepened quickly. I had never had such extraordinary

---

*The word "Christ," in this context, refers to a level of higher consciousness, not to the Christian religion or to Jesus exclusively.

inner visions and wisdom pour forth from deep within. I met many divine teachers, deities, and masters, who became my inner friends and loving guardians. Although I had spent many years dwelling in the silence of consciousness within me, I was now delving into a realm of joy that added a richer tapestry to my experience. There were many spheres of spiritual awareness that I had ignored on my previous journeys to inner space. Now was the time to savor every one of them.

I was so thrilled with the changes in my own life that I was inspired to give this experience to others, so I studied with Dr. Peter Meyer and received bachelor and master of ministerial science degrees and later a doctor of divinity degree from Teaching of Intuitional Metaphysics.

I realized that in order to bring this teaching to many people, a new format and approach might be helpful. Specifically I desired to demystify the teaching, making it accessible to those of all backgrounds and religions. While many of the basic concepts, techniques, terminology, and definitions coincide with Peter Meyer's writing and teaching, the Divine Revelation® methodology was developed so anyone could learn it, and so those who might otherwise not be attracted to it could discover it for themselves.

To what do I attribute my ability to develop these methods and bring them to people from all walks of life? Thirty years of personal research into consciousness and inner exploration of higher levels of awareness have contributed to the development of this teaching, which can reduce many pitfalls in your own quest for inner truth and greatly shorten the time required for your pathway to God. I give the credit not only to my own experience but also to the personal training with my East Indian guru.

My spiritual path has been very enriching and amazing. I continue to study as the years go by, learning from spiritual teachers whom God sends to me. Although I have embraced Divine Revelation, I have not in any way closed myself off to new knowledge. I consider every day to be an adventure in spiritual awakening and every person I meet to be a guru for me. I am still developing my consciousness and my ability to love and open my heart day by day. And, hopefully, I am becoming a better person as a result.

I have been on a spiritual path my entire life and have practiced meditation regularly since 1967. But only after thirty years of deep meditation and prayer did I feel ready to write this book.

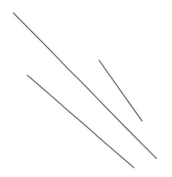

HOW TO USE THIS BOOK

This book is a guide to help you contact your higher self and learn to listen to the divine voice within, the "still small voice" of God. It is also a text about higher states of consciousness and levels of inner identity. It contains the essential information to develop your innate, natural, normal intuitive abilities that are called "super" normal.

Within its pages are keys for opening the doors of your perception and awakening awareness of your divine self. It is an open highway and complete road map for establishing and maintaining your connection to Spirit in the most effective way I have found in thirty years of spiritual seeking.

It is not a primer on parapsychological phenomena or an adventure into exotic, esoteric curiosities. Neither is it a stroll through a parlor of the occult and supernatural. It is not a journey into unfamiliar territory without a map or a guide. All that is presented here has been known, studied, tested, and proven by thousands of students.

This book presents a scientific approach to intuition, which must necessarily deliver what the word "scientific" implies. "Scientific" is defined by *Webster's* to be "systematic and accurate." Indeed this science of intuition is both.

A science, systematic and accurate, should be useful to those who are unconvinced but willing to test it themselves. The science offered here happily stands up to that definition. Even if you have little or no belief in God, in intuition, or in meditation, as long as you are willing to try the techniques suggested in this book, you can achieve the desired results.

This book is organized into seven parts. Parts I and II, "Awakening the 'Still Small Voice'" and "Getting in Touch with God," provide inspiration and motivation for getting spiritually connected with the divine presence within you. Part III, "A Road Map to Your Inner Life," helps you to uncover your true identity and to attain higher consciousness. Parts IV and V, "Opening the Pipeline to the Divine" and "Spiritual Healing and Self-Defense," offer powerful meditation, intuition, healing, and self-protection techniques that unlock the doors to divine contact. Part VI, "Becoming Spiritually Street-Smart," helps you identify the source of your intuitive messages and avoid psychic deception. Part VII, "Waking Up Your Inner Genius," describes many techniques to receive divine intuition, to express divine inspiration, and to awaken your own unique creative genius.

This book also contains a complete glossary beginning on page 247. I recommend that you consult the glossary often, as it provides definitions for any terms in this book that may be unfamiliar to you.

It is best to use this book in conjunction with the "breakthrough intensive" described in chapter 7. To become an expert in the subtle, delicate techniques of intuition offered in this book requires time, patience, and consistent practice. Your "breakthrough" is merely your first opening, which must be cultivated by love and continual care. Once that opening has been made, it is conceivable that a student could excel in intuitive awareness with the help of this book alone. But for many people personal training may be required to fully establish a clear divine contact.

In this book you will learn specific meditation, intuition, and healing techniques. You will receive guidance for developing your ability to meditate and to receive clear intuition from Spirit, even without the help of a teacher. However, it is recommended that along with this book you also take advantage of the personal instruction offered in Divine Revelation classes. You may find out about Divine Revelation classes in your area by writing to Divine Revelation, One New York Plaza #315, New York, NY 10004-1901. Or you can write or call one of the teachers or centers listed on page 271, all of whom are fully qualified to teach the techniques described in this book.

PART I
Awakening the "Still Small Voice"

CHAPTER 1

Getting Spiritually Connected

Is it possible to be directly connected with Spirit?* Can you learn how to hear the "still small voice" of God† as easily as using a telephone? Is it possible to learn to receive guidance from your inner divine voice?

The answer to these questions is a definitive yes. Contacting the divine presence and receiving divine messages is a time-honored tradition in every culture. But psychologists and psychiatrists warn us of the dangers inherent in contacting inner voices without guidance or safeguards.

How can you know "who" or "what" you are communicating with while receiving intuition? Is it safe to develop and use your supernormal powers and psychic abilities? Although intuition has become increasingly popular recently, no book currently available helps you to clearly

---

*Throughout this book the word "Spirit" refers to a life energy or force that underlies and pervades the universe. It is a concept that is multicultural and interdenominational, not confined to any particular religious philosophy or lifestyle.

†Throughout this book the word "God" refers to a personal concept of a higher power, according to your own beliefs about who or what that power might be. Therefore, in this context "God" is not confined to any particular culture, religion, or denomination.

identify the source of your intuitive messages and to test inner voices accurately.

This book was written to help you to hear the "still small voice" of God within you, the voice of inner guidance, comfort, love, healing, and wisdom, and to help you tell the difference between that divine voice and other "voices" (such as those of fear or self-doubt) that you might "hear" in your mind.

Three basic inner voices can be heard through inner sensing:

1. The mental voice (subconscious mind).
2. The psychic voice (extrasensory perception).
3. The divine voice (spiritual awareness).

This book will help you recognize and differentiate these inner voices and contact the divine voice clearly and reliably. It offers a new, systematic approach to intuitive training and will help you establish a spiritual connection with deeper levels of inner being. You will find this direct pipeline to profound wisdom provides a great source of inner strength and self-confidence, which is unavailable via any other technique.

Providing a complete road map to your inner life, this book can lead you safely through the maze of the spiritual path, pointing out signposts along the way. Its field-proven methods have been tested and verified by students from all backgrounds who have had beneficial experiences with these techniques.

For example, Janet Di Giovanna, an exporter from Mill Valley, California, states: "By using the techniques in Susan's book, I became more aware of the silent messages I had always been receiving. I now pay attention more frequently, and the accuracy of these messages has been astounding. I no longer take for granted or disregard this small voice. The techniques in this book are very simple and easy to learn."

To illustrate this further, here is one of Janet's experiences: "As I was on my way to the grocery store, I suddenly heard an inner voice which said, 'Go home. There is an important message on your answering machine.' Even though I figured I was just making this up, I went back home. Sure enough, when I arrived home, there was one message on my machine concerning my finances. Had I not received it that hour, I would have missed a very important, lucrative opportunity."

By using the tools offered in this book, you can develop your ability to receive clear, precise divine intuition safely and avoid the pitfalls of psychic delusion.

What Is Divine Revelation?

Divine Revelation, the technique of intuitional development offered in this book, is a way to develop your innate ability to hear the divine voice within. It is a method of listening, letting go, and receiving from Spirit. This universal technique is a simple, effective way to directly communicate with God, in whatever form you personally believe God to be.

Kera Gill, a homemaker from Ohio, describes her experience with this technique: "I see it as a very simple, powerful, and effective way of communicating with God, but, for me, it's not talking to God. It's listening to God. Before I learned Divine Revelation, I always talked to God. I would read prayers or say prayers, and then I would be done. That was it. Divine Revelation provides a way of listening to God. I ask a question and then I sit and wait, and I listen, and the answer comes—from that part of myself that is connected to God."

Divine Revelation techniques help you experience higher states of consciousness and inner contact with your higher self, the divine presence, and the enlightened ascended masters, also called the "inner teachers." These divine personalities are real, and you can meet them directly. They are eager to welcome you and to enrich your life, ease your burdens, and uplift your soul.

The Divine Revelation meditation and intuition technique is a practical, easy, step-by-step process of awakening true inner divine contact. Its purpose is to help you receive divine guidance in a clear, consistent, precise, reliable way. It enables you to experience direct divine communication without "doing" anything. It is not about trying or effort; in fact, it is completely effortless. Divine Revelation is not psychic-mediumship or spirit-channeling. It is direct contact with God-awareness and your higher self rather than entities from the astral world.

By uniting your conscious mind with the divine mind, you can directly contact the source of wisdom, healing, intelligence, inspiration, peace, and happiness within. This is not a daydream or out-of-body experience. It is a practical way to receive answers to everyday problems and inner healing, love, wisdom, and understanding.

Sandy Roth, a writer from Michigan, describes what Divine Revelation did for her: "I felt that I had a great deal of wisdom within, and I wanted to directly tap into that wisdom to make use of it in my life. This was the first benefit that I received, and it has continued to provide a source of knowledge and wisdom to me. Any situation or challenge that comes up in my life, I only need to go within, to my God self, and the right direction or the right decision automatically comes to me."

Practical Solutions

Throughout thirty years of teaching meditation and intuition techniques to thousands of students, I have often heard the following ten complaints, to which this book provides practical solutions:

1. **"I have little or no confidence in my intuitive abilities. Even when I have inner experiences, I tend to deny or refute them."**
This book offers a systematic method for receiving intuition consistently and reliably. It helps you recognize, categorize, and understand your spiritual experiences.

2. **"I occasionally receive intuitive messages or visions, yet I feel great uncertainty about 'who' or 'what' is the origin of these messages."**
In this book you will learn a unique system of spiritual discernment that can help you identify the source of your intuitive messages.

3. **"I have been discouraged by meditation, because I do not receive the spiritual experiences that I seek."**
Chapters 8 and 9 provide meditation instruction, including practical solutions to problems preventing clear meditation experiences. Chapters 7, 10, and 11 help you break through resistances to having recognizable, tangible spiritual experiences.

4. **"I have become disillusioned by New Age philosophies and feel confused by a maze of paranormal offerings and occult practices."**
In this book you will learn the distinction between spiritual and psychic experiences. Chapters 13 and 14 will help you test the authenticity of various methods of intuitive exploration.

5. **"I have played a dangerous game of 'psychic roulette'—a trial-and-error approach to intuitional development—following the advice of inner voices or psychic readers unquestioningly, with damaging results."**
In this book you will read anecdotes about the perils of following psy-

chic guidance without testing its accuracy. You will learn reliable safe-guards for testing inner voices and for differentiating one voice from an-other.

6. **"I feel overly sensitive to negative internal or environmental in-fluences."**

In chapter 10 you will learn specific techniques for healing negative influences and for preventing harm from future influences.

7. **"I am offended by rules and regulations, cults, and coercive or-ganizations."**

The universal techniques in this book impose no restrictions and are compatible with other forms of meditation and religious philosophies, lifestyles, and personal beliefs.

8. **"I don't want to work at difficult, strict, hard-to-follow disciplines."**

This book is easy to understand, logical, and practical, with simple-to-learn methods that require no previous experience, background, train-ing, or knowledge.

9. **"I don't want to be dependent upon psychic readers and as-trologers."**

This book helps you take control of your destiny by developing your own spiritual intuition rather than depending on others for advice or counseling.

10. **"I desire to live a spiritual life, yet I have no idea how or where to begin."**

This book can help you directly experience the divine presence within, in whatever form you personally believe it to be. Chapter 17 con-tains remarkable stories of those who follow and trust their intuition. These can inspire you to develop faith in your inner voice and follow its spiritual guidance in your everyday life.

Benefits You Can Expect

Here are just a few of the many benefits you will gain by reading this book and practicing its techniques. Included are quotations from stu-dents who have used the methods described in this book.

1. **Learning to listen to and trust your inner divine voice.**

"I am indebted to Susan Shumsky for helping me, through Divine Revelation, gain more self-confidence in listening to my divine Self and finding that I already *know* the answers deep inside. I am growing ever faster as my divine Self teaches me."—Mark Schoofs, seminar leader, Santa Cruz, California.

2. Enjoying life more and being happier through experiencing God within.

"Divine Revelation has transformed my life on all levels. I have gained a new profound connection with God within myself that has brought immense love and happiness into my relationships and more energy and creativity to my daily activity."—Susan Silverman, minister, Malibu, California.

3. Experiencing greater peace of mind and trust in the divine.

"I feel very peaceful and best of all I *know* I am going to be all right. I feel more peace inside and a knowledge of divine order in my life."—Pier Landman, homemaker, Greenwich, Connecticut.

4. Attaining spiritual discernment and overcoming illusions of your mind.

"I have been involved in psychic and channeling groups for over a decade. I've seen many people make mistakes that were deleterious to their health and happiness. Susan knew all of the precautionary steps to take."—Luke Pearson, polarity therapist, Iowa City, Iowa.

5. Healing negative beliefs, habits, and false conditioning.

"Divine Revelation has helped me train my mind so that if I have a negative thought or am completely immersed in a negative mood, I can clear that negative feeling quickly and simply, and it's very powerful."—Nancy Maurice, homemaker, Des Moines, Iowa.

6. Receiving vital energy from universal Spirit.

"I had always needed a lot of sleep, and if I didn't get a certain number of hours a night, I was tired all day. Now I find that no matter how much sleep I get, I have lots of energy. I feel much more full of vitality and energy and dynamism than ever before."—Connie Huebner, homemaker, St. Louis, Missouri.

7. Improving your personal relationships.

"A certain level of peace, joy, and ease has enabled me to be with myself and with other people and not anticipate, expect, or judge as much as I used to. I feel a greater opening of my heart, and a greater closeness with people in recognizing a oneness that we share."—Thom Fesperman, sales manager, Asheville, North Carolina.

BENEFITS OF DIVINE REVELATION
• Clearer intuition
• Supernormal abilities
• Greater happiness
• Greater freedom
• Greater peace of mind
• Spiritual discernment
• Clarity of mind
• Expansion of mind
• Better decision-making
• Greater energy
• Better relationships
• Greater creativity
• Greater direction
• Greater purpose
• Greater self-love
• Greater self-respect
• Greater responsibility
• Greater self-reliance
• Greater effectiveness
• Greater success

8. **Developing and expressing greater creativity.**

"Divine Revelation has set me free to draw on creativity as never before. I have been trying to be a creative painter for several years but only occasionally could touch on spontaneous expression. Using this system I am able to invite the creativity in as I wish."—Donna Miller, retired, Kansas City, Missouri.

9. **Taking personal responsibility and gaining greater self-acceptance.**

"For most of my thirty-seven years I had looked outside myself for happiness, love, approval, guidance, and security. Now I recognize and accept that I am fully responsible for my experiences in life, that I created them and that I have the power to change anything I don't like. This discovery of self-authority grows daily and fills me with a great sense of freedom. I am in control of my life. I don't seek outside approval as much and am much less concerned about what others think."—Barbara Hearn, teacher, Sunset Beach, California.

10. **Taking command of your destiny and increasing your effectiveness.**

"It just seems to make life a lot easier. Things I do in my career now, I once considered to be impossible. I don't really think about how I do it. I just do. I've almost doubled my income. My ability to create what I want in my life has gotten a lot better."—Jay Reynolds, contractor, Chapel Hill, North Carolina.

Invitation to Inner Discovery

This book can help you discover the richness and texture of your inner divine nature. It can help you realize your own identity and your connection with God-Spirit. You have heard that "the kingdom of God is within you."[1] You may grasp this concept intellectually, yet how many of you have the tangible experience of God within? How many actually feel the divine presence at the center of your being?

Many people believe that such an experience is impossible, but those students with no prior knowledge or training who have practiced the Divine Revelation techniques have proven that they can experience it.

For example, Dorrie Rosen, a landscape architect from New York City, describes her very first experience with using these techniques: "I feel the love and presence of the divine. I feel a sense of calmness, centeredness, and wholeness, as if I am being carried by divine parents who will take care of every need!"

The emphasis in this teaching is on personal experience and finding the answers within yourself. Therefore, you become your own guide, your own teacher, on this path to spiritual fulfillment. The tools offered within this book are simply a do-it-yourself kit for understanding and experiencing your own higher nature.

You have within yourself a hidden treasure trove to discover and explore. Once you find this fortune, you can use it to enrich every aspect of your life. You are invited to begin this journey of inner discovery—locating and tapping this treasure within. At the center of your being is the source of all wisdom, all knowledge, power, healing, light, and love. All the answers lie inside of you, deep within your own heart of hearts. Through the techniques offered in this book, you can open your heart to that inner light and discover the truth of your being.

"Seek for God within thine own soul."
—*John Smith the Platonist*

CHAPTER 2

The Sound of Stillness

Miracles can happen when you are connected with Spirit, and magic occurs when you trust your intuition. By following your heart and listening to your inner voice, the extraordinary can become ordinary. Your life takes on a new dimension—a dimension of grace—when you live in the divine presence. Your full potential is to bask continually in this grace and to express greater power than you have ever imagined.

Until you realize your full potential, life continues to be a struggle. When you come home to the divine, you live the miraculous, magical life. God's protection enfolds you. You are divinely inspired and guided in your daily life. You no longer live in doubt and fear. Your faith becomes tangible. Cares and worries disappear. Struggle becomes foreign to you. This is a life worth living, the life divine.

Up until now, only saints and prophets had the opportunity to live this life. The rest of us had to muddle along in ignorance. But now times are changing. Our planet is experiencing a vibrational transformation. Gradually people are waking up to who they really are. This process of planetary lifting will lead eventually to an earth filled with men and women of wisdom. Many seers and prophets will move among us.

The time is at hand for this transformation. With the tools contained in this book, you can ride the crest of the spiritual wave, rather than drowning in the tidewaters of psychic delusion.

You Are on an Exciting Journey

The divine voice is within you, the voice of inner guidance, love, healing, and wisdom, and you are capable of listening to it. All that is required is to quiet your mind enough to hear it. This loving voice of God wishes to speak to you, to bring you comfort and blessings. All that you need to do is open yourself up to it. With the methods offered in this book, you can make progress in this endeavor.

Steve Ziebell, a mental health care professional from Iowa City, Iowa, writes: "Divine Revelation has opened my mind to the reality of the God self within and the guidance that comes from my own Self."

This voice that I speak of can be received in many ways. For each person it is different. Some people are naturally more visual (seeing), some are more auditory (hearing), and some are more kinesthetic (feeling). In whatever way it is natural for you to receive, that is the way you will receive divine inspiration from deep within yourself.

You need not fear this inner exploration. Throughout this book are many safeguards that will assure steadiness and safety in your progress. Once you make contact with the divine within, you are beginning a grand journey. There are many adventures ahead of you and many places to explore. But you need the proper map and the tools for navigation. For this reason this book contains all the techniques and procedures needed to ensure safety on this voyage.

What has brought you to this supreme journey, this step toward God realization? You may think you have done nothing to warrant this. Perhaps you have never prayed or meditated. Maybe you don't like the word "God" or even believe that such a being exists. Yet you may have a deep sense of more possibilities to life than what you have experienced so far. Perhaps you feel a great depth of untapped wisdom within.

Your intuitive sense about a greater potential within human beings is indeed accurate. Psychologists say we are using but a small fraction of the potential of our brains. You have, hidden within yourself, an unlimited source of love, power, and energy just waiting to be uncovered. The gap between your innate unexplored abilities and your present capacities can be bridged.

Drawing upon your inner power is like operating a television. Once you know how to turn on the switch, you can experience myriad visions, sounds, and feelings that were previously unavailable to you. This book is an instruction manual for turning on the switch to unlimited possibilities.

Your Innate Intuitive Abilities

Have you ever had a flash of creative inspiration? Have you felt an inexplicable attraction to someone you just met? Have you ever received an inspiring message from within? Have you told a friend some profound wisdom and then wondered, "Where did that come from?" Have you experienced "coincidences" of thinking about people and then suddenly hearing from them? Have you sometimes regretted ignoring your hunches? These are times when you have been open to and touched by Spirit. The fact is, you are already connected with Spirit. How much you live the spiritual life depends upon how conscious you are of this connection.

At this time many of you are realizing that you are *yourself* the source of knowledge, wisdom, love, and inspiration. You may already be manifesting natural intuitive abilities. You can augment your intuitive gifts and become self-sufficient in receiving inner guidance, rather than depending on others for counseling.

For example, Claudia Rainford, a student at Pepperdine University in Malibu, California, states: "I would say that this experience of the higher self has always been there, at least as long as I can remember, but as a result of learning Divine Revelation, it is much clearer, and I have much more confidence in the truth and validity of my own intuition and inner guidance and experience of my own higher self."

Intuitive powers and divine inspiration have been expressed by extraordinary people throughout history. Great artists, composers, playwrights, scientists, as well as spiritual leaders and prophets, have been in contact with their inner genius. For instance, Beethoven, Schubert, and other great composers did not compose the music themselves, but *heard* the music within and then transcribed it. Mozart reported that he heard compositions with his inner ear when he was alone and happy, such as walking after a good meal, traveling in a carriage, or in the middle of the night. He heard the music as finished compositions and then simply wrote them down.[1]

This inner genius, or ability to be a channel for God, used to be reserved for a select few geniuses, saints, and prophets. But now the vibratory level of the earth has been lifted to such a degree that *anyone* can awaken his or her inner genius. You have heard that you are using a limited portion of your brain, but you may not have been taught how to use the vast portion that has remained dormant. How can you learn to awaken your intuition and open the door to the spiritual realm?

Listen to Your Heart

The first step to piercing the veil covering the divine is to listen to your heart. The heart is the seat of your soul, the place where God can be heard when your mind is still. The incessant chatter of your surface mind battles clear communication with your divine self. You may have heard the expression "You think too much." A mind that thinks too much, that ruminates ad infinitum, is too noisy to hear God's voice.

The "still small voice" is a delicate sound that can be heard by a placid mind in quietude. This does not mean that you must stop thinking in order to hear the voice of God. For it is the nature of the mind to think continually. What it does mean is that the ego has to let go of its stranglehold on the mind so you can hear your heart speak.

In order to listen to your heart, you must learn to "let go and let God." Let go so the noise of the surface mind can settle down to a peaceful state. Letting go or surrendering to God is not the big dramatic deal that you might think it is. It just means relaxing and getting comfortable. Meditation is a way to quiet your mind so you can hear your heart speak.

Glory Fiorente, a therapist from Boston who has learned Divine Revelation, says: "All I need to do is just take a moment and sit down and be quiet, go within myself, and just let go and let God. It's a very personal, intimate kind of experience, but I found that it was exactly what I had been looking for to enrich this need for a personal communion with God."

You may find it necessary to attain a meditative state in order to receive divine messages, at least in the beginning stages of your practice.

There are many ways to enter a meditative state. One recommended method will be covered in chapter 8.

Once you are deep in meditation, the most important thing is to *trust* what you are receiving from your divine voice. How many of you block your abilities by self-doubt or fear! You think, "It can't be this easy" or "I can't do it right." It *is* easy to hear your "still small voice."

For instance, Rae Aranander, a fashion designer from New York, describes: "When I first began to listen to the inner voice, my biggest conflict came from a fear of making a mistake. Even though I heard the words in my heart, I doubted whether they were the 'right' words. I thought I was just hearing my own mind and tended to deny the experience. I wasn't sure whether I was receiving true messages from Spirit or thoughts from my surface mind. Sometimes, when I spoke the inner messages out loud during group meditations, I spoke haltingly and hesitantly, with little confidence. However, with practice I began to trust my inner voice."

From nearly thirty years of teaching, I have found that such experiences of self-doubt are common in the beginning stages of practice.

"Be Still and Know That I AM God"

"Be still and know that I AM God."[2]

How many people have heard these words? Most, however, do not comprehend their true meaning. They live in a materialistic world, a world that never thinks of being still, let alone knowing God. But you are desirous of a deeper reality—a reality of inner knowingness, of knowing the truth within yourself.

Many of you are limited by defensive walls that shield you from influences of people around you. These walls have served you well. But if you want to live a truly spiritual life, these defenses must go. They must be healed. How, then, can you prevent yourself from being unduly influenced by others? You can learn how to protect and heal yourself by using the affirmations and prayers in chapter 10 of this book.

Tom Coté, a radio station owner from Nevada City, California, says: "With the help of this knowledge I came to the realization that there's really no obstacle other than those I may place there myself, even if I do it unconsciously. But then comes the realization that if I put it there, then I can also remove it, and I'm the only one who can. Whereas before

I was thinking, 'Oh, well, it's out of my power. I can't do anything about it. I guess I just have to feel like this.' Now I have come to the realization that I have the power to heal or dissolve any seeming block that is in the way of my fulfillment."

It is time to realize that you are an all-powerful being. You are not restricted by anything. You have an unlimited capacity to heal yourself and to live in the glory of your inner beingness. You can "be still and know that I AM God" in the midst of the turmoil of this world. How? By practicing meditation and by asking for help.

It is difficult to "be still and know that I AM God" if you have not achieved inner peace. The first step is to "be still." By quieting your mind and allowing your body to settle down in a natural way, you can "be still."

"Commune with your own heart upon your bed, and be still."[3]

Being still doesn't mean being asleep or being in a "trance" (out of the body and absent). It means being fully in the body, completely awake and alert. Being still means being quiet enough to hear the voice of God within you—and eventually to "know that I AM God." For you are not separate from your "still small voice." Your mind is united with the divine mind on that supreme level of awareness. "Be still and know that I AM God" and that "in him we live, and move, and have our being."[4]

Andrea Hsu, a restaurateur from Jersey City, New Jersey, writes: "Divine Revelation has been one of the most helpful tools I've ever used on a spiritual path to God. It has dramatically changed my life and brought me closer to God and to myself. The meditation is very inspiring, uplifting and fun."

"Seek and Ye Shall Find"

You are never alone. You have an inner teacher, the divine presence within, to guide and comfort you in times of trouble. But you must remember to ask.

"Ask, and it shall be given you; seek, and ye shall find; knock, and it shall be opened unto you."[5]

When you are in need, call upon your inner divine presence. Ask, ask, ask. It is only by asking that you receive. For God, as near and dear to you as your own self, is always listening.

Wake up to the sound of stillness. Within your heart is a solution to every problem. Your answer will come to you, but you must be quiet enough to hear it.

The message is received in many different ways. You may:

- See or envision the message (clairvoyance).
- Listen to or hear the message (clairaudience).
- Feel, sense, taste, or smell the message (clairsentience).
- Meet the message in the form of a person, a sign, or an omen.

The sound of stillness is very loud once you begin to listen. Your divine messenger desires to contact you but will not communicate unless you request it.

"Behold, I stand at the door and knock; if any man hear my voice, and open the door, I will come in to him, and will sup with him and he with me."[6]

You cannot hear the message unless you open the door, but beware: identify the messenger before you open. Many anxious voices of untruth are knocking continually, desiring for you to listen. Only one voice speaks with authority and truth—the divine voice within.

There are four basic categories of voices that you might hear inside:

1. The divine voice, the "still small voice" of God (the true voice of God-Spirit).
2. The voice of your own subconscious mind (the voice of memories, beliefs, habits, and conditions).
3. The voice of environmental influences (the voice of influences from other people).
4. The voice of an astral entity or spirit.

The Silent Sound of God

Perfect stillness is the sound of God, dwelling within your heart as love. Listen to the sound of this stillness, the true voice of Spirit. Within your heart dwells divine consciousness, your supreme Self. That is who you really are. That is the voice to listen to. All other voices are saboteurs.

You have within yourself all that you need. You do not need a guru or psychic adviser. You are the source of your own wisdom. How many of you continue to frequent these advisers? The supreme Seer is within *you!* You are the *rishi*. No one can tell you anything you don't already know. Be the power and the authority, take command over your life.

Patrick O'Hara, an electrician from northern California, experienced this using the methods in this book: "I've felt more of a sense of my own power and self-authority and I'm reminded that I'm the one in control of my life—no one else. For me that's particularly important, because in the past I had an idea that someone or something else out there should tell me what is appropriate or best for me. Now I'm taking more responsibility for my own life, for my own decisions, knowing that what I feel is appropriate for me *is* appropriate for me, and no one else can tell me something that would be wiser than that."

You are not a limited being, a slave to circumstances, upbringing, beliefs, habits, and conditions. You have a divine gift given to you by God, the gift of freedom of choice, which you can use to express yourself in joyful and fulfilling ways, ways that you may never have believed possible. With this gift you can realize your dreams and your true soul desires, the purpose that you were born to fulfill. That purpose is hidden deep within your heart and can be awakened, activated, and expressed.

Be Led by Spirit

Inspiration and revelation from your divine voice can become as commonplace as receiving a message on your answering machine. You can be guided by Spirit in your everyday life. You needn't think that only special or gifted people can do this. I am not a special or gifted person. I practiced and learned to do it. So can you.

You are seeking this knowledge for a reason. You have a purpose and a divine plan for your life beyond your mortal self. God knows this plan and can reveal it to you. Just ask. "Ask, and it shall be given you."

After her very first experience with Divine Revelation, Prentiss Taylor, a businessperson from New York City, wrote: "I'm feeling different— more of a sense that Spirit is unfolding a plan for my life."

Listen to the sound of stillness. It can guide and heal you. You can be led by this divine voice to greatness. Only it requires faith to follow the voice. It requires less faith to hear this voice than to actually follow its guidance, which may be difficult or challenging. But I have discovered that following this voice is the most fulfilling, extraordinary adventure I have ever undertaken. You can discover this, too. Listen to the sounds of stillness, which are the whispers of eternity, the murmurings of God.

> *"Consult thy heart, and thou wilt hear the secret ordinance of God proclaimed by the heart's inward knowledge, which is real faith and divinity."*
>
> —Muhammad (Islam)

PART II
Getting in Touch with God

CHAPTER 3

God Is Within You

As a child I desired to hear the "still small voice" of God, yet my attempts to hear that voice met with failure. My childhood dilemma is not unique. In the heart of humanity burns a longing to know and to realize God. The beloved voice of God is sought in every part of the globe. Poets write about it. Scientists ponder it. Religions dwell on it. Philosophers reflect on it.

But so much seeking has been in vain. Many seekers with a spark of faith in their youth gave up their quest, succumbing finally to cynicism and despondency. They concluded that God either does not exist or cannot be reached.

Others with greater determination continued their search. Many renounced everything—family, home, wealth, and prestige—with the faint glimmer of hope that one day God would be revealed to them. Without evidence that their longing would ever be fulfilled, they moved onward blindly with one goal in mind—to realize God.

There is evidence, in great scriptures and literature, of prophets, saints, and sages who actually reached their goal. Who were these fortunate God-realized souls? Were they angels or emissaries of God, visiting earth temporarily? Or were they humans who somehow managed to get their foot in the door of the Most High? Is God reserved for a select clique of saints and prophets? Is God the property of religious institutions? Or can ordinary people like you or me meet God?

Many would answer with a resounding no, declaring that God cannot be known directly. They believe the higher power to be far away and unattainable. Millions pray to God and attend religious services, yet think that God never hears their prayers. They assume that they will never see God until they are dead. Perhaps not even then.

Yet the experience of thousands of students of Divine Revelation has demonstrated that any person can learn to hear the "still small voice" of God without setting foot in any church, practicing any religion, reading any scripture, relinquishing any possession, or having any special innate gift.

One of these Divine Revelation students, Mary Glenn, a nurse from Chicago, states: "I feel it's a beautiful opportunity to develop a personal relationship with God and know that I am one with God, to experience that the temple resides within my own heart. That's where God is. I don't have to look outside myself to a church to find God. I don't have to look to a priest to be a channel for the divine power to come through. I can have that direct experience myself."

God in an Age of Science

Why do so many believe that God cannot be found? Was it always this way? One reason humanity has lost faith in God-realization is due to its habitual focus on external "things." People look outwardly to fulfill their desires and in turn believe God to be located outside themselves. God has become a commodity, another "thing" in the external world. God is conceived as an anthropomorphic entity living at a great distance from us. People pray to a faraway God, in the sky, not to a God within. How could such a remote God be located or hear our prayers?

Religion is stagnant due to the belief in most creeds that its founding revelations were complete, eternal truths available only to the exalted prophets who first cognized them. The assumption is that from then on, God can be known only through study of these ancient revelatory scriptures. Religious leaders proclaim that there is nothing more to learn and no contemporary prophets. God is an abstract concept owned by seers of the distant past rather than a living, breathing reality of today.

Few overcome the erroneous opinion that God is located only in the scriptures. Of those who believe that revelatory truth is present, progressive, and continually unfolding, most presume that they are not worthy to receive the word of God *themselves*. They place an intermediary between themselves and God in the form of a religious leader, guru, faith healer, channeler, psychic, or another person deemed saintly.

Another reason for God's elusiveness is that it is customary in this scientific age to seek truth in the outer world through experimentation rather than within. Yet God cannot be found externally or scientifically. Even though God pervades every particle of the universe, your own connection to God can be reached only through a deep inner awakening. God is here within you.

The teaching of Divine Revelation presented in this book is a revival of an ancient forgotten ability alluded to in the sacred literature of all religions—the capacity to hear the "still small voice" of God within. This ability, common during past "Golden Ages" of enlightenment, has been rediscovered and is available to you now. This profound, valuable teaching can help you fulfill that universal archetypal longing that lies deep within our collective human unconscious—the desire to know and to realize God.

Helena Roberts, a graduate of Divine Revelation from Toronto, Canada, says: "It's a way of being open to letting God fill me up with love and light, and to get very clear and specific guidance from God, just like Elijah and all these people in the Old Testament and the New Testament who would actually communicate with God and get messages and answers, and it's available. It's so easy. I guess I've been experiencing this type of phenomena for years, but it was very sporadic and not very specific. I just learned to listen to these messages from inside."

Who Is God?

God means many different things to different people. If you were to ask a Chinese person what God is, you would get a different answer than if you were to ask an Arab. Many people don't even believe that God exists, so defining God is tricky at best. The following definition is therefore an agreeable starting point:

God, in a universal sense, is an energy or force that gives life to the cosmos. Eminent physicists have theorized that an underlying field of energy pervades and unifies all known energy fields (such as the gravitational and electromagnetic fields). These scientists may not call that energy "God," but they may believe in a wholeness definable as "energy" or the "unified field."

According to major religious scriptures of the world, God seems to have two aspects: the personal and the impersonal. The *impersonal* concept of God is described in all major religions as Absolute, Omnipotent, Omnipresent, Omniscient, Invisible, Energy, Life Force, Being, Infinite, Unbounded, Unlimited, Universal, Oneness, Wholeness, All-Pervading, Indivisible, Formless, Nameless, Endless, Transcendental.

The nature of the impersonal God, as defined by scriptures of East and West, is everywhere present, within everything and everyone. If God is everywhere and within everything, and if you are a part of everything, then aren't you also a part of God? How can God be omnipotent and omnipresent and not be within you?

The *personal* concept of God differs from place to place and person to person. This aspect of God is known by many different names to different people in different cultures. As the prophet Muhammad said in the *Hadith:* "There are as many ways to God as souls; as many as the breaths of Adam's sons."

Here are just a few of the many names, according to scriptures of various major religions, of the personal aspects or attributes of God: Lord, God, Yaweh, Jehovah, Christ, Jesus, Great Spirit, Sri Krishna, Vishnu, Brahma, Shiva, Allah, Buddha, Divine Mind, Atman. You will worship whatever idea of God is suitable to your temperament, personal experience, and religious beliefs.

You may also enjoy a concept of God that has a less "religious" connotation but that still could be defined as personal, such as: Consciousness, Awareness, Higher Power, First Cause, Higher Self, Higher Mind. Even without a belief in the concept of a personal God, you might accept the possibility that an underlying Intelligence organizes this complex universe.

Because the personal aspect of God is personal by definition, it has qualities of a somewhat anthropomorphic nature. This is because human nature seems to have the need to personalize and to name attributes of God. We deify and develop a devotional relationship with an anthropomorphic God, since it is difficult to feel devotion to an abstract, attributeless, impersonal, transcendental being.

Colin Maxwell, an astrologer from Louisville, Kentucky, says: "What was missing in my spiritual experience was a personal, meaningful relationship with Being. Being is the absolute, without attributes. How do you have a personal relationship with something that has no attributes or qualities? Well, you personalize it, and it becomes God. And that's what Divine Revelation did. It made the absolute personable and meaningful to me, so that I could relate to it and have a personal relationship with Being."

God as Consciousness

Let us now consider where God is located and what God's relationship is to human beings. According to the definition of the impersonal aspect of God, God is found everywhere and within everything. So the impersonal God is within you. Can we also say that the personal God is found everywhere? Is the personal God within you? If God's impersonal, universal aspect is everywhere, then why can't the personal attributes of God be found everywhere as well? The ancient Egyptian scriptures say: "For the Lord manifests himself ungrudgingly throughout all the universe; and you can behold God's image with your eyes, and lay hold on it with your hands."[1]

The Vedas, the most ancient scriptures of India, state that the imperishable consciousness, the spark of life at the basis of every living thing, is the source of all life, all substance, all matter, all intelligence, and all the aspects of divinity itself.* According to the Vedas, consciousness is the ultimate definition of the impersonal God. And the impersonal God gives rise to the personal God, and both are everywhere present.

Even modern physicists have come to the conclusion that consciousness is the ultimate reality. The Uncertainty Principle, formulated by Werner Heisenberg in 1926, changed profoundly the way scientists view the world. Quantum physics has proven that there is no matter without consciousness. The subatomic world is dependent on the conscious awareness of the experimenter. The world is as we believe it to be.

---

*"Richo akshare parame viyoman yasmin deva adi vishve nishedoo." This Sanskrit phrase means, "The hymns of the Vedas, which are the imperishable primordial vibrations that structure the entire universe, are created out of consciousness, wherein all the Gods reside."

Sir Arthur S. Eddington, renowned British astronomer and astrophysicist, said: "Modern physics has eliminated the notion of substance. . . . Mind is the first and most direct thing in our experience . . . I regard Consciousness as fundamental. I regard Matter as derivative from Consciousness."[2]

If matter and consciousness are linked in such an intimate way, it is important to look at how our own conscious awareness affects our material life.

Perhaps you believe that consciousness has power and therefore your thoughts have the power to affect your life in some way. But do you have any idea to what extent your thoughts affect your life?

Every thought has energy, and the energy contained within that thought is composed of vibrations that affect the entire universe! You have power beyond what you could ever imagine. In fact, you have cooperated with God to create your mind, body, and environment. You have contributed to your life by your thoughts, speech, and action. You are fully responsible for what you have created, and this creation is your own.

If you were to drop a pebble into a bowl of water, you would notice ever-widening concentric circular waves radiating out from where the pebble entered the water. When the waves reach the outer limit of the bowl, they immediately start back to the center. This is exactly how your every thought, word, and action act upon the universe. Everything that you think, speak, or do sets up vibrational waves that radiate to the farthest extent of the universe and then immediately return to you, just as they have been sent. Every seed idea that you plant into the universe eventually sprouts into physical form. If you plant beautiful, loving seeds of perfection, then you will reap perfection. If you plant seeds of imperfection, then you will materialize imperfection. Exactly that which you ask for by thought or desire, you receive.

Lord Buddha has said, as recorded in the ancient scriptures: "All that we are is the result of what we have thought. . . . If a man speaks or acts with an evil thought, pain follows him, as the wheel follows the foot of the ox that draws the carriage. . . . If a man speaks or acts with a pure thought, happiness follows him, like a shadow that never leaves him."[3]

Think for a moment about some plans in your life that you know will be successful and other plans that you feel might fail. Your failures and your successes are determined by your attitude. By transforming your thoughts, beliefs, habits, and patterns, you can transform your life into whatever blueprint you desire. I am not saying that this can happen instantaneously or that there is no effort involved, but with concentrated effort and discipline (yes, discipline!), you can make conscious, demonstrable changes in your mind, your body, and your environment.

José Gomez, a salesman and Divine Revelation student from Santa Fe, New Mexico, says: "I am in control of my life. Taking responsibility for every feeling, every thought, everything that's happening in my life is a great feeling. It's nice just knowing that I can create my world just by choosing what I want."

Direct Experience

The definition of God as consciousness seems logical to you, right? Or does it? Have you gone beyond the old concepts of God and accepted this new idea of God within everyone and everything? Or are you still operating under the assumption that God is "out there somewhere" beyond your grasp?

God "out there somewhere" can only be replaced by God "within" by having the *direct experience* of and *direct communication* with God within. Let's face it, many of us were brainwashed to believe that God is a big man in the sky who punishes us when we are bad and rewards us when we are good. Temples, churches, synagogues, society, and parents begin teaching this idea from birth. Such an idea cannot necessarily be easily eradicated by just hearing about a God within or by reading a few books about it. It may take a lot more than that to eliminate centuries of brainwashing by the powers of society.

"Knowledge is of two kinds, that which is heard, and that which is felt directly in the heart; The heard yields not full fruit until it comes home to the soul by some experience."[4]

I spent twenty years practicing deep meditation before I could even begin to grasp the concept of a personal God within. Even though I enjoyed daily experiences of direct unity with the divine consciousness within, the concept of a God outside of myself was so deeply ingrained that I still considered God to be a faraway object, elusive, impossible to attain. It was not until I learned to communicate directly with the inner divine voice that I began to realize that God dwells within my heart.

Still, I have struggled with God's being an intimate part of my being. And I can testify that many of my students have gone through the same struggle.

Your concepts of God, of life, and of yourself are about to be transformed by the direct experiences of Divine Revelation that you are about to undergo.

For example, Janet Rubenstein, a holistic health practitioner from Marin County, California, states: "I had been practicing meditation for twenty years and had been a spiritual healer for ten years. I had also been teaching seminars in the human potential field. Then I had a 'breakthrough session' using the techniques in Susan's book. This was the very first time, in all these years of experience and all those practices, that I felt and saw this divine Spirit that was inside me and at my service. I realized I could use this any time I chose. This was a great relief to directly experience that, in fact, God was inside me and not just out there."

An Argument for a God Within

Let us study the concept of a God within by reading scriptures of various religions, speaking about God as consciousness, the supreme Self, or, at least, God near at hand.

CHRISTIAN:

"Know ye not that ye are the temple of God, and that the Spirit of God dwelleth in you?"[5]

"The kingdom of God cometh not with observation: Neither shall they say, Lo here! or, lo there! for, behold, the kingdom of God is within you."[6]

"[The Lord] be not far from every one of us: For in him we live, and move, and have our being."[7]

JUDEO-CHRISTIAN:

"Whither shall I go from thy spirit? or whither shall I flee from thy presence? If I ascend up into heaven, thou art there: if I make my bed in hell, behold, thou art there. If I take the wings of the morning, and dwell in the uttermost parts of the sea; Even there shall thy hand lead me, and thy right hand shall hold me."[8]

ISLAM:
"I am in your own souls! Why see ye not? In every breath of yours am I."[9]
La ilaha illa Ana" ("There is no God other than I my Self").[10]

SUFI:
"He who is absent far away from God—His heart can only say: 'God is,' somewhere; He who has found the Loved One in himself—for him God is not He, nor Thou, but I."[11]

BUDDHIST:
"This very mind is the Buddha."[12]
"Every being has the Buddha Nature. This is the self."[13]

ZEN BUDDHIST:
"Why not seek in one's own mind the sudden realization of the original nature of True Thusness? . . . If we understand our minds and see our nature, we shall achieve Buddhahood ourselves."[14]

SHINTO:
"The human mind, partaking of divinity, is an abode of the Deity, which is the spiritual essence. There exists no highest Deity outside the human mind."[15]

TAOIST:
"Find the Tao in yourself and you know everything else."[16]

SIKH:
"Why do you go to the forest in search of God? He lives in all and is yet ever distinct; He abides with you, too. As fragrance dwells in a flower, and reflection in a mirror, so does God dwell inside everything; seek Him, therefore, in your heart."[17]

JAIN:
"May He abide always within my heart, the Supreme Self, the One God of all gods; Transcending all this world's ephemera, by deepest meditation reachable!"[18]

HɪɴDU:

"I, O Gudakesha, am the Self, seated in the heart of all beings; I am the beginning, the middle, and the end of all beings."[19]

"I am the True, the Real, Brahma. That thou art also. The heart of man is the abode of God."[20]

The Mighty "I AM" Presence

The "I AM" self, otherwise known as the mighty "I AM" presence, is the indwelling God at the core of your being. It is your divine self, the aspect of yourself that is one with God. For "God created man in his own image."[21] The perfect image of God is the "I AM" self, your individual divine consciousness. It is God's perfect image of you—your perfect self, the oneness of Spirit within you.

Your "I AM" self is your own truth. You are that light, that power of God. You are basically pure, divine, ecstatic, and radiant. Behind all the coverings and identifications of the ego, you are that divine self, the mighty "I AM."

"I AM" means "I exist and I know myself to be." It is the most simple, profound statement, with unlimited power. It is the OM, the creative word of God. The use of the words "I AM" releases unlimited cosmic energy *(purusha)* into universal substance *(prakriti)* and, as a result, forms come into existence.

When you use the words "I AM," you set into motion the power of God to fulfill what you speak. That is because "I AM" is God in action. The words "I AM" define, identify, and limit you by whatever you place after those words. For "I AM," by definition, is who you are.

Every thought you think and every word you speak has tremendous creative force. Your thoughts and speech, which are under your control, determine your actions and therefore your destiny. Because of the inherent power in thought and speech, it is essential to pay meticulous attention to what you are thinking and saying. Thinking and speaking pessimistic ideas can manifest failure, while optimistic ideas can manifest success.

Some of us habitually follow the words "I AM" with negative, pessimistic definitions. Common thoughts and speech are those such as: "I AM sick, I AM unhappy, I AM a failure, I AM broke, I AM dying, I AM unworthy." Such creative statements bring about their inevitable result. Thoughts or decrees with the power of the "I AM" vibrate in your mind, then your body, then travel into the atmosphere by your life energy, reverberating and eventually returning to you.

By using the creative words "I AM," you activate your life energy and then give birth to whatever follows these words. These words continue to work until their result manifests on the material plane, especially if you have a force of conviction behind the words. For example, if you say "I AM sick," and if you really believe that you are, you will become sick, for "as thou hast believed, so be it done unto thee."[22]

Jesus was a great exponent of the creative use of the "I AM." He was a living example of the law of the "I AM" and an inspiration to others. The miracles he performed were the practical use of God's law of the "I AM" in action. This supreme law is stated as follows: "With God all things are possible."[23] This great law of life was present in every statement he made, for he continually spoke the word revealed to him by God from the level of his "I AM" self.

Realizing the "I AM"

"I AM That, Thou art That. All this is That. That alone is." So say the ancient Upanishads of India. This statement is the ultimate reality according to Vedanta, an ancient but very advanced philosophy. Brahman Consciousness, the highest level of awareness, is attained when a seeker has peeled away all illusion and realized this supreme truth. Its meaning is simple:

"I AM THAT."
The "I AM" self, my individual expression of God, called the Atman, is "That" Brahman, the oneness of life, the impersonal universal aspect of God.

"THOU ART THAT."
Your Atman, your "I AM" self, is also "That" Brahman. God is not only within me, but also within you. I see the preciousness of life in you. What I am, you are also.

"ALL THIS IS THAT."

There is nowhere that God is not. "That" Brahman is everywhere present and within everything. Therefore, everything is as precious to me as my own self.

"THAT ALONE IS."

God is all that is. There is nothing that is not "That" Brahman.

This realization of God within is the ultimate supreme knowledge to be attained by a human being. Yet even without this ultimate state of enlightenment, it is possible for any person to experience these ancient truths by direct cognition. Through the Divine Revelation technology you can have glimpses of and communicate directly with the divine presence, in whatever form you believe that presence to be.

> *"God is the real Self in me, I AM That; He is the Self of all beings, I AM That. All-pervading like the sky, I AM That. Spotless pure consciousness, I AM That."*[24]
> —The Avadhuta Gita 1:6 (Hindu)

CHAPTER 4

Your Inner Teacher

The mighty "I AM" presence is your inner teacher, your true guru. The meaning of the Sanskrit word "guru" is one who destroys darkness and illusion and brings light and truth. The syllable "gu" means darkness and the syllable "ru" means light. The guru is one by whose light true knowledge arises. The true light-giver is the "I AM" Self.

A scripture from India called the Guru Gita states that "the Guru is none other than the true Self."[1] Your real anchor is your God self. Turn to the inner presence of God, your true guru.

Many people think it is necessary to have a human guru in order to make spiritual progress. But it is rare to find an enlightened saint worthy of being such a guru. Even if you find one, human foibles may preclude the God nature within him or her. Every living saint, although God-realized, is still limited by a human body.

After finding a proper guru, you may eventually be dismissed once you are strong enough to stand on your own feet. A guru's purpose is to raise your level of awareness to self-reliance. Eventually you will make your own connection to God directly and leave your guru behind. The guru is a guide to bring you to God, not God himself.*

Jesus, one of the greatest gurus in history, stated: "It is expedient for you that I go away: for if I go not away, the Comforter† will not come unto you; but if I depart, I will send him unto you."[2]

Jesus' intention was for his disciples to become fully self-sufficient, connected to the Holy Spirit within, capable of receiving divine wisdom without his physical presence.

"[Human beings] have spontaneous wisdom and wisdom without teacher."[3]

You may think I am arguing against having a human guru, but, believe me, I know the value of having one. I lived in the presence of a saint for many years and have enjoyed the holy presence of other great masters. But few gurus are capable of bringing a person to enlightenment, and few people have the time, ability, desire, and opportunity to live with a true master.

But do not lose hope. With this book you will enter an extraordinary world where you can meet your "inner guru," the supreme self at the core of your being. This enlightened master within you has all knowledge, all wisdom, all understanding, and can heal you and bring you divine guidance. This inner divine teacher can lead you to your ultimate goal, inner communion with God.

Your inner teacher is free from impatience, intolerance, anger, criticism, judgment, domination, coercion, egotism, limitation, greed, and lust. Your inner teacher can bring comfort, unconditional love, and inner happiness twenty-four hours a day. No human guru can ever give as much love and attention as your inner teacher. No human guru is free from all limitations of embodiment. Your inner guru is ultimately your true guru.

Divine Revelation brings you direct contact and clear communication with your inner guru. As if you have an in-house counselor, you are never alone or at a loss with your inner guru to guide you.

Sarah Levine, a retired woman from Miami, Florida, describes her in-

*Although you could argue that everyone has God within, because the higher Self is the supreme Brahman, the ultimate reality, the wholeness of the absolute and relative existence together.
†The inner guru, the Holy Spirit.

ner guru: "In this meditation we get in touch with our higher self, as if there were another personality there, and I really feel I have some friends that are with me. When I meditate I'm in touch with them, and I get advice and encouragement."

Who Is Your Inner Teacher?

You may think of your inner teacher, the guru within, as a guardian angel, ascended master, saint, inner comforter, wise one, personal God, divine Spirit, higher self, or inner guide. Whatever you personally believe your inner teacher to be, so it shall be.

The personal God, discussed in chapter 3, is one of the two aspects of God you can contact through Divine Revelation (the other is the impersonal God). The personal God can be defined as your inner teacher. That inner one could also be thought of as an emissary, a messenger, an angel of God—or a master, saint, or teacher guiding you to God. Or you might envision your inner teacher as an aspect of your higher self.

George Fitzgerald, a New York ad agency vice president, sees his higher self this way: "In Divine Revelation meditation, I experienced my own soul. I saw and sensed my higher self as a magnificent blue being with a visage both powerful and benign, with stars in his brow, imparting wisdom and unconditional love. I know that my higher self is in me and with me always, bestowing support, guidance, and protection. It is an experience that is liberating, exhilarating, and comforting on the most profound level."

The teaching of Divine Revelation is universal, for it helps you contact your inner teacher in whatever form you personally believe that teacher to be. All possibilities are open to you. Your only limitation is your own faith or lack of faith. You can directly communicate with your beloved personal God, your higher self, inner teacher, sage, or prophet of God. It is within your grasp.

Jean Gambee, a great-grandmother and Divine Revelation graduate from Kihei, Hawaii, describes it this way: "I don't think you can go much higher when you can find your guidance from God within or Christ within or whatever you want to call it. I used to think that God was sort of out there somewhere, but I am finding out He is just within everyone, and that's quite something to become aware of, I think."

The personal aspects of God are those inner teachers with whom you can communicate directly, from whom you can receive inner messages, revelation, guidance, healing, love, upliftment, and inner happiness. The "still small voice" of God is heard through your inner teachers.

Susan Christine Reid, a child care professional from Makawao, Hawaii, states: "It wasn't until I learned Divine Revelation that I developed a personal relationship with God, with the personal aspect of God, where I could speak to God and have Him speak back, and ask questions and have them answered—all kinds of questions of a deep spiritual nature— and to really feel that I'm one with God, to feel His unbounded love, to feel vibrational lifting, and to feel healed."

During the Divine Revelation "breakthrough intensive," you will meet at least one of your inner teachers by name and receive a particular experience, called a "vibrational signal," that helps you to identify that teacher in the future. You may think of that teacher as part of your higher self or outside of yourself. In either case you will learn to communicate with your inner teacher whenever you desire, day or night, to receive inner guidance, healing, or whatever you wish to receive.

Your inner teachers are aspects of God within, the most sublime attributes of yourself. When you begin to identify with your true divine nature, then you recognize yourself to be one with God. Frequent contact with your inner teachers helps you establish God consciousness, the supreme goal of human life.

Linda VanDervort, an attorney from Auburn, California, tells of her experiences: "I have really gained an intimate contact with God, with Jesus Christ, and with the Christ aspect of myself, the divine beingness of myself. I have really come to know what it is to be one with God and to have that aspect manifest in my everyday life."

The Myth of "Enlightenment"

Nearly twenty years of my life were spent seeking an entity called "enlightenment." I believed that if I would meditate long and hard enough and be celibate, obey my guru, and be good, my guru would eventually consider me worthy to be enlightened.

Undoubtedly you have heard or read about "enlightenment." Many people believe a romantic notion that they will be struck with a profound insight that causes them to instantaneously jump off the "wheel of birth and death" or "*karmic* wheel."* This sudden realization is attained by their guru striking them on the head or another such fantasy. Then their life is miraculously transformed and their problems are over.

Although many people have an unrealistic view of enlightenment, the concept of *nirvana*† or *nirvakalpa samadhi*‡ is well documented in Eastern texts. This ultimate state of illumination is not imaginary, but the concept of biding your time in expectation of a sudden mystical realization is as preposterous as "waiting for Godot."

"Enlightenment," according to traditional Eastern thought, is the state of *jivan mukti*, liberation of the soul. The result of this liberation is that you are free to live with your personal God or to merge with the impersonal Godhead, the absolute Brahman. In this theory it is believed that you are bound by past actions or *karma* to take a body again and again. Once you have attained a desireless state with no further impulses to action or *sanskaras*, then you are no longer compelled to reincarnate. After death your soul merges with God and never returns.

Many misinterpret this as a philosophy of absolute determinism, in which past *karmas* keep you revolving on an unending cycle life after life. Those who subscribe to this belief think it is rare indeed for anyone to attain liberation from this cycle, and such a person is elevated to the pedestal of worship.

What the believers in this philosophy have forgotten is three important factors:

1. You have the power to make choices and to change your destiny. You can choose, at any moment, to live with God, to incarnate into any form, or to remove yourself from incarnating into human form.

2. The law of grace overcomes the law of *karma*. At any moment you can allow God's grace to annihilate past actions.

3. You are already enlightened and don't have to "attain" anything. Enlightenment is not a goal. It is not an accomplishment, reward, or possession. Its purpose is not to puff up your ego or to place yourself above

---

*In Buddhist philosophy, life is believed to be like a wheel that cycles repeatedly in reincarnation. This is called the "*karmic* wheel."

†Sanskrit word meaning "extinction of individuality and absorption by Spirit."

‡*Nirvakalpa* is a Sanskrit word meaning "changeless" or "permanent"; *samadhi* is a Sanskrit word meaning "a state of perfect tranquillity of mind and body."

others. There is nothing glamorous about it. It is a process of choosing to remember God and live in the presence of God. This remembering process happens over time and requires patience. It takes place gradually and is rarely like a sudden bolt of lightning.

You Are Already Enlightened

For twenty years I believed my life could not begin until I had attained enlightenment. I was anxious to win the "prize," the goal of life. But the harder I worked to serve my guru, the more I denied my own desires, the wispy trophy eluded me all the more.

Many cults promise enlightenment. Inevitably followers hope to attain this state by obeying the rules prescribed by the cult. They believe that if they are good little boys and girls, one day they will be rewarded—their leader will cast a magic spell and then, poof! They will see the light.

However, waiting for Santa to come down the chimney can be a disappointing experience. Disillusionment eventually sets in. This is because no one else, other than yourself, is going to give you enlightenment. Many of you seek a carrot continually dangled in front of your face by a cult leader. But you never get it. The more you try, the further the carrot recedes from your vision.

That is because self-realization, enlightenment, *jivan mukti, satori, nirvana*, or whatever you want to call it, is *not about trying. It is about being.* The Zen masters have discovered a great truth in their simple teaching of "chop wood, carry water." They teach that enlightenment is not about attaining a goal in the future. It is about being here now, present in the moment, living life to its full. It is about joy, loving, and expressing who you really are. It is not about austerities or renunciation or about being a scholar. It is about laughing, being happy, and spreading your bliss to others. It is about uplifting humanity and bringing joy to others' lives.

You are, in fact, already enlightened now. There is nowhere for you to go. Right here, right now, *you are enlightened.* Your true inner nature is a God-realized being. Your higher self knows and lives the truth now and always. It is just a matter of peeling away the mask you have been wearing that covers your true, loving, joyous, natural God self.

"With no hindrance of mind—no hindrance therefore no fear. Far beyond all such delusion, Nirvana is already here."[4]

"Liberation and bondage is the game of the mind, the Atman is always free. With the mind, it looks like bound, but the Self is eternally free."[5]

Enlightenment is not a goal. It is a process, a process of living in the presence of God. As you read further, you will come to understand that deep within you are aspects of yourself that are in contact with God at all times. By making those parts of yourself a conscious experience, you are realizing, or I should say "recognizing," enlightenment.

"As one not knowing that a golden treasure lies buried beneath his feet may walk over it again and again, yet never find it, so all beings live every moment in the city of Brahman yet never find him because of the veil of illusion by which he is concealed."[6]

Who Is Enlightened?

Many spiritual leaders are venerated for attaining a state of consciousness that is considered to be higher than "ordinary" people's. Catholics revere the pope and other leaders in their organization. Nuns and monks are also scored with high marks on the spirituality scale. Hindu devotees worship gurus and try to get into their physical proximity, touching their feet, believing that even their *darshan* bestows a blessing. Buddhists venerate lamas, who are considered to be on a higher plane of awareness. Native Americans honor shamans, who seem to have direct contact with Spirit.

In nearly every religion those who seem to have a direct link to God are put on a pedestal. Often these "enlightened" are placed between the laity and God as intermediaries. They are lifted to the status of worship by their followers, who idolize them.

Let us begin to examine who these religious leaders are and what makes them different from you or me. Let us try to understand who is really "enlightened" and who is not.

The reality is that everyone on earth is already enlightened. You are in perpetual contact with God, which is the very breath and blood that flows through your body. There is no one who is not one with God now. There is no one who is not already a saint now. For the saint within you, your inner teacher, dwells within your heart.

"In every heart there dwelleth a *Sajin;** only man will not steadfastly believe it—therefore hath the whole remained buried."[7]

The only difference between an ordinary person and an enlightened person is that the enlightened one recognizes who he or she really is, and the ordinary person does not. The enlightened one sees the Self everywhere. The ordinary person sees separateness.

"One who has realized Brahman sees Brahman everywhere and in all."[8]

If you think you are capable of recognizing who is enlightened and who is not, you may be mistaken, because a person's inner status cannot be determined by any outward signs or marks. Just because a person is called "Swami," "Cardinal," "Pope," "Babaji," "Sister," "Brother," "Father," "Rabbi," or even "Saint" does not mean that person recognizes who he or she really is. Just because one radiates a lot of power or has a large auric field does not mean he or she has realized God.

Conversely, the homeless man who approaches you, begging on the street, dirty and disheveled, with missing teeth, may be a divine being, even one who has been sent by God to teach you.

"Be not forgetful to entertain strangers: for thereby some have entertained angels unawares."[9]

In the Bhagavad-Gita, one of the most profound scriptures of India, the student Arjuna asks the teacher Krishna, who is God incarnated into human form: "O, Krishna, what is the mark of a God-realized soul, stable of mind and established in *Samadhi?* How does the man of stable mind speak, how does he sit, how does he walk?"[10]

Lord Krishna, in answering this question, completely ignores the outer signs, such as how a person sits or walks, because such superficial things have nothing to do with the inner status of a person's consciousness. Instead he replies: "Arjuna, when one thoroughly abandons all cravings of the mind, and is satisfied in the self through the self, then he is called stable of mind. The sage, whose mind remains undisturbed in sorrows and pains and indifferent amidst pleasures, and who is free from passion, fear, and anger, is called stable of mind. He who is unattached to everything, and meeting with good and evil, neither rejoices nor recoils, who neither likes nor dislikes, his realization is stable."[11]

Krishna does not refer to any outward material sign to determine a

*Sage.

person's inner state of consciousness. How can anyone judge what is going on inside another person? Only that person can judge. You alone know what level of consciousness you have attained by measuring yourself against the scale that Krishna has demarcated.

A guru might have one million followers who may worship that guru and call him or her an *avatar.** Yet that guru may not have established the state that Krishna describes in the Bhagavad-Gita.

On the other hand a person living in an ordinary house with a conventional family may be a fully realized enlightened saint. Lahiri Mahasaya, who was Paramahansa Yogananda's guru's guru, was married with a normal job. No one in his neighborhood recognized his spiritual status. He was completely unassuming and lived in utter humility. Yet he was one of the greatest God-realized souls of the nineteenth century.

You Are the Authority

If you think someone has more wisdom than you or should be adulated due to a supposed spiritual status, if you are considering joining an organization with a figurehead as a supreme authority, if you think that a supposed enlightened guru will solve all your problems, then beware. Before you know, you might find yourself in a situation similar to this one: A woman from Danbury, Connecticut, went to India to find a miracle cure for her paralyzed godson. After weeks of waiting to see a world-famous guru, she finally received an audience with him. He "materialized" an amethyst ring and gave her instructions to hold it against the boy's severed spine. He promised the boy would be totally cured and walking within fifteen days. Regretfully, when she returned home, she told the boy the guru's promise. When he did not recover as expected, the boy took it as a rejection by God.[12]

Remember, you have within yourself all the healing energy, love, power, wisdom, and enlightenment that anyone could ever desire. The fulfillment of every dream is right here within you now. Never look to anyone else as your authority. Your supreme self is the only authority in your life and the only teacher you need. Remember the words that my guru once said to me (thank God!): "Don't look to anyone. If you don't look to anyone, then everyone will look to you."

*An incarnation of God.

Patricia Hannah, Divine Revelation student and store manager from Detroit, describes her experience: "I have more self-authority now. I look inside for guidance instead of looking to someone or something outside of myself who seemed to be a better authority than myself, because I know that my own God self is the greatest authority."

The habit of most of humanity is to seek knowledge from others and to deify those with special powers. When you seek outwardly for truth, then you rob yourself of inner wisdom. When you seek for God without, then you deny the power within. When you look to others as your authority, then you become a part of their dream and don't fulfill your own. You have a divine purpose to fulfill and you have within yourself all you need to fulfill it. Your inner knower is the knower of all that is to be known.

You can learn much from the knowledge and experience of humanity and do not need to reinvent the wheel. But your outer life can work together with your inner life to produce a symphony of great harmony. You may not have been aware that there are inner teachers from whom you can receive knowledge and guidance. So you felt compelled to receive all instruction and advice from the outer world. It is, after all, probably the way your predecessors behaved.

However, a world within is waiting for you to explore, a marvelous world that contains such magic! The inner one is in continual communication with you anyway, although you may be unconscious of it. Why not make this divine self a part of your conscious waking awareness? Your inner teacher already guides your life and destiny. Why not be conscious of its guidance?

"His throne is in heaven who teaches from within the heart."
—*St. Augustine*

PART III
A Road Map
to Your Inner Life

CHAPTER 5

Discovering Who You Really Are

Physicists say that everything in creation is simply a bundle of vibrations—a mass of energy accumulated into form. Scientists of the most ancient scriptures of India, the Vedas, say that every package of energy, called a "form," has a unique rate of vibration called a "name." The name or sound is the seed vibration of the form that has coagulated into a package of vibrations.

As a physical entity, you are a bundle of energy with a name and a unique form. But the nonphysical parts of yourself, such as your emotions and thoughts, are also composed of vibrations. Your identity also includes invisible aspects, such as your mind, intellect, ego, and emotions, and deeper aspects of yourself, which comprise your "higher self."

As an entity, you are a stream of consciousness, reaching from the divine level to the gross physical level. You possess myriad inner identities within your one recognizable identity, and many subtle bodies comprise your inner form. Subtle bodies are not necessarily confined to the space occupied by your physical body; inner bodies may even exist in more than one place at a time.

Vibrational Levels of Identity

Your inner bodies vibrate at specific frequencies and have different functions. For example, the vibratory rate of dense physical matter is slower than the vibration of light, the highest frequency. Thus your physical body vibrates at a slower pace than your subtle bodies, while your subtlest body vibrates at the highest frequency. Some of your inner bodies are more individualized and some are more universal. The more subtle and abstract the level of inner identity, the more universal it is. Inner bodies on higher levels of vibration are less subject to laws of time and space than bodies of denser vibration.

Please refer to the chart labeled "Road Map to Your Inner Life." This chart is a representation of the various levels of identity within yourself. These levels should not be taken as rungs of a ladder. In truth, there is no "higher" or "lower." All life is one life, all Spirit is one Spirit.

ROAD MAP TO YOUR INNER LIFE

Outer Life (Material World)	Body	Environment
		Physical Body
	Mind	Conscious Mind
		Subconscious Mind (Façade)
		Subconscious Mind (Feeling)
		Façade Barrier (False Belief in Separation from God)
		Etheric (Soul) Self
Inner Life (Spiritual World)	Spirit	Christ Self
		"I AM" Self
		God Self
		Cosmic Self
Present Everywhere		Absolute Pure Consciousness

Your life is composed of two aspects, the Inner Life and the Outer Life. Three basic categories exist within these: Body, Mind, and Spirit. Your Outer Life consists of your Environment, Physical Body, Conscious Mind, and Subconscious Mind. Your Inner Life includes your Etheric or Soul Self, Christ Self, "I AM" Self, God Self, and Cosmic Self.

The Body consists of the dense material world of the environment and the physical body. These aspects of life are perceived through your five senses. The Mind contains your conscious mind, subconscious mind, and your etheric soul self. These are invisible to the outer senses but visible to the subtle senses (clairvoyance, clairaudience, and clairsentience). Spirit consists of the *personal* aspect or aspects of God. These aspects of divinity can be perceived by attuning your conscious awareness to God.

Absolute Pure Consciousness pervades your inner and outer life and is the *impersonal* aspect of God. This aspect of life cannot be perceived by the sense faculties. It can be experienced only by direct union of your conscious mind with transcendental consciousness. It is beyond the forms and phenomena of creation.

It is important to understand that all the vibrational levels of your inner identity can be experienced directly by practicing Divine Revelation. You can enhance these experiences by familiarizing yourself with the unique faculties and qualities of each of these levels. You can locate the aspects of your higher self, otherwise known as the aspects of God or inner teachers, on these levels and receive the names and signals that vibrate on each level. The remainder of this chapter is a detailed explanation of these vibrational levels of identity. Please refer to the glossary to understand any terms that are unfamiliar to you.

Your Environment

Your Environment is the most dense level of existence. The experience of the environment is one of physical limitations and laws. The environment is the material world, composed of five elements, listed in order from the densest to the subtlest: earth, water, fire, air, and ether. The body of the environment is the physical universe. It is the thought of God made manifest in physical form. Its movements and evolution are directed by God's intelligence. It is so vast that it is beyond human comprehension.

Your Physical Body

Your Physical Body is made of the five elements of earth, water, fire, air, and ether and the five senses: smell, taste, seeing, feeling, and hearing. It was originally intended to manifest a perfect form, symmetrical and beautiful. However, the form of your physical body is usually distorted by negative beliefs of limitation, illness, aging, and death. Your body is immortal by design but can become mortal by unconsciously implanting the belief in death into it.

Your Conscious Mind

Your Conscious Mind is that intangible aspect of yourself that makes you aware of your existence, feelings, desires, thoughts, environment, and experiences. Your conscious mind allows you to be awake and identify yourself and your environment. It is your perceptive mechanism and uses your senses in order to experience. Most people experience the continual fluctuation of the conscious mind without fixing on any one point.

The embodiment of the conscious mind is called the "mental body." This body consists of thoughts projected from the mind. Your mental atmosphere can be discerned by intuitive people who can read these thoughts. Clairvoyants often see the mental body as an aura around the body with unique colorations and fluctuations.

Your Subconscious Mind

Your Subconscious Mind consists of two parts: the Façade Mind and the Feeling Mind. Your façade mind generates your ego body, and your feeling mind creates your emotional body.

The subconscious mind differs from the conscious mind in many ways. The conscious mind makes choices and creates actions. The subconscious mind receives and retains the memories from sensory experience. The conscious mind is the objective, active part of your mind, while the subconscious mind is the subjective, passive part.

The embodiment of the subconscious mind is the "astral body," also known as the "causal body," because your past history is the seed cause for future action. Without this "causal body," containing the seeds of action (*sanskaras*) promoting future action (*karma*), there is no need to reincarnate.

The astral body may look like the physical body, or it may be gray or blue. It survives death as a ghost or spirit. It can travel as quickly as thought and pass through solid objects. Although it may feel dense or heavy, it is not subject to the laws of gravity.

Your Façade Mind

The façade mind is your ego with which you identify yourself, composed of encrusted thought-forms and habit patterns. Its experience is self-consciousness, inner discomfort, and discontent.

The embodiment of your façade mind is called your "façade body," made of illusory thoughts so deeply ingrained that they have crystallized into form. These thoughts manifest themselves as conditioning, habit patterns, beliefs, memories, thought-forms, and ego identity. Your façade body consists of false, limited constructs of your ego, built from past experiences and influenced by the race-mind consciousness.* The façade body is sometimes perceived as an armor, a protective covering of defensiveness. It is entirely illusory and can be healed through prayer and love.

Your Feeling Mind

The feeling mind is that aspect of yourself that senses and feels emotions. Its experience is fluctuating, depending on moods. The embodiment of your feeling mind is called the "emotional body" or "feeling body," made of feelings and emotions, either negative or positive.

Your feeling body is the link between your soul and your conscious mind. Through your emotional body you can be receptive to sublime feelings of joy, truth, and fulfillment from Spirit. The feeling body may be seen clairvoyantly as an aura. It may be a variety of colors, depending upon your mood.

The emotional body can project out of the physical body and travel at the speed of thought anywhere it is directed. This body continues after death and may be felt as loving, protective feelings by remaining loved ones. This body has no heaviness or mass. It can be located, although it occupies no space, and it is not subject to gravity.

*The collective thoughts and beliefs of the entire human race.

The Astral Plane

The subconscious mind is so complex and contains so many levels that it is worthy of further study. Please refer to the chart labeled "The Astral Plane." This chart shows the aspects of the astral world, also known as the "subconscious mind." This world consists of illusory thoughts and feelings.

THE ASTRAL PLANE

Subconscious Mind (Individual)	Façade Mind (Ego)
	Feeling Mind (Emotions)
	Psychic Mind (Mental Powers)
Subconscious Mind (Collective)	Race-Mind Consciousness (Collective Thoughts)
	Entity World (Lower Beings)

There are two basic parts of the astral world. The first is the subconscious mind of a person, the Individual Subconscious Mind, and the second is the subconscious mind of the human race, the Collective Subconscious Mind. The individual subconscious mind includes the Façade Mind or ego, Feeling Mind or emotions, and Psychic Mind, or extrasensory mental powers. The collective subconscious mind consists of the Race-Mind Consciousness or collective thoughts of the human race, and the Entity World or collection of lower beings.

The façade mind and feeling mind, the two aspects of the subconscious mind depicted on the chart "Road Map to Your Inner Life," have just been described. The following is a description of other aspects of the astral world.

The Psychic Mind

The Psychic Mind consists of the faculties of extrasensory perception. This aspect of mind displays extraordinary talents that are not necessarily understood or accepted. However, these talents, such as psychic reading, mental impressions, mind reading, fortune-telling, psychic mediumship, astral projection, and mind direction, can be developed.

These psychic abilities are well developed in certain individuals. Some police departments use psychics to find missing persons or to solve crimes. Readings done by psychics can be very accurate. But the mental states read through psychic abilities are nothing more than that—mental states, continually fluctuating with no lasting reality. Therefore, reading your future based on present thought-forms cannot be done accurately, since changing your beliefs will change your destiny.

The embodiment of the psychic mind is the façade body.

The Race-Mind

The Race-Mind Consciousness comprises the collective thoughts of the human race. These thoughts are a collection of societal beliefs, habits, and conditions born of communal, social, religious, political, and national thought-forms. Often these beliefs are shared by almost the entire earth's population. The embodiments of the race-mind consciousness are collective façade bodies and collective emotional bodies.

The Entity World

The Entity World consists of astral beings invisible to the outer eye. These beings have a slower, denser vibration than spiritual beings. The entity world is often experienced by those sensitive to subtle vibrations. But it is important for sensitive people to learn how to deal with astral beings.

The entity world has been ignored by countless religions and philosophies that deny its existence out of fear. People often don't want to give energy or credence to the negative side of life. However, the entity world is not frightening, nor is it necessarily negative. It is simply illusory. It is vital to learn how to heal experiences of the entity world, since such experiences exist and cannot be denied. That is why an entire chapter of this book, chapter 10, is devoted to healing.

The embodiments of the entity world are bodies of astral beings, such as discarnate entities and earthbound spirits.

The Façade Barrier

Please refer again to the chart "Road Map to Your Inner Life," on page 68. Now that the subconscious mind has been studied, let us examine the Façade Barrier in the center of the chart. The façade barrier is composed of crystallized beliefs of separation from God. This illusory experience of duality is the cause of all suffering.

The façade barrier is also called the "psychic barrier," an illusory mental barrier dividing your ego identity from your true self. The ego is like a façade or mask. The true self of love, harmony, and Godlike qualities gets hidden by this false ego.

Your Etheric Self

The Etheric Self or soul self is the true expression of yourself as an individual. Its purpose is to fulfill your heart's desires and soul purpose for this incarnation. Your etheric self is your true identity, your unique individual expression. You are that light, that love, that expression of God, incarnated in human form. Although your physical body may change with time, the immortal etheric soul is ever youthful and effervescent with divine love. The experience of the etheric self is joy, self-confidence, and self-empowerment. It uses the faculties of clairvoyance, clairaudience, clairsentience, and intuition.

The embodiment of the etheric self is the etheric soul body, an immortal body of pure light, ever youthful, with perfect symmetry and divine radiance. The soul body is the same sex as your physical body during any particular incarnation. Therefore, your soul body's appearance may change from incarnation to incarnation. The soul body is flawless, vibrant, luminous, and beautiful.

The soul body is the true incarnation of the individual, and it wears the mental body, astral body, and physical body as distorted masks covering its true glory. This effulgent being, when seen clairvoyantly, displays beautiful pastel colors radiating light. This etheric body can visit a person in a form that looks like the physical body.

Your etheric self is working out your true purpose and pathway. On the level of the soul, your life is flawless, without imperfection. All limitations of the outer mind and body are an illusion. Your etheric self lives in paradise, even if your body and mind experience distortion or suffering. From the viewpoint of your etheric self, untouched by the material world, your life is perfect.

Your Christ Self

When defining the Christ Self it is important to realize that in this context the name "Christ" is not synonymous solely with Jesus. Here the word "Christ" means a universal level of consciousness not bound by any particular religious tradition. The "Christ self" is a level of inner identity within people of all backgrounds. The word "Christ" comes from the Greek word *christos*, meaning "the anointed." After Jesus's death he was given the title "Jesus the Christ" out of adoration and respect.

Your "Christ self" is your inner Christ, the "anointed one" who lives in Spirit within you. The Christ within you, known as your "Christ consciousness," expresses the most ideal qualities of human life.

Jesus performed miraculous works when he walked the earth, and yet he said: "He that believeth on me, the works that I do shall he do also; and greater works than these shall he do."[1]

Your Christ self within you can perform the works of Jesus and even greater works, if you would have enough faith. Your Christ self expresses through direct knowing. It is both individual and universal, so it assists both you and all of life. The experience of the Christ self is comfort, love, peace, and joy, and it brings teaching and lifting of consciousness.

The embodiment of the Christ self may appear with various forms and names. You probably have several Christ selves that reveal themselves as you progress on your path, specializing in areas of life that you are working on at the time. Your Christ selves may appear male or female, depending on which is more appropriate for a particular area of learning. Your Christ selves may work with you and others at the same time or different times.

Your Christ self body may be seen above your head as a divine protector. Many people who see the Christ body perceive it as a guardian angel or a celestial being. However, it is an aspect of your higher self, rather than a power outside yourself. The Christ selves are composed of Spirit and are subject to no physical laws.

Your "I AM" Self

Your "I AM" Self is the most basic component of your individuality. "I AM" or "I exist" is the most fundamental characteristic of self, yet it has no particular uniqueness in itself. It is the most abstract part of yourself as an individual. Universal consciousness, the impersonal God, manifests as individual consciousness in order to communicate or express through human beings. Your "I AM" is an individualization of the universal God.

The "I AM" self knows all through direct revelation and is universal wisdom, love, and truth made manifest. The purpose of the "I AM" self is to fulfill God's purpose through you as an individual. The inner experience of the "I AM" is power, wisdom, and beingness.

The embodiment of your "I AM" self is the "I AM" body. It usually appears in both male and female form and has two names, male and female. The "I AM" self can be in many places at one time, working with many different people.

Your God Self

The God Self is your direct connection to the almighty personal God in whatever form you believe God to be. The purpose of your God self is to unify your individual consciousness with God. Your God self is the personal form of God realized as your higher self.

Your God self may be any beloved form of God, whether Krishna, Jesus, Mother Mary, Jehovah, Allah, or another form. The God self is universal, without characteristics associated with you as an individual. However, you can own these characteristics as a God-realized being. The inner experience of the God self is devotion, wholeness, unity, and sanctity.

The embodiment of the God self is the body of the personal God in a universal form, either male or female. You probably have one male and one female God-self name and form. Your God self works with many different people at the same time on a universal and personal level.

Your Cosmic Self

Your Cosmic Self is wholly universal in nature. It is the universal "I AM" presence, unbounded consciousness, the omnipresent intelligence of the universe. As vast as the universe, it contains all the stars, galaxies, and space of the cosmos. All life is contained within the cosmic self, and the cosmic self is within every person. Your cosmic self experiences itself as being as large as the universe, with all galactic life contained within it.

The embodiment of your cosmic self is the body of the universe, and its nature is universal consciousness. It is neither male nor female, and you probably have one cosmic self name and one form. The cosmic self works with cosmic life, and its function is universal.

Absolute Pure Consciousness

Absolute Pure Consciousness is beyond other vibrational levels of identity and also permeates all levels. It is the ultimate principle of life, the basis of the entire creation. It upholds the universe by its very being. The impersonal aspect of God, beyond time, space, limitation, and causation, it is infinite and has no characteristics whatsoever.

This level of consciousness is pure universal awareness. It is the silent witness of all creation and contains no activity.

The experience of absolute pure consciousness is pure silence without thought, activity, or fluctuation—"One without a second."[2] Its inner state is called *samadhi* in Sanskrit. It can be experienced in deep meditation.

Absolute pure consciousness has no embodiment. It is beyond the universe, nameless and formless, so it has no personal name or identity. It is without light, color, form, or phenomena.

Understanding the vibrational levels of your identity gives you a complete road map to your inner life, providing a basis for recognizing and categorizing your own spiritual experiences.

> *"He who knows others is wise; He who knows himself is enlightened."*
>
> —Tao Te Ching 33 *(Taoist)*

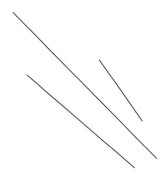

CHAPTER 6

Developing Higher Consciousness

As you deepen your study of Divine Revelation, you will discover the names, forms, feelings, and experiences of your unique vibrational levels of identity. During the Divine Revelation "breakthrough intensive," you will contact at least one aspect of your higher self.

Each of your higher selves has a unique individuality, just as your human self is unique. And your expression of a higher self, even if it has the same name as another person's, may be completely different. Your higher selves have specific characteristics. They are like various flavors, each with a unique, distinct taste to the palate.

One Christ self may specialize in financial abundance. Another may deal with spiritual growth. Yet another may assist in your ability to experience love. Your inner teachers work together to assist your overall evolution of consciousness. On higher levels of being, individuality does not merge into an amorphous wholeness but instead expresses a distinct nature at every level. Each of your inner names and forms has specific characteristics, powers, abilities, experiences, joys, and fulfillments.

Stephanie Grayson, a college professor and graduate of Divine Revelation from Los Angeles, describes her experience: "What I experience during these wonderful meditations is whatever I ask for. And generally the experience is one of great lifting. I feel great joy, great communion with the many wonderful Christ teachers. Each one has his or her own special feel, own special gift that they come to bring us."

As you work with your inner teachers, a wondrous transformation takes place. Whereas before you identified with your limited ego and defined yourself by past history and physical and mental characteristics, now you can identify with something new and extraordinary. You can experience the characteristics of your higher self.

You can begin to realize and appreciate who you are on deeper, higher levels of being as you gradually emerge as a fully God-conscious, enlightened being. The process begins the day you start to contact your inner teachers. You can see glimpses of the truth of your being, beyond the limitations you had imposed upon yourself.

A minister from northern California who practices Divine Revelation says: "Having the courage and confidence to claim and accept what I truly am, and begin to be more of myself, is the greatest thing for anyone to do, because we're all wonderful expressions of God. It's such an incredible feeling to know that within yourself there is the source of all love, wisdom, joy, and perfection."

The practice of Divine Revelation meditation, of direct conscious contact with God, is a profound technology for developing God-realization.

Camille Zaloren, a lawyer from Los Angeles, says: "Experiencing God within myself has been a really profound development. I have been doing spiritual practices for twenty years, and I've had tremendous success. But I was really feeling the need to establish a personal relationship with God. Divine Revelation fulfilled my prayers—I'm experiencing God within myself and am communicating with God directly. It gives me a feeling of total love and support."

Levels of Consciousness

What is God-realization, and what are the levels of consciousness available to you? What does it mean to experience a higher state of consciousness? This section enumerates and describes all the states of consciousness you are experiencing now and all the states of higher consciousness you can experience:

DEEP SLEEP, DREAM, AND WAKING STATES

In Deep Sleep State the mind is completely unconscious and the body is resting deeply. The Dream State is known to sleep researchers as REM sleep because of the characteristic rapid eye movements during dreaming. In the Waking State you are awake yet ignorant of your true nature, your God self within. You have identified yourself with your ego, mind, and body and have not realized that you are much greater than these. You are in the waking state now as you read these words.

TRANSCENDENTAL CONSCIOUSNESS

With the practice of meditation you may begin to experience a state called *turiya** in Sanskrit. Sometimes this level of consciousness is called *samadhi, satori,* or *nirvana.* On this level you are awake to the impersonal God, the absolute bliss consciousness (*satchitananda* in Sanskrit). This state is called Transcendental Consciousness. As you experience this state frequently, you can begin to identify with inner wholeness rather than with your limited ego.

To find out whether you have experienced this state, ask yourself this:

- Have I ever been in a state without thought, completely silent, yet fully awake inside?
- Have I ever felt completely whole, unified, integrated, and composed within?
- Have I ever experienced absolute perfection within?
- Have I ever experienced the mind without boundaries of time or space?
- Have I ever been in a state without breathing, with complete stillness of body?
- Have I ever completely lost awareness of my body and environment, absorbed in inner bliss alone?

---

*Sanskrit word for "fourth state," beyond the three states of waking, dreaming, and sleeping.

If you can answer yes to these questions, then you probably have experienced the fourth state, transcendental consciousness.

COSMIC CONSCIOUSNESS

Once you have developed your consciousness to encompass all three states of waking, dreaming, and sleeping, together with the fourth state of transcendental awareness, then you have attained Cosmic Consciousness. In this state you are in continual contact with the impersonal God. Whether asleep, dreaming, or awake, you experience *satchit-ananda*, fully identified with absolute pure awareness. You no longer identify with your ego, and you fully identify with inner wholeness. You are not overshadowed by outer experiences, for you are in a state of eternal evenness. Nothing can disturb your inner joy, happiness, love, and fulfillment.

To test whether you have fully attained cosmic consciousness, ask these questions:

- Am I fully identified with absolute bliss consciousness?
- Am I in continual contact with the impersonal God?
- Am I in a state of continual harmony, balance, evenness, and inner peace?
- Can nothing disrupt or ruffle my state of inner pure, blissful awareness?
- Do I witness all my experiences without attachment or ego identification?
- Am I conscious and awake inside during deep sleep and dream states?

If you answer yes to all of these questions, then you are probably experiencing cosmic consciousness.

GOD CONSCIOUSNESS

The experience of the personal aspect or aspects of God is called God Consciousness. In this state both the personal and impersonal God are realized within you. Experiences of God consciousness can come at any stage of development. They may come before or after you are fully established in cosmic consciousness.

To know whether you have had experiences of God consciousness, ask yourself:

- Have I ever experienced something I could describe as divine grace?
- Have I ever had a message from a personal aspect of God?
- Have I ever seen a vision of a personal aspect of God?
- Have I ever felt the presence of a personal God?
- Have I ever experienced the thrill of God's love?
- Can I say that I know who the personal aspect of God is?

If you can say yes to even one of these questions then you probably have had a glimpse of God consciousness. If you are in continual daily contact with the personal aspect of God, you might be fully established in God consciousness.

UNITY CONSCIOUSNESS

The seventh state of consciousness is called Unity Consciousness, otherwise known as Brahman consciousness in Sanskrit. In that state you realize yourself as absolute bliss consciousness, the impersonal God, Brahman. You also realize that the personal aspect of God is that Brahman, and that everything in creation is that Brahman. You realize that your supreme Self, the impersonal God, is one with all creation.

Ask these questions to test whether you have experienced unity consciousness:

- Have I ever felt one with the personal God?
- Have I ever felt one with creation?
- Have I felt that something other than myself was myself, yet had its own identity?
- Have I ever experienced that what I do affects the entire cosmos?
- Have I ever felt completely connected to everyone and everything around me?
- Have I ever experienced my body as large as the entire universe?
- Have I ever felt a sanctity in all of life?

If you have answered yes to any of these questions, then you have had glimpses of unity consciousness. If you can answer yes to every one of these questions twenty-four hours of every day, then perhaps you have attained Brahman consciousness.

Higher States of Consciousness

How can you rise to a higher level of consciousness? Higher consciousness can be developed by alternately experiencing the silence of deep meditation and then engaging in activity. My Indian guru often used an analogy to explain this: In India cloth is dyed by dipping it into a vat of dye and then setting it out in the sun to dry. Once it is dry it is dipped into the dye again and then placed in the sun. By repeating this process, eventually the cloth becomes colorfast.

You can develop cosmic consciousness by experiencing transcendental consciousness for a few minutes daily (dipping into the dye) and then experiencing waking, dreaming, and sleeping states (fading in the sun). By alternating deep silence with dynamic activity, eventually your mind becomes so saturated with transcendental consciousness that it "sticks" even when you are fully active.

This process is explained by Lord Krishna in the Bhagavad-Gita. He states: "Established in yoga, perform action, O winner of wealth, abandoning attachment and balanced evenly in success and failure, for equilibrium of mind is called yoga."[1]

Mark Schoofs of Santa Cruz, California, a graduate of Divine Revelation, says: "In meditation itself I feel very attuned to my inner divine nature, but what is probably even more gratifying is that I also feel it during my daily activity. It's nice to go through the day feeling anchored to the inner divine being. It really changes your perspective on life. It makes you feel much more secure, much more confident. I've come to expect the best in my life."

The cloth-dyeing analogy also applies to other higher states of consciousness, such as God consciousness and unity consciousness. By spending a few minutes in communion with God every day and then confronting the day's activity, God consciousness and unity consciousness can eventually be fully established.

A Divine Revelation graduate, Julie Stein, from Atlanta, describes her experience: "The results of this meditation don't wear off. It's as if you are lifted to a certain level of vibration, and you engage in your daily activities operating on that level. Like being plugged into a divine socket, you are continually being replenished with energy, love, happiness, peace, and creative inspiration. It never gets used up."

It is important to realize that the seven states of consciousness are not necessarily attained in any particular order. You may not experience the growth of higher states of consciousness as stepping into an elevator and getting out on distinct floors, one after the other. You may visit floors at random, or you may visit an upper floor first and a lower floor last. Therefore, it is not a good idea to place numerical values on these states, such as fourth, fifth, sixth, or seventh.

Divine Revelation can help speed up the process of developing higher states of consciousness. A retired woman from South Africa expresses her experience with Divine Revelation: "It has affected every part of my life. I don't even think the same way. My life now feels limitless—I've eliminated all boundaries. It's very exciting. I feel like my spiritual growth is moving at lightning speed. It's the best, to know God within yourself, to be guided by God. You think you would have to go a pretty long way to find that kind of teaching, and it's right within yourself."

It is God's desire to express through you, and the more you familiarize yourself with your divine self and inner teachers, the more you can express divine Spirit. Your inner contact with the vibrational levels of identity is the expression of the truth of your being and the glorification of God. The spiritual power and presence of the divine radiate from deep within as you make conscious contact with your divine self. This not only elevates your consciousness but also blesses the entire creation with vibrations of peace. For you are intimately connected to the whole of universal life.

The more you open your awareness to God, the clearer your connection becomes, until you are eventually in constant contact with Spirit. This leads the way to full God-realization, the fulfillment of your life on earth. Your destiny is to realize God and to live heaven right here on earth.

"The soul is not like God: she is identical with him."
—*Meister Eckhart (Christian)*

PART IV
Opening the Pipeline to the Divine

CHAPTER 7

Ways to Have a Spiritual Breakthrough

Your God self is deep within, beckoning you to come into its presence. Our longing for God is demonstrated by a continual hunger for things of the material world, a craving that can never be satisfied with anything less than complete communion with God. No matter how much worldly wealth, power, affection, learning, admiration, possessions, success, or pleasure you may acquire, you will feel incomplete until you have fully awakened God's eternal love within your heart.

There is nothing your soul yearns for more than to experience God, even if you are unaware of it consciously. It is the home for which you are homesick, for which your heart cries out continually. But that home is not far away or unattainable. It is at the center of your being, waiting for you to open the door to its magnificent radiance.

"And ye shall seek me, and find me, when ye shall search for me with all your heart."[1]

A time comes when you are ready to open to Spirit. At that time you will find a way to achieve the "breakthrough." God will assist you, and all that you need do is ask.

The entire Divine Revelation methodology is based upon a single principle: "Ask, and it shall be given you; seek, and ye shall find; knock, and it shall be opened unto you."[2] It is by asking that you receive. It is by making your request, by "placing your order" with God, that you find what you are seeking.

You have the power to experience the inner one whom you seek. You need only to open your heart to let that divine one in. Then your life will be filled with light and your being will be filled with joy. Never again will you feel lost or alone. For you will open the floodgate to paradise, heaven on earth, right here, right now. Not in some future "heaven" in the sky, but the rapture of divine union in every moment.

Kevin Dunn, a motivational speaker from Mount Shasta, California, describes this: "Divine Revelation lifts me into a state of heightened consciousness of divine love, light, and truth. It opens my heart center to the divine inmost nature within me. It aligns my thoughts and attitudes more clearly to divine truth, and stimulates and nurtures a greater sense of personal power. I now feel less lonely and as though I'm 'having a party' or communion with myself when I sit to meditate. It is cozy, warm, comfortable, delicious, nurturing, and like having company, as well as high and at times ecstatic."

Are you ready to take a step toward God-realization? There is nothing to fear in taking this step. It is as natural as eating a meal or walking down the street, as ordinary as a daisy. Yet it is profound and sublime. Many are willing to have a brief experience of their God self. Fewer are ready to follow through with daily practice of meditation. Fewer still are willing to listen to the divine voice. Even fewer are ready to follow divine guidance on a daily basis. Rare indeed is a person who desires to be led by God's voice all the time.

One of the main goals of Divine Revelation is for your inner divine contact to become so well established that you have the capacity at any moment to contact your divine voice at will. This means that you are in continual contact with your true God self.

Resistances to Breaking Through

The reason so few are willing to listen to their intuitive voice is due to many fears: fear of the unknown, fear of possession or loss of control, fear of unalterable life changes, of isolation from normal society, of persecution by others, fear of confusion about reality and fantasy, of making a mistake, of misusing powers, of misguiding others, and so forth.

These are fears rooted in historical race-mind thought patterns shared by all students of spiritual knowledge. Often students are terrified of developing supernormal powers due to persecution of religious and spiritual leaders suffered in past times, such as the horrors of Christian martyrdom, the Inquisition, and medieval witch-hunts. Even in today's society of relative freedom, those following an unusual spiritual path are often fearful. And with good reason—nearly all spiritual pioneers were systematically scoffed at by their peers, disinherited by their families, scorned by their communities, and beaten, lynched, imprisoned, tortured, or brutally murdered.

Here are some cries of fear expressed by those beginning to develop their intuitive abilities:

1. **"I don't want to change."**
"By listening to my intuition I might change. Who wants to change? Change may mean giving up something I need. My cart will be upset, my status quo disrupted."

2. **"What will other people think?"**
"I might be criticized and laughed at for being weird. Cherished, comfortable parts of my life might be affected. I could be rejected by a person or institution that I hold dear. Who wants the aggravation?"

3. **"Ignorance is bliss."**
"What if I am told something that I don't want to hear? What if I am guided to do something I don't want to do? How can I take the risk?"

4. **"I don't want to face my weakness."**
"What if I see something uncomfortable that I don't want to look at? Maybe it is more comfortable to live with pain and frustration than to do the work of healing."

5. "Yes, but . . ."

"I would do it, but . . ." "I could do it, but . . ." "I should do it, but . . ." "One day I'm gonna do it, but . . ." "I can't do it until . . ." "I tried once and I failed." "Let me get ready first." "I need————first." "Yes, but . . ."

These excuses are cries of weakness. They are your limited ego-self trying desperately to hold on to past habit patterns of limited identity. Defensive walls have served it so well that it cannot imagine operating without them. It struggles for dear life to hang on to the past by fighting anything threatening it.

Why work so hard to maintain your grip on limitation? Has it given you your heart's desires? Has it created lasting happiness, love, and joy in your life?

It is time to step outside your comfort zone and discover who you really are. By staying in the encrusted past, you could be doomed to a life of "quiet desperation." By taking a risk, you can open to the possibility of fulfilling your dreams!

Karlene Main, an employment agent from Fairfield, Iowa, states: "I definitely would recommend Divine Revelation to anyone that wants to know themselves better, that wants to know more who they are, who they *really* are, not just how to do the job better. But anyone who wants to face the challenge of having that inner knowledge of what is really, truly theirs. And I don't think that everybody in the world is ready for that. I think that it's a very special person that has to be ready to want to know who they really are."

Don't be afraid to take the first step toward opening the door to God. You will never know what is behind that door unless you open it. What you will find on the other side is greater than you could ever imagine. It is freedom, power, fulfillment, and glory. It is the extraordinary, which is the ordinary state of divine grace, your God-given birthright. You were born to live in the paradise of God's grace right here on earth. You were not born to suffer. You were born to be happy.

As Sally Farnsworth, a student of Divine Revelation from Nebraska, describes it: "The connection with God within me is constantly a source of joy, happiness, freedom, ecstasy, and knowledge. I've realized that my relationship with my God self is the most important thing in my life, and that all answers come from there, all joy comes from that, all of my happiness."

Simplicity, love, and devotion are the stairways to God's doorway. Saint Francis and other God-realized saints demonstrated this in their lives. You can prove it yourself. The "Be-attitudes," or attitudes of being, are the steps on the stairway of devotion. By practicing these attitudes, you prepare the ground to invite God into your heart.

Daily exercise of such attitudes as nonjudgment, unconditional love, faith, trust, patience, guilelessness, sincerity, responsibility, self-reliance, humility, nonresistance, forgiveness, kindness, and gentleness can help you attain greater awareness of yourself as well as compassion for others. Be-attitudes of contentment, inner peace, serenity, tranquillity, joy, happiness, balance, harmony, wisdom, and freedom, which are cultured through meditation, help to fill your mind with divine light and invite more of God's presence into your life.

The following is an exercise that can help you develop these attitudes of being:

Take a walk through a crowded street or shopping mall. While you are walking, look into the eyes of every person who passes you. See God within each soul. Let go of all critical judgments about race, sex, physical characteristics, and so forth, and just see the divine beauty in each person. By doing this, you will realize how your condemning judgments have blinded you to the truth. By practicing this often, you will open your heart to God's love.

Breaking Through Your Inner Barriers

Breaking down the wall to the God-presence at the center of your being—this is how you might define the breakthrough experience. This wall may be made of gossamer or brick. It is made of habits, beliefs, and thoughts that have convinced you that you are separate from God. These thoughts of fear, judgment, guilt, and confusion have become so crystallized that they have coagulated into form.

Please refer to the chart on page 68, "Road Map to Your Inner Life." The Façade Barrier in the middle of this chart is an illusory division between matter and Spirit. It is a false barrier of error-thoughts that cuts you off from your true nature, a veil of subconscious beliefs preventing you from experiencing God-Spirit at the center of your being and keeping you from developing your innate intuitive abilities. The façade-wall is created by human freedom of choice. That is, your habitual thoughts can become so deeply entrenched that they mask your clear, radiant, true self.

With this protective façade-covering, you could feel so comfortable and secure in old habits that you have no incentive to change. You may resist the idea of healing old fears and worn-out beliefs. Remember, this barrier is made of memories stored in your subconscious mind, which comprise your ego identity, who you think you are. Who you *think* you are and who you *really* are, most likely, are two different things, for you probably identify yourself by your past history.

"Breaking through" means walking through the façade barrier and experiencing who you really are. When you have your first breakthrough, the divine self that you contact is so different from your ordinary human self that you might think it is another person! But this perfect spiritual being is the *real you*, the true self beyond boundaries.

When you lift above false human beliefs and penetrate the barrier, you return to a state of pure innocence—the original divine being that God intended you to be, living in paradise, heaven on earth. At that moment you are one with God and your own love-nature. You find no limitation, fear, frustration, and confusion there—only peace, love, truth, and wisdom.

Brigitte Dulac, a Divine Revelation graduate and homemaker from Minnesota, describes her experience: "It has filled aspects of my personality and my life that were very sad, that were hurting and in pain. There were parts of me that I accepted, that would feel spiritual, and then there were parts of me that felt very unspiritual. The breakthrough spiritualized my whole body, my life, every aspect of my being."

Each time you break through the ego-façade and experience the true nature of your being, you identify with your divine self. By contacting your God self daily, you gradually develop a rapport and create a deeper identification with it. Eventually the day may dawn when you realize, "I AM that oneness, I AM that wholeness, I AM that God-being. THAT is who I AM!"

Breakthrough Experiences

The breakthrough experience is entirely unique for each of you. It may be as smooth as a sailboat gliding over a silent lake or as tumultuous as a large vessel in a storm, and then after the storm, perfect quietude. It may be like dancing in a waterfall with rainbows all around, or it may feel like taking communion in church.

You will break through to Spirit in your own dramatic way or your own quiet way or something in between. You may notice one or more of the following experiences during your breakthrough:

1. A rush of energy going through your body
2. Tingling or chills in your body
3. Deep, labored, or rapid involuntary breathing
4. Feeling of light-headedness
5. Trembling or shaking of the body
6. Involuntary laughter
7. Deep emotional feelings
8. Emotional release in the form of crying
9. Tears of relief or joy
10. Deep inner peace
11. Deep relaxation
12. Inner joy and freedom
13. Surges of ecstatic love
14. Feelings of being loved and protected
15. Desire to express love to others
16. Visions of light
17. Celestial fragrances or tastes
18. Swaying or rocking of the body
19. Twitching or involuntary movements of body parts
20. Vibratory lifting or quickening of the body
21. Feeling of power or strength being fed into you
22. Feeling of divine love being fed into you
23. Feeling of warmth or cold
24. Feeling of electrical currents running through the body
25. Cleansing and clearing of the emotional body
26. Inner ecstasy or rapture

All these experiences are normal and no cause for alarm. They are the natural outcome of a process known as "vibrational lifting," purification of your body and mind to clear the way for greater power and love. In order to sustain new levels of consciousness, you will be transformed in your body, mind, and emotions. God is in charge of your breakthrough, so you will experience what is for your highest good.

The Breakthrough Intensive

During the experiential session known as the "Divine Revelation breakthrough intensive," students are guided into a deep meditation and receive direct contact with aspects of God within them. During this class remarkable vibrational liftings,* healings, and inner messages come from Spirit.

Anna Valenti, a holistic health professional and Divine Revelation student from Plainview, New York, describes her experience: "The best part for me was the breakthrough session. I had a very incredible experience. It was very spiritualizing and deep, intensified, and concentrated. I felt as if my whole body was just filled with God. It was very powerful."

Most people taking the class desire to develop their intuitive abilities. Some wish to directly communicate with their higher self, with God within, or with a guiding angel or ascended master, in whatever form they believe. And they are surprised at how easy it is to receive this blessing. This experience is truly extraordinary and very spiritual.

The communication with the divine comes in three basic ways:

1. Receiving divine visions
2. Hearing divine messages
3. Receiving divine feelings

These experiences for most people are on the inner level. So, for instance, they may see a vision of Jesus or Buddha or Krishna or another master in their inner vision, or they may see an angel or dazzling, brilliant light. Others may receive messages on a verbal level and "hear" words of comfort or wisdom with their inner ear. Some may receive ecstatic feelings or promptings within them. These are ways that Spirit communicates with our human selves.

Students learn how to read these inner experiences and how to hear the divine voice. They also learn how to "speak-through"† the messages

---

*Raising the vibratory level of the mind and body to a higher level.
†Speak aloud while hearing the messages coming from the inner divine voice.

coming from Spirit. Everyone who has completed the course received messages from the divine voice successfully and spoke these messages out loud.

Comforting messages from Spirit are accompanied by feelings of joy, happiness, peace, serenity, and ecstatic unity. Students are amazed at how inspiring and freeing this divine contact can be. They are astounded by the profundity of their thoughts and inspirations when their conscious minds unite with the divine mind. Beautiful poetry and scripture pour from the mouths of ordinary people in that deep state of awareness.

Maureen Schneider, a schoolteacher from Bethel, Connecticut, describes her experience of receiving messages from Spirit during her breakthrough: "I felt light and inspired when words were flowing through my heart. It touched the deepest part of my being and gave me hope and possibility, and a connected sense of reality. The course was inspiring."

When Peter and Ann Meyer (Makeever) first began to teach and give breakthrough sessions in 1963, the earth was clouded by negation and pessimism. A dense cloud of "astral dust," composed of erroneous thoughts and feelings, enveloped the earth. Because of the negativity present at that time, it took eighteen weeks of classes before students were ready for their breakthrough.

Today much of this negative dross has been cleared by the efforts of people meditating, praying, healing, and clearing the atmosphere surrounding the earth. In 1963 there was "static on the line," preventing clear reception from Spirit. Today there is less static and messages are clearer. Now students can receive their "breakthrough" within just a few minutes, whether they are American, British, Russian, or Turkish; Jewish, Hindu, Moslem, or Christian.

I personally possessed no special abilities in the field of intuition, clairvoyance, or clairaudience before I learned Divine Revelation, yet I learned to do it effectively. If I can learn it, then you can learn it, too.

Nancy Aurelia of Greenwich, Connecticut, describes her breakthrough: "At first I felt very nervous, not so much about the messages I would receive, but over the idea that I might not get any. (Am I really good enough for God to talk to me?) After Susan said her healing prayer, the nerves quieted down. I felt at peace but still 'tingly.' I heard words, not so much like a voice, but more like a thought. Only not coming from my head, but from my center. The message I came away with is that I don't have to worry about ever being okay and will I connect with God, but that these things are already so, and I will be lifted up in that knowledge. I feel relieved, encouraged, and delighted that I have finally started on my path to spirituality."

Goals of the Breakthrough Session

The Divine Revelation breakthrough intensive includes a meditative experience in which you receive a personal breakthrough to Spirit.

This meditative experience has three basic goals:

1. Inner Vibrational Name

The first goal is to receive and verify at least one inner vibrational "name" that identifies an aspect of your higher self or a divine teacher within. Inner names are sound vibrations of various aspects of God. These names are important signposts of contact with true Spirit rather than with aspects of your mind or entities from the astral world. Once you identify these names, you know whom you are contacting and receiving messages from.

2. Inner Vibrational Signal

The second goal is to receive and verify an inner vibrational "signal" corresponding to each inner name. Signals are subtle feelings, visions, sounds, body movements, fragrances, or tastes. By receiving a specific signal corresponding to each inner name, you can later identify each name by that signal.

For example, Charlotte Liss, an artist from New York City, describes her own unique signal received during her breakthrough: "I was becoming aware of my inner divine signal—a rush of tingling energy coming from above that washed over the back of my neck, down my shoulders and across the back, down my arms. As it intensified I felt it go down my thighs into the legs and feet."

3. "Speaking-Through" Messages

The third goal is to receive and verify a message from Spirit and speak the message that you receive out loud. This message is either a thought, a vision, or a feeling, which you speak aloud as you receive it within your mind or heart.

For instance, Arlene Krieger, a pharmacologist from Greenwich, Connecticut, describes her first experience of speaking-through: "I saw a grayness, then a blueness, and then a golden lightness. I received a message, 'I am the light. I am the only light. I am the only way.' I felt the peace of the light. I presently feel a strong energy throughout my body. I feel a deeper relationship with my higher self. I feel confident in this relationship."

How You Can Have a Breakthrough

This book can offer some steps to help you have your own breakthrough. Since the entire Divine Revelation process is based upon the principle "Ask, and it shall be given you," your breakthrough can come about simply by asking for the experience!

By getting quiet, comfortable, going into deep meditation, and then asking God, it is possible for you to experience a breakthrough. Begin your meditation with an opening prayer. Then, as you go deeper, you will pass through various levels of consciousness, step by step, outlined on the chart on page 68. First, notice the environment. After that, become aware of the body, the conscious mind, and the subconscious mind. Then walk through the façade barrier and experience Spirit within, your divine self.

This state is not a trance or leaving the body. It is a state of deep meditation and relaxation in which you are fully alert and awake. Walking through the door of the façade barrier may be very inspiring or it may be very ordinary. You may feel you are in deep meditation or not deep at all. It depends upon your makeup and past experiences.

Once you are in meditation, you can call upon aspects of God and inner teachers, such as the Holy Spirit, Jesus, Jehovah, Krishna, Buddha, Babaji, Saint Germain, to help you contact inner names and signals and receive messages from Spirit. The important thing is to let go and allow the process to happen. If you fight the process or try too hard, it might take longer to have your breakthrough. You can deal with any resistances to breaking through by using the healing prayers in chapters 10 and 11. These prayers help you let go so you can break through more easily. You can also take deep breaths any time you feel "stuck" during the process.

You might now be thinking, "I know that I won't be able to relax. It will be difficult for me." Or "I know that I will try too hard. I never have spiritual experiences. I will just sit there like a log and nothing will happen."

If you have such doubts, then answer this question: Even with these doubts in your mind, are you still able to think a thought? Anyone who can think can receive divine messages. If you can think a thought, then you can receive a thought from divine Spirit. It is simply that easy.

It is natural to have doubts about something you have never done before. But be assured that you *can* have a breakthrough experience. It just takes a willingness to learn. It may take longer for one person to break through than another. But I have never encountered a willing person who was unable to break through.

For example, Frankie H. Davis of New York City describes her breakthrough: "I really thought that nothing was going to happen for me because of my lack of experience and knowledge, listening to everyone share what Spirit was doing for them. Well, I really see that I *must* let go my *fears* and being afraid of communicating with Spirit. I really enjoyed what took place with me and look forward to other new signals and experiences in the future. I'm really happy with what my body is feeling. Peace and quietness within my being. Lots of good energy running up and down my body. I think on a scale from 1 to 10: Ten + + + + +."

Your inner experience of breaking through can be very enjoyable. Most people have feelings of joy, bliss, happiness, relief, inner peace, deep relaxation, fulfillment, wholeness, inner strength, self-authority, and self-confidence. It is usually a moving, emotional experience, as God welcomes you with open arms.

Darryle Smith, a social services supervisor from New York City, explains: "I felt moved to tears and I felt touched by God. There was a wonderful feeling of relief, and later peacefulness. I felt warm and tingly and tears were flowing. I had a sense that all is well now."

You may receive a message of unconditional love and acceptance that speaks personally to you. This message might be an inner vision, or visual experience that tells a story. Then you can describe this vision out loud. Or it may come as thoughts or words in your mind, which you can speak audibly as you receive them. Or you may receive an inner feeling or emotional experience that you can describe out loud.

Your Inner Connection

Once you have passed through the façade barrier, regular conscious contact with your divine self can bring rapid spiritual growth in your life. As you meditate daily, it becomes easier to connect with your God self. Your true feeling-nature can begin to open, and your actions may be perceived by others to be more loving, genuine, and natural. You might drop false personality mannerisms and begin to give more freely and fully to others.[3] Your sphere of influence may expand as you become more powerful.

A graduate of Divine Revelation, Terry Melikan, a biologist from Colorado, states: "I have felt more more at ease with other people and I have stopped trying to be someone who I am not in order to please others."

With practice you can develop your intuitive abilities to such a degree that you can receive messages or answers from Spirit even outside of meditation. The flow of intuitional guidance can become continual and constant.

Dr. Richard Ford, a dentist from northern California, writes: "I 'talk' to my Self all the time now, not only in my Divine Revelation meditations, and I am growing ever faster as I, or my God-self, teaches me."

You may receive wonderful inspirations of truth, vibrational liftings, love feedings (receiving divine love from Spirit), energy feedings (receiving divine energy from Spirit), and power feedings (receiving divine power from Spirit). You may remember deep soul memories and previously incomprehensible spiritual revelations that you can now understand.

With regular divine contact your inner life can become rich and your outer life joyous. Your inner teachers can guide you to fulfill those heart's desires most beneficial to your spiritual growth and material happiness. You can begin to live your true purpose for the greatest attainment in this incarnation.

Laura Gold, a Divine Revelation student and masseuse from Los Angeles, writes: "I now feel supported by life more than ever before, and with each new day, with each meditation, come increasing waves of joy and upliftment and movement toward my soul's true purpose."

After meditating for some time with your inner name(s) and signal(s) that you received in your initial breakthrough, you might be ready for new breakthroughs in consciousness, other levels of inner identity or divine teachers. When you receive new inner contacts, remember that this aspect of God that you have just contacted is not "new." It was always within you—you have just now become aware of it. When you receive a new contact, you may continue to receive teachings from your old contact as well, or that older contact might fade into the background.

Every time you break through to a new inner contact, you can record it on the chart labeled "Personal Inner Divine Identities." This way, you can refer to your inner names and signals when you wish to call upon an inner contact in the future. (If you are experiencing any difficulty receiving breakthrough experiences, you can check with a qualified teacher of Divine Revelation. Please refer to the list on page 271.) Inner Divine Names are names of your inner contacts. Each inner contact has a Sex, either male, female, or neuter. Inner Divine Signals are signals that correspond to the inner names. Levels of Identity are the vibrational levels discussed in chapter 5, such as Christ selves, "I AM" selves, etc. In addition to your own higher selves, other inner teachers may come on these levels of identity, such as Christ teachers, master teachers, deities, divine beings, angels, archangels, etc.

PERSONAL INNER DIVINE IDENTITIES

Inner Divine Name	Sex	Inner Divine Signal	Level of Identity

Yogananda's Breakthrough

In his book *How You Can Talk with God*, the great saint Paramahansa Yogananda (1893–1952) describes his first experience of God's voice. His description is very similar to many of the breakthroughs that I have witnessed in Divine Revelation students:

> I have written in *Autobiography of a Yogi* about some of the numerous occasions on which I have talked with God. My first experience in hearing the Divine Voice came when I was a little child. Sitting on my bed one morning, I fell into a deep reverie.
>
> "What is behind the darkness of closed eyes?" This probing thought came powerfully into my mind. An immense flash of light at once manifested to my inner gaze. Divine shapes of saints, sitting in meditation in mountain caves, formed like miniature cinema pictures on the large screen of radiance within my forehead.
>
> "Who are you?" I spoke aloud.
>
> "We are the Himalayan yogis." The celestial response is difficult to describe; my heart was thrilled. The vision vanished, but the silvery beams expanded in ever widening circles to infinity.
>
> I said, "What is this wondrous glow?"
>
> "I am Iswara (the Lord). I am Light." The Voice was as murmuring clouds.[4]

"And they were all filled with the Holy Ghost, and began to speak with other tongues, as the Spirit gave them utterance."
—Acts 2:4 *(Christian)*

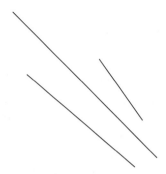

CHAPTER 8

Meditating Your Way to the Spirit

Practicing Divine Revelation meditation has many benefits, such as receiving divine guidance, healing yourself, taking responsibility for your life, and gaining self-confidence. But the most important benefit is self-realization and self-love. That means experiencing who you really are on the deepest levels of your being. In order to love yourself completely, it is essential to know who you really are. And who you really are is not the limited ego whom you may have believed yourself to be.

You have heard that you have a divine self, that God is within you, and that you are a child of God. But how many actually *experience* these truths from the deepest level? In order to really *own* this knowledge, you must first *feel* it. It is not enough to know it intellectually.

Tricia Fesperman, a homemaker from Asheville, North Carolina, says: "Divine Revelation has brought into my awareness direct contact with God. Through contacting my own divine self, I experience peace, trust, and faith that I am God's child and I am in His loving hands. All is well."

Divine Revelation meditation is a way to *experience* who you are and identify yourself with divine qualities, so you can begin to recognize yourself as divine love, light, healing power, energy, wholeness, oneness, and peace. Identifying yourself with these divine qualities promotes greater self-worth and self-acceptance.

"Speaking-Through"

"Speaking-through" is a method of listening to the inner voice and simultaneously speaking the inner message out loud. The Divine Revelation method of speaking-through is unique and produces untold benefits for the practitioner.

The brain waves of Divine Revelation students were measured while speaking-through. Every time these students "spoke-through" from Spirit, their EEG produced sharp spikes of theta band coherence. Coherent spikes of theta band brain waves are associated with the highest levels of consciousness in EEG measurements by many researchers. Some enlightened *yogis* display theta coherence at all times.

Why did brain waves displaying higher states of consciousness appear when students spoke-through? Because speaking-through is a powerful technology for developing God consciousness.

When you speak-through, you are no longer the small ego-self that you were before you began to speak. In this state you are not limited human consciousness. Your human identity has become divine identity. You are hearing God's thoughts and speaking God's voice. You begin to identify yourself more with expanded, positive qualities and less with limited, negative qualities.

James Addison, a business owner from Naples, Florida, says: "The first time I spoke-through, it was as if the Spirit within me was growing and expanding and coming out and being out more and more. All of a sudden it felt like this part of me *must* speak, must come out. People can laugh, cry, I don't care. It was me on a divine level. It wasn't some spirit overtaking me or something. It was actually a divine aspect of my own Self which had a chance to speak out and had a chance to be *real*, had a chance to be *me*, really *me*."

Speaking-through has power because divine truths are spoken out loud. Thus the potency contained within the resonance of the words is released into the universe, producing a profoundly positive effect upon you and the environment. It is a technology of affirmation from the deepest level of consciousness.

The technique of speaking messages aloud also provides a focus during meditation. When you speak-through there is no danger of drifting into a state of lethargy. Even when you meditate alone it is beneficial to speak-through messages out loud.

Preparing for Divine Revelation Meditation

In preparing for Divine Revelation meditation, it is important to remember that this technique is different from other forms of meditation you may have tried. One main difference is that many other meditation techniques are based on *doing* something—you are instructed to think or chant a *mantra*, stare at a candle, or contemplate the meaning of a phrase. Or you may focus your attention on a certain part of the body or on your breathing. All of these techniques require *doing*.

Divine Revelation meditation is unique in that you are not *doing* anything. With this technique you are *being* receptive to Spirit. In *being*, you are open to receiving. If you spend your entire meditation *doing* something, time goes by and what have you gained? The way to receive from Spirit is to be open to receive rather than to be busily doing.

Many who practice meditation spend their meditation period thinking run-of-the-mill thoughts that they would normally think during the day. Sometimes meditations are not very deep, especially when the meditator is straining to concentrate or drifting into daydreams. The experience of inner stillness, silence, and perfect peace, which is the goal of meditation, is rarely achieved.

Divine Revelation meditation is a technique that helps you move your conscious mind into the awareness of Spirit, or God consciousness. This level of awareness is different from the mental level. When your attention is on the level of divine Spirit, a distinct shift takes place. You will have different experiences than the experiences you have on the mental level.

If you are going to take the time to meditate, it is essential that you achieve the goal of meditation, which is to experience inner peace and eventually gain enlightenment through direct communion with God.

This goal *cannot* be achieved by:

1. Floating around in whimsical thoughts or daydreams.
2. Drifting in undirected, scattered thinking.
3. Leaving your body and gliding in an unrealistic state.
4. Going blank or into a blackout or unconscious state.

On the other hand, this goal *can* be achieved by:

1. Allowing Spirit to guide your meditation.
2. Praying for clarity and divine order in meditation.
3. Using the power of prayer to heal all the way.
4. Being rested and clear when you meditate.

Practicing Divine Revelation Meditation

The Divine Revelation meditation technique is very easy to practice. By using the procedure described in the rest of this chapter, you can begin to experience your inner divine contact. The first part is an explanation of the practice. The next part contains a guided meditation that you can record onto an audiotape to use at home.

1. BEGIN WITH AN OPENING PRAYER OF UNIFICATION.

You may use a familiar prayer, such as "Our Father," or read a prayer from a book. I recommend reading the scriptures, or *Science of Mind*, by Ernest Holmes. Once you are more experienced at receiving clear revelation, you may speak-through your prayer from the divine voice within. If you wish, in the initial stages of practice you may use a prayer similar to the one in Point 1 in the sample meditation on page 111.

It is important to begin your meditation with a prayer. You may find that your experiences are better if you pray before meditating. If you have trouble going deep into meditation, no matter what form of meditation you practice, you can go much deeper by praying before meditation. During prayer you are lifting your vibration to the level of Spirit, which automatically sets up a higher state of awareness from which to begin your meditation.

2. STATE YOUR INTENTION OR GOAL FOR THE MEDITATION.

Just as in any other endeavor in life, you have a better chance of succeeding if you set clear goals. It is important to set a theme or goal for your meditation. If you meditate with no intention in mind, then your results will be as vague as your intention. Your theme could be something very general, such as:

a. Unconditional love.
b. Inner peace.
c. Deep relaxation.
d. Deepening of inner contact.
e. Inner power.
f. Ascension.

Or your theme could be something more specific, such as:

a. Answer to a specific question.
b. Creative ideas for a specific project.
c. Healing a relationship.
d. Healing a specific bodily ailment.
e. Divine guidance about your profession.
f. Divine guidance about a love relationship.
g. Wisdom about your living situation or property.

Some examples of ways to state your theme for your meditation are as follows:

a. "The theme for this meditation is Divine Light."
b. "I claim that in this meditation today I receive the answer to the following question: How can I best deal with my child's drug problem?"
c. "In this meditation I ask that I receive highest wisdom concerning finding the perfect apartment to live in."
d. "Today my theme is healing of my relationship with my husband."
e. "In this meditation I receive healing of the pain in my back."

The theme is usually stated just after the opening prayer.

3. CALL UPON THE DIVINE.

Call upon God or a higher power in whatever form you believe God to be, and call upon your higher self in whatever form you believe that to be. Calling upon divine beings, teachers, saints, sages, prophets, angels, and God will raise the vibration of the atmosphere and immediately bring you to a higher level of consciousness. For example:

a. "I call upon beautiful Mother-Father God to help me in this meditation."
b. "I call upon the mighty 'I AM' presence to be with me at this time."
c. "I call upon beautiful Lord Krishna and Lord Shiva to be with me now."
d. "I call upon all the beautiful many Christ beings and the ascended masters to be with me now: beautiful Babaji, Jesus, Mother-Father God, the Holy Spirit, Saint Germain, the angels and archangels of the Christ."
e. "I call upon all the saints, sages, and prophets of God to be here with me now. I call upon beautiful Jesus Christ, Mother Mary, and Saint Francis to be with me now."
f. "I call upon Allah and Muhammad the Prophet to be here in this meditation."
g. "I call upon God the Father to be with me now."
h. "I call upon Lord Buddha and all the bodhisattvas to assist in this meditation."

Call upon your own inner teachers, your own Christ and "I AM" selves, your God self, or whatever aspects of God you wish to assist in your meditation. These are just examples. You may call upon other divine personalities.

4. CLOSE OFF YOUR AURA.

It is important to close off your aura any time you are going into a subliminal state, such as meditation or sleep. In order to close off your aura, I recommend the Self-Authority affirmation on page 131. You may also visualize a white light surrounding you, sealing off your aura. You may see a golden or white sun above your head coming down like a column in the center of your body and radiating outward from that center.

Close off your aura near the beginning of the meditation and any time during the meditation that you feel out of control or in need of divine protection.

5. DO ANY HEALING PRAYERS THAT ARE NEEDED.

Before you meditate, it is a good idea to heal anything needing healing. If you do not take time to heal, then you may find it difficult to go deep in meditation. Therefore, check to see whether any healing prayers are needed.*

You may feel the need to say one or more prayers to heal thought-forms, psychic ties, entities, façade bodies, etc. Once you have completed these healings, you should be clear and ready to go deep into meditation. You may do these healings at the beginning, before the prayer of unification, or you may do them at any stage during meditation. Any time that you feel the need to heal, "heal first and ask questions later."

6. GO INTO DEEP MEDITATION STEP-BY-STEP.

Look again at the chart on page 68, "Road Map to Your Inner Life." On this chart are listed the levels of consciousness of the outer and the inner life. It is recommended that you go into meditation step-by-step, through each of these levels, taking deep breaths to relax between each step.

Begin by being aware of the Environment and relaxing your attention on that level. Then take a deep breath and go deeper and become aware of the Physical Body. Relax every part of the body, and then take another deep breath and go deeper. Then become aware of the Conscious Mind and relax it and allow it to become still. Then take a deep breath and go deeper to the level of the Subconscious Mind. Relax this level and then take another deep breath and go deeper and pass through the Façade or Psychic Barrier and go deeper to the level of Spirit within.

On each level of awareness you can receive divine messages to bring you deeper into the meditation. In other words, going into meditation is not done by rote. You can receive the words to speak that will take you deeper.

7. PRACTICE THE PRESENCE OF GOD IN SILENCE.

Take a few minutes to "be still and know that I AM God." Go into the deepest silence, the state of pure divine consciousness, without thought.

*See chapter 10 for more information about using healing prayers.

This absolute pure consciousness is the basis of all life, love, and existence itself—that "still point of the turning world."[1] Spend several minutes in this state of silence, known as pure intelligence, *satchitananda, samadhi, nirvana, satori,* absolute bliss consciousness, wholeness, oneness, peace. It is a place beyond time, space, and causation, a state of equipoise, nameless, formless, and motionless. It is the impersonal aspect of God, transcendental consciousness.

In that state your body is deeply relaxed, yet your mind is completely alert. Your body may become completely still, without any perceptible breathing.

8. CONTACT THE PERSONAL ASPECT OF GOD.

Now contact personal aspects of God and aspects of the higher self in whatever form or forms you believe. Call upon the names of God or saints, ascended masters, Christ teachers, master teachers, angels or archangels, and get a clear signal from each one whom you contact. Use the nine tests outlined in chapter 13 to verify these contacts.

9. PRACTICE SPEAKING-THROUGH, SINGING-THROUGH, OR ONE OF THE OTHER "ECSTATIC EXPRESSIONS OF GOD."

To maximize the time that you spend in Divine Revelation meditation, it is not enough to just sit in the silence. It is beneficial to bring that silence into activity and stabilize it through one or more of the ecstatic expressions of God described in chapter 16.

During this portion of the meditation, practice speaking-through, singing-through, and so forth. Be sure that you have a clear name and signal and that you use the nine tests in chapter 13 to verify that the message is clear and coming from Spirit. "Speaking-through" provides a way for Spirit to resonate on every level of your being. It also is a method of focusing your attention on Spirit and developing an inner identification with divine aspects of your being.

10. ASK WHATEVER QUESTIONS YOU WISH TO ASK OF SPIRIT.

After you have spoken-through your message, you may wish to ask specific questions of the "still small voice" within. Use the format for asking questions detailed in chapter 14. Ask and receive the answers to your questions and problems. No question is too small or too great for the divine voice to answer. You may ask for any healing or inspiration that you desire. Your only limitation is your own imagination, for "every one that asketh receiveth."[2]

11. COME OUT OF MEDITATION STEP-BY-STEP WHEN YOU ARE READY.

Come out of meditation the same way that you went in, step-by-step. Begin by thanking God for all that you have received in the meditation. Then affirm that you are bringing back what you have received into your waking consciousness. From the level of Spirit begin to bring your conscious awareness back, step-by-step, through all the levels of consciousness. Take a deep, vigorous breath between each level and pretend that you are blowing out a candle when you exhale. First take your awareness back from the deep level of Spirit to the level of the Subconscious Mind. Then take a deep breath and move your awareness to the level of the Conscious Mind. Then take another deep breath and bring your awareness to the level of the Physical Body. Then take another deep breath and become aware of the Environment.

12. COME ALL THE WAY BACK TO OBJECTIVE/SUBJECTIVE BALANCE.

Take four deep, vigorous breaths, as if you were blowing out a candle on each exhale. Come all the way back to objective and subjective bal-

---

**DIVINE REVELATION
MEDITATION PRACTICE**

1. Begin with an opening prayer.
2. State your intention or goal.
3. Call upon the Divine.
4. Close off your aura.
5. Do any healing prayers needed.
6. Go into meditation step-by-step.
7. Experience God in silence.
8. Contact the personal God.
9. Practice speaking-through.
10. Ask questions of Spirit.
11. Come out of meditation step-by-step.
12. Come back to objective/subjective balance.

ance. Then open your eyes and speak the affirmation in Point 12, pages 114–15, in a strong, clear, loud voice.

Example of a Possible Meditation

The following is a sample of the possible statements you might use to guide yourself in and out of meditation. When you are first learning to practice Divine Revelation meditation, it is recommended to record these statements onto an audiotape, which you can later use as a guided meditation. At the beginning of each section is a number and a title referring to the corresponding sections explained above. Don't record the titles or the words in parentheses onto the audiotape, just the statements that are in quotation marks. While recording your tape, speak very slowly. When you come to a blank space, be silent for a few seconds so that when you play back the tape during meditation, you can insert the appropriate words.

1. BEGIN WITH AN OPENING PRAYER OF UNIFICATION.

"I recognize that God is all that is. God is the one power and the one presence in the universe. God is all-loving, all-powerful, and all-embracing. God is the source of my good and the source of my strength. I am one with God now. The all-loving, all-powerful presence of God dwells within me now. I therefore claim for myself the perfect meditation now, which proceeds perfectly with divine order and timing. I claim that I receive all that is wise for me to receive today in this meditation. I claim that I receive the perfect messages from Spirit, the perfect healing, the perfect clear inner names and signals, and the perfect divine guidance. I claim that I go deep in this meditation and receive a beautiful lifting of Spirit. I accept this wonderful meditation today with all gratitude. Thank you God and SO IT IS."

2. STATE YOUR INTENTION OR GOAL FOR THE MEDITATION.

"The theme of my meditation today is _____[theme]_____."

3. CALL UPON THE DIVINE.

"I now call upon dear Mother/Father God, the beautiful Holy Spirit, and all the ascended masters to be here with me now to lift my vibration and the vibration of this place to the level of divine Spirit. I ask these dear beings of light to fill this place with God's love, light, and truth."

4. CLOSE OFF YOUR AURA.

"I AM in control. I AM the only authority in my life. I AM divinely protected by the light of my Being. I close off my aura and body of light to all but my own God self. Thank you God and SO IT IS."

5. DO ANY HEALING PRAYERS THAT ARE NEEDED.

"I know that any dear ones who have come for healing are lovingly healed and forgiven. You are one with your own higher nature, your own divine selves. You are filled and surrounded with divine love. You are filled and surrounded with divine light. You are free from fear, pain, and the earth vibration. I ask the Holy Spirit to take you to your perfect place of expression. Go in peace.

"I invoke _____ [divine teacher] _____ to hear my prayer, to strengthen me and help me eliminate any false beliefs, concepts, thoughts, or vibrations that do not reflect the truth of my being. I discharge all thoughts such as _____ [negative thoughts] _____ and am lovingly healed and lifted in divine love and light. I AM enlightened, strengthened, and forgiven. I AM enlightened, strengthened, and forgiven. I am open and free to embrace positive, life-supporting, energizing thoughts of _____ [positive thoughts] _____ . I AM now in balance. I AM in control. Thank you God and SO IT IS."

(Include whatever healing prayers are needed at the time you are meditating.)

6. GO INTO DEEP MEDITATION STEP-BY-STEP.

"I now begin to take my awareness deep within to the level of divine Spirit. I now let go of the Environment. I let go of all my cares and concerns of the day. I give all my worries over to God. I allow God to be in charge of the circumstances in my life.

"I now take a deep breath and go deeper to the level of the Physical Body. I begin to relax every portion of my physical body step-by-step. I take a deep breath to relax my toes and my feet, my ankles, calves, and knees. I take another deep breath and relax my thighs and buttocks. I relax my lower back, my middle back, and my upper back. I take a deep breath to relax my entire back. Now I sink into the chair and let everything go. I relax my pelvic area, my abdominal region, my stomach, and my solar plexus. I take a deep breath into these areas and let them relax. I now relax my chest, my heart, and my shoulders. I let my shoulders drop as I take a deep breath. Now I relax the neck, the jaw, and the mouth. I take a deep breath and let the jaw and mouth drop. I let everything go. I relax every portion of my face. Now I relax my cheeks, my temples, my forehead, and my eyes. I relax the eyebrows and the space between the eyebrows. I relax every part of this body. I take a big, deep breath and release any tension in any part of my body.

"Now I relax and go deeper to the level of the Conscious Mind. I now let go of the conscious mind and allow it to relax to a state of pure peace and silence. I take a deep breath and allow my mind to settle down. The mind is perfectly serene, like a still, quiet pond. I now take a deep breath and go deeper.

"Now I relax my attention to the level of the Subconscious Mind. On this level I let go of all habits, patterns, and conditions that have caused me to believe that I am separate from God. I let go of all limitations and negations. I am now one with God and one with all life. I am pure divine intelligence. I now take a deep breath and go even deeper.

"I now take my attention deep within to the level of Spirit. I walk through the door of the façade barrier and allow myself to be unified with the truth of my being, God consciousness. I let go and let God give me divine wisdom and strength. I am open to receive a deepening of my inner contact in this meditation. I go deeper now to the level of my God self or better. I take a deep breath and go deeper."

7. PRACTICE THE PRESENCE OF GOD IN SILENCE.

"I now give this meditation over to God and allow myself to sink into the deep silence of my being, the level of pure transcendental consciousness."

(Sit in silence for a few minutes.)

8. CONTACT THE PERSONAL ASPECT OF GOD.

"I call upon _____ [aspect of God] _____ now to come and give me a signal . . ." (signal is fed). "Make the signal stronger, dear _____ [aspect of God] _____. Thank you. Do you come in the name of God? . . ." (Yes.)

9. PRACTICE SPEAKING-THROUGH, SINGING-THROUGH, OR
   ONE OF THE OTHER "ECSTATIC EXPRESSIONS OF GOD."

"Please feed me your message, dear ____ [aspect of God] ____."
(The message is fed and you practice speaking-through.)

10. ASK WHATEVER QUESTIONS YOU WISH TO ASK FROM SPIRIT.

"Dear ____ [aspect of God] ____, please give me the answer to the
following question: ____ [question] ____ .

(Example: "Dear Holy Spirit, I wish to know how to heal the relationship between myself and my son." Answer is fed and you speak it out.)

11. COME OUT OF MEDITATION STEP-BY-STEP
   WHEN YOU ARE READY.

"I thank God for this meditation and for all that I have received today.
I thank God for the divine messages from Spirit and the healings I have
received. I now begin to come out of this meditation step-by-step. I
come out bringing with me all the love, light, joy, power, and healing that
I have received in this meditation. I bring with me the presence and the
power of God.

"I begin by taking a deep, vigorous breath and bring back all this divine energy from the level of Spirit to the level of the Subconscious
Mind. I release all past conditions and habits, and my subconscious mind
is healed by God's love. I now take a deep breath and come out to the
level of the Conscious Mind. I know now that my conscious and subconscious minds are one with the divine mind. My individual will is united
with the will of God. I now take another deep, vigorous breath and come
out to the level of the Physical Body. The physical body is filled with energy, love, ecstasy, vitality, wholeness, and perfect health. This physical
body is one with my divine etheric body of pure light. I am becoming
more and more youthful as my body is raising its vibrational frequency. I
now take another deep, vigorous breath and come out to the level of the
Environment, knowing that on this level I am living the presence of God
in every moment. I know now that I am the living, breathing, walking,
talking temple of God. I am living my true divine purpose now."

12. COME ALL THE WAY BACK TO OBJECTIVE/SUBJECTIVE
   BALANCE.

"I now take four deep, vigorous breaths and come all the way back to
objective and subjective balance." (Take deep, vigorous breaths as

though you were blowing out a candle, and then open your eyes.) "I AM alert. I AM awake. I AM objectively and subjectively balanced. I AM in control. I AM the only authority in my life. I AM divinely protected by the light of my Being. Thank you God and SO IT IS!"

How to Use Your Meditation Tape

Once you have recorded the appropriate statements onto an audio-tape, you can use this tape to lead yourself into and out of meditation. This tape is to be used only in the beginning stages of your practice, to familiarize yourself with the Divine Revelation meditation technique. After you become practiced at this format, you can receive the words to speak from your own inner revelation rather than from a tape.

The tape is mainly for the purpose of leading yourself deep within at the beginning of your meditation and bringing yourself out of meditation at the end. Therefore, after you feel that you have achieved a deep state of silence within, it is a good idea to turn off the tape and allow yourself to experience the silence. When you feel that it is time to receive messages from Spirit, check your inner name and signal and the other nine tests (see chapter 13), and then receive inner revelation from your divine voice within. Then ask inner questions according to the format in chapter 14.

After you have enjoyed your meditation experience, turn your tape back on to lead yourself out of meditation. Be sure to use the tape to come out of meditation slowly, rather than just jumping out of meditation. Coming out of meditation too fast can have very negative results. You may feel disoriented, off balance, or headachy.

By following the suggestions in this chapter, the practice of meditation can become simple and easy, even commonplace, and your daily meditation experiences can become a thrilling adventure into the realms of inner space.

> "In returning and rest shall ye be saved; in quietness and in confidence shall be your strength."
> —Isaiah 30:15 (Judeo-Christian)

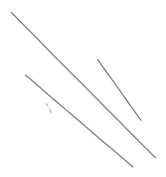

CHAPTER 9

Fine-Tuning Your Meditation Practice

A typical Divine Revelation meditation takes only a few minutes. You may enjoy meditating for ten minutes, or you may wish to take forty-five minutes to experience a deep meditation. It is not necessary to go into deep meditation in order to receive divine guidance, answers to questions, or healing. All you need to do is call upon your divine self, get your inner signals, use the safeguards, check the nine tests, and ask for what you desire. This can be done anytime, anywhere. The divine teachers are always present. But be sure you are clear by following the tests and safeguards outlined in chapters 13 and 14.

It is advantageous to have a regular time and place for deep meditation and to maintain that time and place without disturbances. In this way regular contact with the divine voice becomes habitual. In order to achieve a clear, consistent, reliable connection with your God-awareness, it is beneficial to meditate every day. In this way you can quickly deepen your inner contact and develop your ability to receive divine guidance.

When you first begin, it is better to focus more on receiving inner experiences than on receiving answers to your questions. Establish a clear, profound inner contact with the divine first. Then later you can learn to receive guidance from Spirit.

Divine Revelation deep meditation, revelation, healing, and prayer treatment are a four-pronged program for a balanced, graceful life with growth in God consciousness. Deep meditation means experiencing deep silence of the mind and relaxation of the body. Revelation means receiving messages from Spirit. Healing means practicing the healing prayers in chapter 10. Prayer treatment means creating goals and fulfilling your desires through the principles of manifestation.* With these four, practiced regularly, your life can soar to new heights of inner joy, fulfillment, and the glory of God.

THE FOUR FACETS OF FULFILLMENT

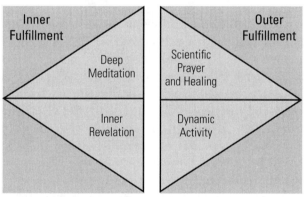

Four facets of fulfillment compose the diamond of a balanced life. Your inner life is enriched through practicing Deep Meditation and Inner Revelation. Your outer life is enhanced through using healing prayers, setting goals, practicing Scientific Prayer, and engaging in Dynamic Activity to fulfill your aspirations.

Be Innocent

There are no "right" or "wrong" experiences of meditation. Experiences will be different for each of you, and it is wise not to expect partic-

*Prayer treatment requires involved study and intensive practice. I recommend books by Ernest Holmes or Catherine Ponder to develop your prayer treatment skills.

ular results. God is in charge of your meditation, so you will get exactly what you need every time you meditate. By aligning yourself with the divine will, your meditation will be in divine order and timing.

The richness of inner experience grows with greater depth of inner contact during meditation. With the highest intent you can experience sublime realms of radiant joy and delight, known as the "celestial realms," or the bliss of divine union with God in the impersonal form, *satchitananda*. In any case, there is no "wrong" or "right" way to meditate or to experience God.

Joan Ashley, a therapist from Omaha who practices Divine Revelation, says: "I can tell you from the very first meditation that I had, I was filled immediately with bliss, and ecstasy of oneness with my own higher nature, with the Christ level, and this isn't a mood, because this same experience happens to me *every time* I sit down to have a Divine Revelation meditation."

God is always at the door, waiting for you to open it. Divine Revelation meditation technique is a wonderful way to invite God into your life. Your inner experience of God consciousness is a joy to yourself and the entire creation. For the deities, masters, and angels rejoice and celebrate whenever a human being breaks through the boundary of the façade barrier and experiences the supernal light of God. There is bliss and rejoicing at the opening of the heart of the devotee of God.

Frederica Sharf, a graduate of Divine Revelation from Burlington, Ontario, says: "It has been very uplifting to be able to close my eyes and go within and experience the radiation of my own God self in myriad ways. It's almost like this inner life that I had before ignored is now there, so lively and so thrilling to be a part of, and I look forward to my meditations, because my experiences have been so fun, exciting, enjoyable, filled with love and beauty, and a great sense of unity with all of creation, and that sense that my Self is the unifying factor of all of creation. So as far as particular spiritual experiences that I had before read about or heard about, I now find that they're frequent. Every time I practice Divine Revelation I have some *very* concrete beautiful spiritual experience."

Your first breakthrough may be a dramatic experience or it may be quite ordinary. In your subsequent meditations your experiences will always be different. Therefore, have an innocent, nonexpectant attitude. You may have an experience of opening to the heavenly realms one day.

Another day you may receive simple, ordinary messages from your inner voice. In every case be open to receive the highest wisdom and experience. Ask for what you want, then let go. It is not helpful to compare your meditations each with the other, to compare yourself with other students, or to judge your experiences against theirs.

Meditation Experiences

What experiences might you have on your path to God's presence? How can you recognize when you are in contact with the divine? You may have new experiences during meditation that you are unfamiliar with. Here are a few of them:

VIBRATIONAL LIFTING

You may experience a quickening of your vibration during meditation. This may manifest as an increase in your heart rate or breathing. Or it may be tingling of the body all over or in some area. You may receive rushes of energy throughout your body or a feeling that your cells are being speeded up. This is no cause for alarm. Your physical body is being transformed into the finer, more rarefied material of the light body, preparing you for ascension.

THE HOLY BREATH

You may find that you begin to spontaneously breathe in a quick, rhythmical pattern or another unusual pattern. Your breath may become fast or slow, shallow or deep. Just allow this spontaneous breathing to take place. It may be a vibrational lifting of your body, a quickening, a purification, or a clearing of blockages.

THE HOLY FIRE

You may feel that your spine or one of your *chakras* is on fire. You may experience intense heat, pleasure, or even pain, if there is resistance. This may be an awakening of *kundalini shakti* rising up your spine. *Kundalini* is the energy in the body that creates the inner awakening of bliss consciousness and self-realization. There is nothing to fear about this experience. It is quite natural and a result of your attainment of higher consciousness. You may feel your head being lifted or moved back, or you may notice your eyes rolling upward during this experience.

You might feel disorientation during the Holy Fire experience. If you feel you are getting out of control any time during meditation, simply affirm "I AM in control," and, if necessary, come out of meditation and do healing prayers before going back in. You will never receive more energy than you can handle. God is in charge of your meditation and will give you exactly what you need and what you are capable of safely experiencing.

PHYSICAL MOVEMENTS

Your body may shake, tremble, or rock during meditation. This is nothing to worry about. It is natural. Don't try to stop or resist it, neither try to encourage or perpetuate it. If it happens, just let it happen. The Shakers, Quakers, and other religious groups who have received divine experiences for centuries, can confirm that there is nothing to fear. God may move your body in specific ways to lift your vibration, to assist in your healing process, or to purify your mind or body.

LOVE FEEDINGS

The inner teachers may feed you ecstatic divine love to bring healing, comfort, or to heal your wounded heart. Love Feedings consist of unconditional love, pouring into your heart, mind, and body. You may feel ecstatic, rapturous feelings of love and unity with God during a Love Feeding. If the love energy becomes too powerful at any time, then consciously send out this energy to all of humanity. This sending out of the energy will help to dissipate its intensity and also assist in healing the planet.

POWER FEEDINGS

Power Feedings are feedings of inner power and strength that come from the divine teachers. These feedings lift your consciousness and bring inner power, strength, self-confidence, and self-authority. Power feedings are often feedings of spiritual power that assist you in expressing your true divine purpose. Usually such feedings are related to the healing, teaching, and lifting of humanity. By becoming a channel for God, you are taking on a responsibility to heal yourself and also the planet.

Power feedings may be pleasant, if there is no resistance, or they may be uncomfortable if you resist the added power being pumped into your mind and body. If you feel discomfort during a Power Feeding, then simply take some deep breaths and let go. Allow the power to be fed to you without resistance.

These feedings may be associated with the violet flame of Saint Germain, a violet-light feeding purifying your mind and preparing you to be a spiritual leader. It is your birthright to ascend, and the violet-flame feeding can be a part of this process. The lifting of humanity and cleansing of the planet to clear the way for ascension is facilitated by the violet flame. Call upon Saint Germain to assist you.

SAMADHI

During meditation, when you are very deep in silence, your body and mind may become very still. This is nothing to be frightened of. It is a sublime experience that has been sought for centuries—*satchitananda*, absolute bliss consciousness.

During this experience you may feel that your heart rate is slowed down, your breathing is so quiet that it becomes imperceptible, and you lose awareness of your body. You may feel completely absorbed in the self, in deep union with inner peace and quietude, a state of absolute tranquillity and serenity. You may have no thoughts in your mind and no awareness of your environment. You may feel one with the universe, expanded, unbounded. You may lose track of time and space. This is union with the impersonal aspect of God, called the transcendental (*samadhi*) state of consciousness.

Trouble-Shooting Meditation Problems

You might encounter a number of problems as you begin the practice of any form of meditation. Divine Revelation meditation is no exception. However, with the healing technologies in chapter 10, there is no reason why you cannot have successful meditations. Here are a few common problems that can easily be solved with the right knowledge.

PROBLEM:

You cannot go deep in meditation. You are stuck on the surface mental level and cannot experience Spirit within you.

SOLUTIONS:

1. Call upon an aspect of the divine to help you go deeper. For instance, "Jesus, take me deeper." Or

2. Take some deep breaths and relax and go deeper. Or

3. Take some deep breaths and with the release of each deep breath, imagine yourself getting out of your head and sinking into your heart. Or

4. Stop the meditation and speak out a healing prayer until you feel clear. Then take some deep breaths and go deeper.

PROBLEM:

You don't feel clear. You cannot get your signals clearly.

SOLUTION:

Stop the meditation and speak out whatever healing prayers are needed to purify your mind. Then take some deep breaths and go deeper.

PROBLEM:

You cannot settle down to meditate. You feel restless, and it is even difficult to begin.

SOLUTIONS:

1. Begin by praying. If you don't know how to pray, then read a prayer aloud from the Bible or other scriptures. Prayer helps to focus and settle your mind so that you can begin meditation from a deeper level. Or

2. Lie down and take a rest or a nap before you begin to meditate.

PROBLEM:

You fall asleep in your meditations. You can't seem to stay awake.

SOLUTION:

Take a nap before you attempt to meditate. If you still fall asleep, then it is okay. Sleep is not a disgrace. It is a sign of successful deep relaxation during meditation.

PROBLEM:

You get interrupted during meditation.

SOLUTIONS:

Before you meditate decide whether you wish to deal with interruptions when they occur or whether you wish to remain undisturbed. If you decide you wish to deal with interruptions, handle them quickly and then resume your meditation. *Never* break your meditation without later going back to finish it. If you decide that you wish to remain undisturbed, then take some of the following precautions:

1. Take the phone off the hook, turn off the phone ringer, or turn down the volume on the answering machine.
2. Put a do-not-disturb sign on your door.
3. Tell your children that you do not wish to be disturbed for a certain length of time.
4. Get a baby-sitter or a friend to watch your children while you meditate.
5. Close the door so that pets cannot jump into your lap while you meditate.
6. Have a regular time and place for your meditation.
7. Consider your meditation time sacred and treat yourself with the utmost respect.

PROBLEM:

You feel as if you are getting out of control.

SOLUTION:

Immediately stop your meditation and speak out loud the Self-Authority affirmation on page 131. Then take a few deep breaths and go deeper into meditation.

PROBLEM:

An experience alarms you and you feel afraid.

SOLUTION:

Immediately stop your meditation and speak out loud the Astral Entity Healing prayer on page 142. Then speak the Self-Authority affirmation on page 131. Then take a few deep breaths and go deeper into meditation. Repeat this process again if necessary.

PROBLEM:

You get an uncomfortable feeling in your body.

SOLUTIONS:

1. Say whichever of the healing prayers in chapter 10 you feel are needed. Then take a few deep breaths and go deeper. Or

2. Quietly put your attention on the area in the body that is giving you discomfort. Don't try to concentrate on the area or try to do anything. Just feel it quietly until it dissipates. Or

3. Call upon a name or aspect of God to heal that area for you. Example: "Mother Mary, please send a beautiful golden healing light to the area of my stomach now."

PROBLEM:

You are gripped by an intense emotion or thought during meditation.

SOLUTION:

Let yourself feel that intense emotion completely without resisting it. Allow it to run its course. Let your emotions flow. If you begin to cry or to get angry, don't resist. Let yourself feel the emotion without judging it or stopping it. Just feel it until it subsides. Then speak out the Thought-Form healing prayer on page 134. Then take a few deep breaths and go deeper into meditation.

PROBLEM:

You are not receiving the message from your divine self.

SOLUTIONS:

1. Call upon your inner teacher to take you deeper. Example: "Jehovah, take me deeper and feed me the message." Or

2. Take a deep breath and, as you breathe out, sink out of your head and into your heart. Or

3. Say whichever of the healing prayers in chapter 10 that you feel are needed. Then take a few deep breaths and go deeper.

PROBLEM:

You are not sure whether the message is clear.

SOLUTIONS:

Use the nine tests outlined in chapter 13. If you are still unsure about a message, then put it on the shelf and ask about it another day. Never take a message as truth if there is any doubt in your mind. If an answer is of great importance, then meditate on it many times before acting on it.

Be sure that each time you receive a clear, consistent answer. If you are still unsure, then ask someone else who practices Divine Revelation to check your answer with their inner signals.

PROBLEM:
You cannot seem to heal something that you have tried to heal.
SOLUTION:
Ask for help. You may ask a minister or a friend to speak out healing prayers for you. Here are addresses and phone numbers of those who can help:

Silent Unity Prayer Tower, 1901 NW Blue Parkway, Unity Village, MO 64065, 816-246-5400, 800-669-7729; World Ministry of Prayer, 3251 Sixth Street, Los Angeles, CA 90075, 213-385-0209, 800-421-9600 (twenty-four-hour prayer lines). See page 271 for more addresses.

PROBLEMS:
1. You can't get the experiences that you want in meditation, and it doesn't seem to work for you.
2. You don't feel motivated to meditate. You would rather skip it.
SOLUTION:
You would feel motivated if you were receiving experiences of divine Spirit within you. These experiences are so wonderful that you would look forward to meditation. If you are not having these experiences, you may wish to receive personal instruction. Take a class, a refresher course, or an advanced class in the Divine Revelation meditation technique from a qualified teacher. You can receive information on classes by contacting any of the addresses on page 271.

PROBLEM:
You feel spaced out, disoriented, disjointed, unfocused, or headachy after meditation.
SOLUTION:
Take enough time to come out of meditation. Don't jump up without coming out slowly first. Come out step-by-step and then take deep, vigorous breaths before opening your eyes. Say the affirmation in Point 12 on pages 114–15 after you open your eyes.

PROBLEM:
You feel negative emotions after meditation.
SOLUTION:
Do whatever healing prayers are needed for you to become clear.

"Verily, from meditation arises wisdom. Without meditation, wisdom wanes."

—*Dhammapada 282 (Buddhist)*

PART V
Spiritual Healing and Self-Defense

CHAPTER 10

Seven Basic Methods of Spiritual Healing

Learning to heal yourself through affirmation and prayer is central to receiving clear intuition from Spirit. Therefore, before you practice meditation and intuition techniques, it is essential to understand the principles and practice of healing.

Using healing affirmations is a precise, scientific way to keep the pathway to your inner contact clear. It is vital to speak healing prayers whenever you feel the need for healing and to *heal all the way*. The motto of Dr. Peter Meyer, the pioneer of this teaching, is "Heal first and ask questions later."

What exactly are you healing when you speak out healing prayers? It is the façade barrier, consisting of the subconscious mind or astral world, that is in need of healing. The storehouse of impressions of the subconscious mind includes encrusted beliefs that have separated you from your true divine nature. By learning to heal these thoughts, conditions, beliefs, patterns, and habits, you can keep your mind free and clear to receive divine guidance and inspiration.

Seven Keys to Spiritual Healing

In this chapter you will learn seven affirmations and prayers for healing yourself, others, and the planet as a whole. These powerful methods are keys to the door of God-Spirit.

The following are the seven methods:

1. Self-Authority—for closing off your aura to discordant vibrations around you and for maintaining self-sufficiency and self-reliance.
2. Prayer of Protection—for filling and surrounding yourself with God's presence and bringing divine protection into your daily life.
3. Thought-Form Healing—for letting go of discordant thoughts, emotions, and feelings and replacing them with positive ones.
4. Psychic-Tie-Cut Healing—for releasing karmic bonds with things in your environment that hold you back from expressing your true self.
5. Astral Entity Healing—for healing earthbound spirits and other beings who are stuck on the mental plane.
6. Past-Life-Mental-Body Healing—for releasing the limiting effects of past conditioning, habits, and beliefs.
7. Façade-Body Healing—for crumbling and releasing your ego-masks and encrusted, limited beliefs about yourself.

These healing prayers and affirmations, which are thoroughly explained in this chapter, can be very useful to incorporate into your daily life. It is not necessary to use these exact words. You may change the wording to suit your own needs, but be sure to maintain the meaning and feeling of the prayers.

Self-Authority

The first affirmation, called "Self-Authority," helps you maintain self-control and self-authority by closing off your aura. What does it mean to close off your aura? Many negative external influences can impinge upon you and cause disturbances in your aura, mind, and body. What are these influences? Here are a few examples:

1. The people in your family, the people at work.
2. The people whom you live with, the vibrations in your home.
3. The vibrations in places that you frequent.
4. The people on the street or in public places.

Many people might be termed "empathic." An empath is susceptible to feelings of others, particularly feelings of suffering, distress, or illness. Many empaths experience physical ills or emotional disturbances as a result of proximity with people who have such problems. Some empaths are influenced by vibrations and thought-forms around them. Such empaths are called "psychic sponges," because they absorb influences as a sponge absorbs water. As a result they are drained of energy. This is particularly true of some hands-on healers who are affected by diseases of their clients.

Some sensitives find that along with heightened psychic abilities come unpleasant experiences over which they seem to have no control. For example, parapsychological author Martin Ebon reports that a woman from Pennsylvania had successfully developed pronounced clairvoyant powers. But she was constantly plagued by certain odors that she frequently smelled and could not eliminate.[1]

Dorrie Rosen, a landscape architect from New York City, describes her experience: "I've had a lot of problems my whole life being negatively psychic, picking up things that were very negative, and it has affected my life in a negative way. I'm on a healing path now, since I've begun using certain prayers that I learned from Susan to protect myself from harm in a psychic way, to protect my essence from psychic attack. It's working for me, and I really have a lot of hope. This is very, very positive and protecting."

Even if you are not a psychic or an empath, people or vibrations around you, especially domineering or coercive people, may be influencing you adversely.

The following affirmation closes off your aura to negative influences but allows divine influences into your auric field. You are not closing yourself off to God and the spiritual plane. Here is the Self-Authority affirmation to maintain self-authority and integrity in the midst of vibrations around you:

I AM in control.
I AM the only authority in my life.

I AM divinely protected by the light of my Being.
I close off my aura and body of light to all but my own God self.
Thank you God and SO IT IS.

The phrase "I AM" in this affirmation means the "I AM" self. The "I AM" self is your higher self. Speak the words "I AM" as if your divine self within you is saying them. Now say this affirmation aloud with all the power of your "I AM" self behind it.

Do you feel the power of your words? Whenever you speak any affirmation, remember that the "I AM" self is speaking. This adds authority to your affirmations.

When would you use this Self-Authority affirmation?

1. Just before entering meditation or another subliminal state.
2. Just before going to sleep and upon first waking up in the morning.
3. Just before leaving your home.
4. Before entering any crowded place, such as a stadium, a nightclub, a subway.
5. Before meeting an authority figure, such as a boss, parent, judge, teacher.
6. Before any important event, such as a test, athletic competition, public speaking engagement, television appearance, sales presentation, phone call, court appearance.
7. Before entering a place with negative vibrations, such as a hospital, mental institution, prison, courtroom, bar, or a place where people use drugs.
8. Before meeting a client who comes to you for counseling, therapy, or body work.
9. When you feel negatively influenced or out of control, especially during meditation.
10. Any time you feel afraid or threatened.

Before an important event, speak the affirmation several times to gain self-confidence, even for fifteen to twenty minutes, as I did in the following instance.

I first used this affirmation several years ago when I had to appear before an intimidating board of inquiry. I phoned a teacher from Teaching of Intuitional Metaphysics and told him my dilemma. He dictated the Self-Authority affirmation and advised me to say it for fifteen minutes before going to the meeting. As I repeated the affirmation, I became increasingly filled with inner strength and arrived at the meeting feeling wonderful. Events turned to my advantage, and the board members ended up apologizing for any inconvenience.

Do not underestimate the power of this affirmation. It helps you to maintain clarity, balance, self-authority, self-integrity, and self-empowerment and to take responsibility for your life.

Prayer of Protection

This well-known affirmation from the Unity School of Christianity is called the Prayer of Protection. It is used to call upon the presence of God for divine protection. This prayer can be used any time you desire God's assistance:

The light of God surrounds me.
The love of God enfolds me.
The power of God protects me.
The presence of God watches over me.
Wherever I AM, God is, and all is well.

Experiment with speaking out this prayer now.

Using this prayer and visualizing a white light forming a pillar of protection around you is like having an armor of God's love to shield you. Imagine the white light of God as a sun above your head. Visualize a ray of this sun shooting through the top of your head down your body's midline to your feet. Imagine light radiating out from this ray, forming a pillar of white light surrounding your body with divine protection.

Now speak out the prayer and practice the visualization process described above. Feel God's protection washing over you with divine love.

Grace Suzuki, a college student who has been using these prayers of protection, states: "One thing I've experienced is a feeling of invincibility. When we know the healing prayers, we know that we are protected by the light of our own being, then there's no reason to fear, no matter where we go, no matter who we happen to be with. And this is a wonderful sense of security."

Thought-Form Healing

The Thought-Form Healing, as its name suggests, heals negative thought-forms. This powerful prayer can heal anything that needs healing. With this prayer you can heal any physical, mental, or emotional problem for yourself or for anyone else.

The premise of the Thought-Form Healing prayer, as Dr. John Gray, best-selling author and healer, says, is "What you feel, you can heal." In other words, when you identify the negative thoughts, feelings, emotions, patterns, habits, and conditions that influence you adversely, you can heal them. By turning your attention within, you can recognize these limiting beliefs and feelings.

Here is the Thought-Form Healing prayer:

I invoke _____ [divine teacher]
to hear my prayer, to strengthen me by helping me
eliminate any false or negative beliefs,
concepts, thoughts, or vibrations
that do not reflect the light and truth of my divine being.
I discharge any and all thoughts such as
_____ [negative thoughts]
and am instead lovingly healed and lifted in divine love and light.
I AM enlightened, I AM strengthened, I AM forgiven.
I AM enlightened, I AM strengthened, I AM forgiven.
(repeat until you receive your clear inner vibrational signal)
I am open and free to embrace positive, life-supporting,
energizing thoughts of _____ [positive thoughts]_____ .
I AM now in balance. I AM in control.
I thank you God and SO IT IS.

The prayer has three blank spaces. The first is for the name of a divine teacher or aspect of God whom you wish to call upon for help. The second is for whatever negative thoughts and feelings you are having at the moment. The third is for the positive feelings that are the opposite correlates to the negative ones that you just spoke out.

Now, do an exercise of speaking this Thought-Form Healing out loud. When you come to the second blank space, close your eyes and feel what negative thoughts come up for you. Speak these thoughts out loud. Then, open your eyes and read the prayer again until you come to the third space. Then close your eyes and speak positive thoughts that are the opposites of the negative thoughts. When you speak the words "I AM," imagine that your higher self is speaking those words. Do this exercise now.

Do you feel more positive and uplifted by healing negative thoughts and feelings?

The Thought-Form Healing prayer can be used whenever you need physical, mental, or emotional healing. This powerful prayer is a way to take command over your life by reversing negative emotions. Once you know this prayer, you no longer have an excuse to remain in a bad mood! You have the power to change it. If you wish to wallow in depression, sickness, self-pity, or what-have-you, you may choose to do that for as long as you like. But now you have a choice. You can speak out this prayer and begin to feel better. You can use this prayer any time you feel down, either physically, mentally, or emotionally. Do it. It works!

Whenever you feel stuck in thoughts and emotions during meditation, stop your meditation and use the Thought-Form Healing (or another healing prayer appropriate for the situation). Once you have healed, take deep breaths and go deeper in meditation.

When you use the Thought-Form Healing, say your negative thoughts and feelings, release them, and replace them with positive thoughts. For instance, if you feel guilt, the opposite would be forgiveness and self-acceptance. If you feel sadness, the opposite would be happiness and joy.

Here is a chart of thirty-six negative feelings and emotions and their opposites. If you are feeling any negative emotions listed on the left side of the chart, the Thought-Form Healing can help you. Use the left side of the chart for the second blank space in the healing prayer and the right side for the third blank space.

LIMITING BELIEFS	POSITIVE CORRELATES
1. Unworthiness, inadequacy	1. Self-worth, adequacy
2. Sadness, pain, grief, suffering	2. Happiness, joy, comfort, wholeness

LIMITING BELIEFS	POSITIVE CORRELATES
3. Guilt, shame, humiliation	3. Forgiveness, self-acceptance
4. Limitation, poverty	4. Abundance, prosperity
5. Fear, trepidation	5. Courage, faith, love
6. Anger, hatred, hostility	6. Love, forgiveness, friendliness
7. Blame, resentment, self-pity	7. Accepting responsibility, praise
8. Punishment, vengeance	8. Forgiveness
9. Doubt	9. Faith
10. Loss, incompleteness	10. Gain, oneness, wholeness
11. Rejection	11. Self-acceptance, self-love
12. Sickness, ill health	12. Health, wholeness
13. Confusion, disorder	13. Clarity, divine order
14. Inflexibility, stubbornness	14. Flexibility, letting go
15. Attachment, obsession	15. Letting go and letting God
16. Addiction, dependency	16. Independence, self-authority
17. Old age, death	17. Youthfulness, life, ascension
18. Coercion, domination	18. Permissiveness, respect
19. Conceit, egotism	19. Humility, seeing God in all
20. Judgment, criticism	20. Nonjudgment, appreciation
21. Tiredness, exhaustion	21. Vitality, energy
22. Depression, despair	28. Lightness, joy, love, hope
23. Frustration, obstruction, delay	23. Letting go, nonresistance
24. Anxiety, worry	24. Calm, relaxation, peace
25. Evasion, flight	25. Assuming responsibility
26. Manipulation	26. Letting go, allowing
27. Pressure, stress	27. Adequacy, resourcefulness
28. Burden	28. Giving over to God
29. Ego-façade, embarrassment	29. Naturalness, honesty
30. Fight or flight, survival	30. Nonresistance
31. Possessiveness, bondage	31. Release, freedom
32. Jealousy, competition, envy	32. Satisfaction, fulfillment, goodwill
33. Perfectionism	33. Self-acceptance, self-love
34. Impatience, irritation	34. Patience, tranquillity
35. Selfishness	35. Compassion, thoughtfulness
36. Mistake, error	36. Forgiveness, perfection

Psychic-Tie-Cut Healing

The Psychic-Tie-Cut Healing heals psychic bondage or psychic coercion. A psychic tie is an invisible, negative bond between yourself and something or someone in your environment. You may experience a psychic tie as an undue attachment or repulsion to a person, group of people, place, thing, organization, situation, circumstance, experience, or memory. Psychic bondage is on the astral level in the Feeling Mind. A true love bond, in contrast, is on the spiritual level of consciousness.

What creates psychic ties? They are made of negative thought-forms and emotions. For example, after arguing with a loved one, a residue of emotion remains after the argument. That residue manifests as a psychic tie.

A psychic tie is a phenomenon that arises in a subtle body known as the astral body. Psychic ties can be seen by clairvoyants as cords, ropes, or strings. They are often attached to your *chakras*. True love ties can also be seen by people with clairvoyant sight. These love bonds can be seen as golden cords of light. They can never be broken and are true spiritual love ties.

How does a psychic tie feel? You may feel it as a tug, a pull, an undue attachment or repulsion. Or you may feel intimidated, dominated, or coerced. You may experience it as an addiction, habit, or co-dependency. The psychic ties are never in any way positive. Nothing is gained by holding on to any psychic tie. In fact psychic ties can and do destroy relationships.

Under what circumstances would you do a Psychic-Tie-Cut Healing?

1. When you are being negatively influenced or controlled by someone or something.
2. When you are dependent on or addicted to a substance.
3. When you have completed an Astral Entity Healing and yet the entity has not left.
4. When you are overly attached to or obsessed with someone or something.
5. When you are in a coercive or manipulative environment, such as a cult.
6. When you are overly concerned about the opinions of others.

7. When you are under psychic attack or you are being controlled by black witchcraft.
8. On a daily basis to maintain harmony in your relationships with those close to you.

Here is the formula for the Psychic-Tie-Cut Healing:

I call upon _____*[divine teacher]*_____
to cut any and all psychic ties between
_____*[person]*_____ *and* _____*[thing, person, etc.]*_____ .
These psychic ties are now lovingly
cut, lifted, loved, healed, released, and let go
into the light of love and truth.
Thank you God and SO IT IS.

This prayer has three blank spaces. The first space is for calling on a divine teacher or aspect of God to help you. The second space is for naming the person for whom the prayer is being done. The third space is for naming the thing the person is cutting psychic ties with.

Experiment with this prayer now. When you come to the second blank space, put in the word "me." When you come to the third space, close your eyes and say the first thing that comes to your mind. Maybe it is a person or group of people, a place, a thing, or an organization. Perhaps it is a habit or addiction, a memory or experience. When using this prayer, cut psychic ties with just one thing at a time. Now speak out the prayer.

How did it feel to cut psychic ties? Did you feel a release? A feeling of freedom?

It is important to cut psychic ties whenever you feel a pulling from anyone or anything. This prayer can help free you from undue enmeshments and attachments.

Jennifer Long, a dietitian from Iowa, said, after using this prayer for a few months: "I feel less controlled by other people. I feel that if someone is trying to control me that I have a way that I can be detached from that."

It is beneficial to cut psychic ties daily with anyone with whom you have an ongoing relationship, such as a relative or an associate at work. This will not weaken or destroy intimacy. It will not create distance. Instead it will make relationships more loving, intimate, and personal. It will strengthen golden love ties, which are signs of true unconditional love and affection. Relationships improve by cutting psychic ties daily, because without tension and co-dependency, love can grow unhampered. Say this prayer daily and notice people near you responding with greater love and affection!

Astral Entity Healing

The next healing prayer is called the Astral Entity Healing. What is an astral entity? It is a bundle of thought-forms or memories left over after a person has died. This bundle is sometimes called the "astral body" or the "mental body," which remains after the physical body has dropped off.

Descriptions of near-death experiences have certain similarities; that is, they include leaving the body and seeing a brilliant light, often at the end of a tunnel or road. Departed relatives or guiding angels usher the way to the light. This universal description might lead one to believe that a divine light is entered after death.

Some people do not enter this light after death. They may try to return to the material plane, which they cannot do without a living physical body. So they wander about, confused and frightened, sometimes attempting to possess a physical body. These beings are called "earthbound spirits" or "discarnate entities." Some people call them ghosts, poltergeists, or demons.

Why would a person not go to the light? What would make one attempt to return to earth? Some of the reasons might be:

1. The person is very attached to the body, to the earth, or to people on earth.
2. The person's loved ones are very attached to him or her and won't let go.
3. The person does not believe in God or in life after death.
4. The person does not know he or she is dead due to an accidental or violent death.
5. The person committed suicide.
6. The person cannot let go of unfinished business on earth.
7. The person is confused and refuses to accept help from loved ones.

In the case where a person's astral body attempts to return to earth, the normal course of evolution after death does not take place. Astral entities are lost and trapped on the lower mental level. They are aware of people and things around them but have no physical body, so they cannot function on the material plane.

Astral entities are usually not harmful. They are just confused. Often they hang around their previous homes or loved ones. Some are mischievous or can be a nuisance. They may attempt to take over one's body or influence one's thinking.

Highly sensitive people may be influenced by astral entities. If these people leave their auras open, then they may become oppressed by or even possessed by an entity. In the case of "oppression" they are still in control of their faculties. "Possession" means they are so out of control that they forget their own identity.

When possessed people seek psychiatric care, they are given depressant drugs, which dull their nervous systems, and they are no longer aware of subtle experiences. If health care workers would use these healing prayers, they could possibly help those influenced by entities with less use of drugs. Reputable psychiatrists such as M. Scott Peck of Connecticut and Ralph Allison of California believe that many multiple-personality cases involve possession by discarnate entities and that exorcism can be helpful in curing such disorders.

In the Christian tradition entities are sometimes called "demons" or "devils." The Catholic religion uses rituals of exorcism to expel possessing entities. Pentecostals and other charismatic Christians drive out entities through "deliverance ministry" by laying-on of hands. In Judaism entities are called *dybbuk*, which can be exorcised by a *ba'al shem*, a rabbi with healing powers.

Exorcism or deliverance is traditionally believed to be the only way to release astral entities. The word "exorcism" means to "expel evil spirits." This implies that entities are evil and should be condemned and driven out. But exorcism, although it may successfully drive a spirit away, does not necessarily address the welfare of the spirit. The confused soul, wandering in the astral world, is still lost.

When a spirit is removed from one place, it often goes elsewhere. You may have expelled it from your sister, but it then might go to a neighbor, a child, or a dog. The spirit, wandering endlessly, just finds another home to inhabit. Our approach to astral healing is to speak lovingly to the spirit and send it to the light. This is effective because it heals the entity and sends it to its highest good, the light of God.

Another shortcoming of exorcism is that an outside agent is responsible for the release of the possessing entity. Ultimately, those overshadowed by entities must free themselves from entity possession by inner conviction and prayer, and disallow further entity possession by maintaining self-authority. Otherwise, when one entity departs, another may immediately jump in. The Self-Authority affirmation and Prayer of Protection can help prevent further entity possession. Only vigilant self-healing and self-authority can prevent an overly susceptible person from repossession after astral healing or exorcism.

"When the unclean spirit is gone out of a man, he walketh through dry places, seeking rest, and findeth none. Then he saith, I will return into my house from whence I came out; and when he is come, he findeth it empty, swept, and garnished. Then goeth he, and taketh with himself seven other spirits more wicked than himself, and they enter in and dwell there; and the last state of that man is worse than the first."[2]

When would you use the astral healing prayer? Here are a few examples:

1. When a person is possessed or you feel the presence of astral entities.
2. When you feel a dense, heavy, negative vibration or get a "creepy" feeling.
3. When you perceive that a person has black in his or her auric field.
4. When a person is mentally ill, suicidal, or displays bizarre behavior.
5. When one receives negative telepathic messages, unpleasant voices, or hallucinations.
6. When a person has depression, bad health, excessive fatigue, or lethargy.
7. When a person is unusually angry or bad-tempered.
8. When a person awakens from a nightmare or bad dream.
9. When a child has a temper tantrum.
10. When a person is addicted to drugs, alcohol, or other substances.

11. When a person suddenly speaks with a different voice, dialect, or accent.
12. When a person exhibits multiple personalities.
13. When a person is under psychic attack.
14. When unusually mischievous or negative things happen.
15. When there is a series of misfortunes or "bad luck."

Who are most susceptible to entity possession or entity influence?

1. Mentally ill, depressed, unduly angry, or out-of-control people.
2. Those dependent on drugs, alcohol, or other addictions.
3. People who meditate too much and are overly subjective.
4. "Psychic sponges," channelers, or spirit-mediums who leave their auras open.
5. People who frequent psychics, spirit-mediums, or channelers.
6. Those who experiment with the occult without proper guidance.
7. People who astral-travel seeking out-of-body experiences.
8. Lethargic, directionless people, or physically ill, unconscious, or comatose people.
9. Practitioners of black witchcraft or those controlled by black witchcraft.

If you fall into one of these categories, you may have had exposure to entities. If you know someone who falls into one of these categories, you can help him or her with the Astral Entity Healing prayer (that is, if that person desires to be healed). This is the format of the prayer:

Dear ones, you are healed and forgiven,
You are one with your own higher nature,
Your own divine selves.
You are filled and surrounded with God's love.
You are filled and surrounded with God's light.
You are free from fear, pain, and from the earth's vibration.
I call upon _____ [divine teacher] _____
To take you to your perfect place of expression.
Go in peace.[3]

In this prayer you are speaking directly to the entities being healed. In the blank space put the name of a divine being who comes in the name of God. Once you have spoken this healing, you may heal the person troubled by the astral entity as follows:

I now call upon _____ [divine teacher] _____
To fill and surround _____ [person] _____
With divine love, divine light, and divine truth.
I know that _____ [person] _____ 's aura and body of light
Are now closed off to all but his/her own God self.
Thank you God and SO IT IS.

This prayer has three blank spaces. In the first blank, place the name of the divine teacher whom you are calling upon to heal the person. In the second and third blanks, put the name of the person being healed. Now speak these two prayers aloud.

How did it feel to use this prayer? Did you feel a shift in consciousness or a vibrational lifting? This prayer should produce the effect of a burden being lifted and a greater lightness, as you feel the entities being healed and taken into the light of God.

This prayer can be used any time you feel astral entities need healing. In cases of heavy possession or mental illness, the afflicted person can use this prayer along with the Self-Authority affirmation, the Prayer of Protection, and Psychic-Tie-Cut Healing (cutting psychic ties with the entity) several times a day. There is nothing to fear when you possess this knowledge of entity healing. You can handle any situation, armed with this prayer.

Past-Life-Mental-Body Healing

The Past-Life-Mental-Body Healing is for healing mental bodies from a person's past. What is meant by this? It heals past memories that have crystallized into form. They may be memories of this present incarnation or a past incarnation. In either case past memories can take subtle form in the astral world and behave like an astral entity.

Some people think of this mental body as the astral body left behind upon a person's transition* from a past life. Others may think of it as a

---

*The term "transition" means death, but it implies a transformation into another state rather than a finality.

memory with no real form or structure to it. In either case the same healing applies.

When is it appropriate to use such a healing?

1. When a memory from a past life comes up for healing.
2. When a person is obsessed with a past life.
3. When a trauma, heavy memory, or other experience from a past
   life adversely affects the present life.
4. To heal the past-life cause behind a negative pattern.

The Past-Life-Mental-Body Healing has the same format as the Astral
Entity Healing on page 142, since the past life mental body is a type of
astral entity.

Façade-Body Healing

The "Façade-Body Healing" is for healing façades or masks that cover
up your true self. A façade body is a subtle body made of crystallized
negative habitual unconscious thought-forms and patterns. These dense
thought-forms can form a subtle body.

The façade body is an armor or mask that identifies you in limited
ways. Your ego and self-image consist of many of these masks. For instance, you may have a façade body comprising a belief that you are a
macho male. This façade makes an impression on others and determines
how they respond to you. But it is not real. It is made of beliefs or
thought-forms that create an illusion of being macho. When people get
to know you better, they realize you are a human being with both weak-
nesses and strengths, just like anyone else. But this façade is an armor of
defensiveness that many cannot penetrate.

If you become aware of a façade or mask, heal it with the following
prayer:

I call upon _____ [divine teacher] _____
To heal any façade bodies of _____ [nature of façade] _____
That are surrounding _____ [person] _____ .
These façade bodies of _____ [nature of façade] _____
Are now lovingly

Cracked open, crumbled up, dissolved, healed, released, and let go.
Thank you God and SO IT IS.

The first blank space is for calling upon an aspect of divinity to help you. The second blank is for naming the nature of the façade body. For example, you may have a façade body of unworthiness, superiority, fear, victimization, or any other negative thought or belief. The third blank space is for naming the person being healed. The fourth space is for naming the nature of the façade body again.

Now speak this prayer out loud, filling in the second and fourth blanks with the façade body that you feel you need to heal. Close your eyes when you come to these blanks to get in touch with what façade needs healing.

Did you experience a feeling of freedom and release from speaking this prayer?

This prayer can be used any time you feel an unreal mask or armor preventing you from expressing your true, innocent self. If you feel the presence of façade bodies during meditation or during the day, then speak out this healing prayer.

"Under shelter of the Supreme Being, not a whiff of hot air touches us—all around us is drawn the mystic circle of divine protection, keeping away all suffering."

—Adi Granth M.5 (Sikh)

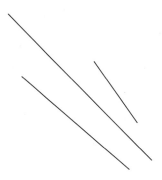

CHAPTER 11

Ways to Heal Psychic Trauma

It has been said by Babaji, one of our inner teachers, through Dr. Peter Meyer, "Man adds fear to God's message." That means that even though you might sincerely desire to receive clear intuition, your own habits, patterns, conditions, and beliefs may prevent it. Also, environmental influences can get in the way.

In the early days of the telephone, there was static on the line. But with the advent of more sophisticated technologies, the static disappeared and now reception is clear. Similarly, with the planetary growth of divine consciousness, messages from Spirit will become clearer. Meanwhile, be vigilant to heal what prevents you from clarity.

The importance of healing cannot be overemphasized. It is vital to use healing prayers, because the consciousness of the earth is not yet free from negativity. Billions of thought-forms and entities are swirling around the atmosphere. These influences prevent clear, precise reception of true divine revelation from Spirit.

Many students learned Divine Revelation and later complained that at first they received clear messages from Spirit, but after a few months their inner signals disappeared and they no longer received clear messages. I asked them, "Have you been using your healing prayers before and during your meditations?"

They would invariably say, "What healing prayers?"

I would say, "The ones that you learned in the course. Healing is essential to receiving clear messages from Spirit."

Doctor, Heal Thyself

In order to maintain purity of consciousness and keep the inner pathway clear, healing is necessary. Few people are entirely immune to lower vibrations of negative thought-forms or entities from the astral world. Therefore, it is common to be negatively affected by outside influences. An entity or a low vibration can disturb the harmony of your consciousness. Here are a few simple guidelines for maintaining a clear mental and emotional state.

1. Any time that you feel "off" or something is "wrong," immediately do a healing.
2. Heal all the way, until the healing is completed and you receive clear signals.
3. If you feel the presence of entities, heal them immediately.
4. If you feel negative, weak, or physically ill, then heal.
5. If you feel something adversely influencing you, then heal.
6. Close off your aura before sleep, meditation, or before entering any crowded place.
7. Maintain self-authority and be in charge of your mind.
8. Never try to receive intuition when you are not clear. Heal first.
9. Close off your aura before seeing a client, an authority figure, or any intimidating person or situation.
10. Don't wallow around in negative emotions. Heal them immediately.
11. Ask for prayer help if you can't do it alone. Don't delay in asking for assistance.

Sabrina Gao, a holistic health practitioner and student of Divine Revelation from Philadelphia, describes her experience: "I think that the as-

pect of healing that this teaching teaches is a wonderful means of healing not only ourselves, but also the people we come in contact with. As
we grow in this inner contact, we learn that all we have to do is ask for
what we want. If we wish to have light and vibrational lifting, and be
filled with truth, and any untruth we may be harboring in our minds,
known or unknown to us, be lifted, we can do this just through these
very special healing prayers."

Ways to Use These Healings

You can use these healing prayers and affirmations in any negative or
uncomfortable situation to heal yourself and those around you, or to
heal others at a distance. Here are examples of how Divine Revelation
students have used these healing prayers effectively.

Jackie Ostrowski, a mother from Grand Rapids, Michigan, says: "I
have one daughter. She is happy most of the time, but two-year-olds go
through something called the 'terrible twos.' I've noticed that when I'm
centered in my God self, she is calm, happy, and doesn't misbehave. If
I'm not centered, that's when she gets cranky or sick. She immediately
reflects what's off in me. I've learned how to do certain healings, to correct negative thinking or behavior within myself. When I correct what's
off within me, she becomes healthy and happy again."

Another mother, Arlene Thompson, who lives in Houston, Texas, describes: "I'm a single mother, and it's a very challenging situation to be
in. A technique that we learned in the course was how to heal negative
thought-form patterns. I very quickly got into the habit—when I started
feeling grumpy, irritable, or tired, then I would use those healing techniques. It didn't take long for my son to figure it out, because I began using them for him, when he was being grumpy. Now, if I'm grumpy, he
says, 'Mom, do your healing!' He's seven years old but he reminds me
regularly if I forget."

Here is how one wife from Idaho uses these healing techniques in her
marriage: "We used to really get into the nitty-gritty of all of the blame
and anger, and everything that blows up into a big argument. Now, as
soon as we notice that there's antagonism, we do our best to go within
and lift ourselves to our God self, doing whatever healing has to be done,
whether it's negative thought-forms we've been thinking about each

other, feelings of resentment or blame or guilt, and actually healing that and elevating it into the light, giving it up to God, and then going back and relating to each other from our God center. We've just found *incredible* smoothing out of situations and a reestablishment of the love and harmony and the connection between us."

There are times when it is necessary to heal intense emotions or deep traumas of the past. In order to get in touch with deeper emotions and the innermost causes of your negative patterns, you can make use of the suggestions offered here.

Forgiveness Healing

The purpose of the forgiveness healing prayer is to forgive those who you feel have wronged you. Without forgiveness, it is not possible to love. Lack of forgiveness restricts the flow of life. Holding on to grudges, anger, and resentment causes mental, emotional, and physical problems. When you forgive, you open to loving unconditionally.

This Forgiveness Healing can be used any time someone needs to be forgiven, for whatever reason. To use this prayer, simply fill in the names of the persons who are healing and forgiving their relationship. "(A)" would be the person for whom you are praying, and "(B)" would be the person whom (A) wishes to forgive.

I now call upon the divine self within (A) and (B) to shine the light of forgiveness on their/our relationship now. I know that the forgiving power of God within (A) and (B) heals this relationship in perfect forgiveness now. The divine self within (A) completely forgives (B) now, for (B) did the very best that he/she could do in every situation with (A). The divine self within (B) completely forgives (A) now, for (A) did the very best that he/she/I could do in every situation with (B). Therefore, there is no reason for guilt or for blame.

I know now that (A) thanks/thank (B) for everything that he/she has done in every situation with (A). I know and accept now that on a deep, unconscious level within (A), (A) asked for everything that happened in his/her/my relationship with (B). Therefore (A) takes/take full and complete responsibility for everything that (B) has done in every situation with (A) now.

So (A) pictures (B) before (A) now and (A) says/say, "Thank you, (B). You have fulfilled my need and my desire. I thank you for being a vehicle for me to fulfill my need now." So the God within (A) forgives (B) completely now and the God within (B) forgives (A) completely now.

I call upon the power of God to cut any and all psychic ties between (A) and (B) now. These psychic ties are now lovingly cut, lifted, loved, healed, released, and let go. (A) therefore accepts/accept fully and completely the healing of his/her/my relationship with (B) now. Thank you God and SO IT IS.

Now speak out this prayer yourself. Fill in the (A) blank with "me" and fill in the (B) blank with the first person that comes to your mind whom you need to forgive.

Did you feel greater love for this person after you spoke out the prayer? As with all of these healing prayers, "What you feel, you can heal." It is very important to feel the prayer as you are saying it, not simply speak it out by rote. These healings can be very powerful if they are FELT completely. While you are praying, it is a good idea to close your eyes and picture the one whom you are forgiving, speaking lovingly to him or her. This prayer can be used any time you wish to heal a relationship, during meditation or during the day.

Fight-or-Flight Reaction Healing

The "fight-or-flight reaction" is an instinctive physiological response to situations of life-threatening danger. Your heartbeat and breathing increase, and your adrenal glands produce more epinephrine, creating faster responses and heightened sensory perception. However, the fight-or-flight reaction can sometimes be triggered in situations of no real physical danger. Such a response takes place when you feel psychologically threatened and enter a defense/attack mode. You may overreact inappropriately to situations that are not actually dangerous by either fighting (becoming excessively angry) or by fleeing (leaving the premises or shutting down emotionally).

Inappropriate fight-or-flight responses are carryovers from childhood situations of seeming danger. For example, a baby whose father shouts abusively at her feels that her life is being threatened. Then, in adult-hood, when her husband raises his voice, she may react with a fight-or-flight response and enter a defense/attack mode. When confronted with this situation, she may react by getting out of control or by shutting down emotionally.

Here is a way to heal this reaction:

Step 1: Acknowledge that you are in a fight-or-flight reaction.

Step 2: Close your eyes and identify the feeling that you are having, whether it be anger, fear, blame, or whatever.

Step 3: Ask your divine teacher to tell you what the cause of this feeling is.

Step 4: Continue to feel your feelings without resisting them until you feel the charged intensity of your emotions begin to discharge and dissipate.

Step 5: Ask your divine teacher to let you know what experience from your past is associated with this feeling.

Step 6: Forgive the person associated with this past memory.

Step 7: Forgive the person associated with the present fight-or-flight reaction.

Step 8. Ask your divine teacher to help you with appropriate healing prayers.

Here is an example of how this healing might be used in a hypotheti-cal situation:

A woman has a date with her boyfriend. She spends four hours driving to meet him. After spending half an hour together, he informs her that she cannot stay overnight at his house that night because he wants his "space." She reacts with anger at his insensitivity and immediately bolts out the door, even though she has to drive another four hours to get home. When she gets to her car, she is completely overcome with in-tense emotions.

Step 1: She acknowledges that she is in a flight response.

Step 2: She closes her eyes and feels intense fear.

Step 3: She says, "I call upon Babaji to tell me the cause of this feel-ing of fear." She receives the message that she is feeling this because she is afraid that her boyfriend will abandon her.

Step 4: She continues to feel her fear of abandonment without resisting the feeling. After some time the charged intensity of the emotion seems to discharge.

Step 5: She says, "I now ask Babaji to tell me what experience from childhood is at the basis of this fear of abandonment, causing this flight response." She receives a vision of herself crying in her crib as a baby. No one comes to pick her up. She feels terrified that her life is being threatened.

Step 6: She says, "I now forgive you, Mother, realizing that you did the best that you could do at the time. I now know that my life was not threatened by this situation and that I was safe. I know that you love me and that you did not abandon me."

Step 7: She says, "I now forgive my boyfriend, and I know that you did not mean to hurt me. I know that you love me and you do not want to abandon me. I know that you are doing the best you can do, and there is no reason for blame. I forgive you."

Step 8. She says, "I now call upon Babaji to cut any and all psychic ties between myself and my mother and between myself and my boyfriend. These psychic ties are lovingly cut, lifted, loved, healed, released, and let go. I now release all feelings of fear of abandonment now. I know that my life is not threatened, and I can now react appropriately to this situation. I am now filled with new creative thoughts of self-love, security, and inner peace. Thank you God and SO IT IS."

Healing of Past Traumas

Most of us have had traumatic experiences that we can or cannot remember. Sometimes these experiences can be difficult to deal with. Should you forget about them or dig them up and attempt to heal them?

My belief is "What you feel, you can heal." In order to heal these experiences, it helps to feel their effects. So while it may not be necessary to remember the details of the traumas, feeling the emotions connected with them can help to heal them.

The following is one way to help heal past traumatic experiences:

Step 1: Begin by getting comfortable. Be in a safe, warm, loving environment—whether your bed, bathtub, easy chair, couch, or backyard.

Step 2: Call upon the divine teachers and God self within you to help you heal whatever pattern needs healing. As long as you put your healing process into the hands of God, it will be taken care of in divine order and timing.

Step 3: Recognize and *feel* a habitual negative pattern you have noticed within yourself. Get fully in touch with that pattern by feeling fully the emotion of it.

Step 4: Ask your inner teacher to show you the experience or memory that is the cause of this pattern. You might then receive a vision, memory, or message.

Step 5: Begin to *feel* this past experience or memory. Feel fully the emotions that come up for you, without holding back. Express your emotions in whatever way is effective for you. If you feel like crying or getting angry, do not hesitate. Do not hold back your feelings, try to push them away, or deny them. Say them out loud if necessary, speaking honestly to the people of the past who have hurt you. Go all the way with your feelings, without any resistance. Once you allow yourself to feel without holding back, the emotions will begin to dissipate.

Step 6: Ask your inner teacher to help you heal this trauma.

Step 7: Ask your inner teacher to speak lovingly to that child or teenager who is your former self. Speak words of healing and comfort to that ten-year-old or whatever age you are in that memory.

Step 8: Now you will be ready to speak out healing prayers. Do not use the healing prayers from chapter 10 to heal intense emotions or traumas without first going through this process. Otherwise you may gloss over problems and not get to the core of your healing.

Here is a hypothetical situation in which this healing prayer could be used:

Step 1: A pregnant woman gets into a safe, comfortable environment.

Step 2: She says, "I call upon Jesus Christ to help me heal my pattern of terror of losing my unborn baby."

Step 3: She now gets in touch with the feeling of this pattern.

Step 4: She says, "Dear Jesus, please give me a vision or memory at the basis of this pattern." She closes her eyes and sees a vision of herself in her bed as a child. She sees herself waking up, coughing and crying.

She then asks, "Jesus, why am I coughing?" She now sees a vision of her mother running into her bedroom, screaming.

She asks, "Jesus, what does this have to do with this pattern?" She now sees herself as a child at her sister's funeral. She is given the message that her baby sister was killed in a fire because her father couldn't get to the baby fast enough. Her divine teacher, in wisdom, doesn't want her to relive the trauma of the actual events of the fire.

She asks, "Jesus, how does this relate to my fear of losing my child?" She now sees a vision of herself at the funeral, making a vow: "I swear that I'll never have a baby, I'll never have a baby as long as I live."

Step 5: Now she speaks to her father the emotions that are coming up for her: "I'm so angry at you, father, for not saving my sister. I feel sad and hurt that you didn't reach her in time, and I feel guilty, thinking that it is my own fault. If I hadn't been there, my sister would have been saved."

Step 6: She says, "Jesus, please help me heal this pattern."

Step 7: She now speaks lovingly to her six-year-old inner child, saying, "Dear child, you are free from blame. You have done nothing wrong. You need not punish yourself for this experience. You did the best you could do in the situation at the time. Therefore, there is no reason for guilt or blame."

Step 8: She now forgives her father. She pictures him in her mind and says, "Dear Father, I forgive you for not being able save my sister. I let go of the guilt and the blame. I know that you did the best you could. I know that I can let go of the idea that I will lose my baby. I let go of the resistance to having children that I created through this experience. I forgive myself completely now, knowing that I did the best I could do with my level of consciousness at the time. I call upon the Holy Spirit to release the belief that I will lose my child now. This thought is lovingly lifted, healed, and released into the light, and it is gone. I know and accept now that I am willing to have children and I am willing to keep my baby. Thank you God and SO IT IS."

During this process, if intense emotions come up, allow them to take place, without resistance. In this way you may begin to heal old habits, patterns, and conditions. With God's help, you can heal anything and create miracles in your life.

The "Healing Consciousness"

It is possible to develop a "healing consciousness," that is, a consciousness so clear and pure that others coming near your auric field are positively affected and cannot remain on a low vibrational level. That is because the purity of your crystalline consciousness automatically heals anyone who comes near it. Even fierce animals can behave like harmless house cats around you, as they did with the *yogis* of India or Daniel of the Bible.

A "healing consciousness" is developed through an attitude of continual, abiding love. It is sustained by self-authority: a state of self-reliance, self-discipline, and dominion over your life. In this state you are unaffected by your environment. Your inner light is so great that it radiates around you, creating a beautiful sphere of protection.

You can begin to develop self-authority by maintaining purity of consciousness through the healing prayers enumerated in chapters 10 and 11. There are many aspects to self-authority. A few of them are:

1. Knowing who you really are on the deepest level.
2. Identifying yourself with your divine self rather than your ego.
3. Maintaining dominion over your mind and emotions.
4. Loving yourself fully, loving God fully, and loving others fully.
5. Being in control of your life and taking charge of your destiny.
6. Maintaining continual divine protection from within.
7. Keeping your aura closed off to all but your own God self.

Here are ten doors through which self-authority can be developed:

1. Healing all the way.
2. Acquiring and maintaining a clear contact with Spirit.
3. Practicing the presence of God through the "ecstatic expressions."
4. Praying, affirming, and decreeing the truth of your being.
5. Setting goals, and praying and working to achieve them.
6. Living in harmony and love with others.
7. Practicing the Be-attitudes, true spiritual qualities.
8. Achieving deep meditation and inner silence.
9. Engaging in dynamic, purposeful, and fulfilling activity.
10. Living your true heart's desires and true purpose.

Healing is a key that unlocks many of these doors. Even doors that have been locked tightly can be opened with the key of healing. Healing is a way to open your consciousness to new levels by breaking through the façade barrier. It is a key to the door of Spirit.

Healing is the seal that protects, secures, and maintains the healing consciousness and the status of true self-authority. It is the glorious jewel on the crown of eternal life on which is engraved *"Shalom."** Ever-abiding and glorious peace in the heart of God is the gift of this seal. Start healing now and live a life of divine glory and fulfillment!

> *"Thy faith hath made thee whole."*
> —Mark 5:34 (Christian)

Shalom is Hebrew for "peace."

PART VI
Becoming Spiritually Street-Smart

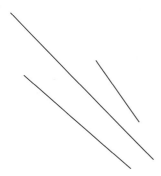

CHAPTER 12

Voices of Self-Sabotage

Why is it important to master the art of spiritual discernment? What is the value in learning to tell the difference between messages from the divine voice and "other voices" you might "hear" in your mind?

As you attempt to receive intuition from your inner divine voice, you may hear false voices of self-sabotage that interfere with and block your ability to receive clearly. These voices fall into four basic categories:

1. The voice of your subconscious mind, past experiences, and memories.
2. The collective voice of society and humanity.
3. The voice of your immediate environment.
4. The voice of an astral entity or spirit.

You are continually bombarded with a massive input of messages and sensory experiences from your environment. These myriad voices and memories can influence you adversely, creating confusion and negativity in your mind. Everyone is influenced by these voices, yet each person experiences them in a unique way.

Let us examine what voices have influenced your life adversely and what voices you hear in your mind.

Voices Influencing Your Mind

In this section are four categories of voices that could influence you adversely. These examples may not describe your situation exactly, and your experiences may not be this negative. Still, many people are influenced to some degree by each of these categories:

1. THE VOICE OF YOUR SUBCONSCIOUS MIND, PAST EXPERIENCES, AND MEMORIES.

a. The voice of negative beliefs and experiences.

You learned negative beliefs about yourself from traumatic experiences and from influential voices of your past. This voice may sound something like: "I'm not good enough. I'm not as good as others. I'm not worthy to be prosperous, happy, loved, etc. I'm addicted to my habits and can't change them. I don't care about myself. I'm afraid, sad, angry, guilty, resentful, etc. I'm sick. I'm a victim. Bad things happen to me. I'm out of control."

b. The voice of your parents.

Your parents taught you to believe what they believed. Even if they were wonderful people, they may have inadvertently taught you conditional love, condemning judgment, reward and punishment. They taught you by their example and their words: "Be like us, do what we say, then you'll get our approval and you'll be safe. If you're bad, you won't be safe. Boys don't cry. Girls don't get angry. If you talk about inner experiences, you are a liar or a weirdo. If we abuse you, don't tell anyone. Obey us and don't think for yourself."

c. The voice of your religion.

Your religion was your ultimate authority, the word of God, and not to be disputed: "God should be feared. God will reward you if you follow the rules. If you don't, you will die and rot in hell in eternal damnation. If you're good, you will go to heaven for eternity. Metaphysical study is the devil's work."

d. The voice of your teachers.

Your teachers filled your consciousness with societal beliefs. They may have taught you to be like everyone else, to follow rules, to passively obey authority figures: "If you don't get good grades, you'll be a failure. You must be like the other children. Don't make waves. Don't think for yourself. Do what we say. Believe us without question. Everything we teach is the ultimate truth."

e. The voice of your community.

Your community was your breeding ground for conformity. If you were different from others, you were ostracized. You may have learned racism and sexism there: "Be like everyone else in your peer group. If you deviate from the norm, you'll be criticized. Stay in your own part of town. You must date boys or girls from your own social status, religion, and race. Other races and religions are inferior."

2. THE COLLECTIVE VOICE OF SOCIETY AND HUMANITY AS A WHOLE.

a. The voice of society.

From society you learned how to fit into its hierarchical structure. You learned fear of being out of the ordinary: "Live a normal life with a nine-to-five job, a new car every three years, a house, a mortgage, and two-point-three children. Political leaders have superior intelligence and should rule over you. They always have your best interests in mind. Give them the responsibility of governing and don't question their authority. Our judicial system gives fair treatment. Law enforcement officers, lawyers, and judges uphold your constitutional rights."

b. The voice of the medical orthodoxy.

The medical establishment taught you to fear sickness, old age, and death, to think that drugs are the only cures to illness, to believe that many diseases have no cures and are therefore "fatal": "The AMA is the only authority. Never trust the quackery of holistic medicine. The only possible cause of your illness is the one your doctor diagnoses. If you are ill, then you need drugs. Prescribed drugs never aggravate your condition. If there is no drug to cure your disease, then you are sentenced to death. As a patient, you don't have the intelligence to take care of yourself. You should obey your doctor's and your insurance company's orders."

c. The voice of the patriarchy.

Men have ruled for so long that their dominance is taken for granted. Steps have been taken toward liberation, but patriarchal beliefs are so deeply ingrained that they may still influence people in subtle, powerful, ways: "Men are more intelligent than women and should make decisions for them. Women should be soft-spoken and never complain or get angry. Women's concerns and careers are never as important as their husbands'. It is taboo for women to marry younger men, but men are privileged to marry younger women. Women should not expect salaries equal to men's. Women who are intelligent, aggressive, dominant, or bossy are unattractive and undesirable. Men who are intelligent, aggressive, dominant, and bossy are attractive and desirable."

d. The voice of the human race.

You learned your most fundamental values and beliefs from the human race. These beliefs seem indisputable: "There is good and evil. You'll be punished for being bad and rewarded for being good. The universe and society are intrinsically evil. Life is a struggle and everyone suffers. Money is the root of all evil. Only the fittest can survive. Fear is the greatest motivator."

3. THE VOICE OF YOUR IMMEDIATE ENVIRONMENT.

a. The voice of people around you.

Your family members, friends, and co-workers may have rigid ideas about you, and you may be negatively influenced by their opinions. People around you may even be coercive or domineering: "Don't do anything out of the ordinary, or we will criticize you. Don't make any changes in yourself, or we will reject you. We know what is 'best' for you. Don't take risks or make waves. Be like us and we will continue to like you."

b. The voice of the media.

This voice is heard every day through the newspaper, television, and radio: "Buy this product or service and you'll be beautiful, glamorous, exciting, wealthy, young, vibrant, and attractive to the opposite sex. Cigarettes and alcohol are glamorous and desirable. Youth is to be valued."

c. The voice of telepathy.

You can pick up people's thoughts or receive messages telepathically if you are very sensitive. You may be influenced by vibrations of people or places around you. You might even be plagued by audible telepathic mind reading. These experiences can arise from experimentation with drugs or the occult.

4. THE VOICE OF AN ASTRAL ENTITY OR SPIRIT.

You may hear voices or messages from spirits of the astral world, either audibly or inaudibly. These spirits may communicate with you, and you may pick up their messages. They may attempt to control your mind or use your body. Opening your mind through drugs, meditation, or mediumship can cause such experiences.

HOW THESE VOICES INFLUENCE YOU.

Voices from these four categories may subconsciously influence your mind daily. Understanding where these voices come from helps you to realize the importance of spiritual discernment when delving into intuitive study. Thoughts, visions, and feelings received through spiritual sensing vary dramatically from those received in the "normal" thought process. The divine voice differs profoundly from these subconscious voices.

Now let us examine the dangers of opening yourself to inner voices indiscriminately.

"Channeling"

"Channeling" seems to be a trendy idea, but this practice is not new. From the *rishis* of ancient India to prophets of the Bible, from the oracle at Delphi to the Spiritualist Church, mediums, psychics, and soothsayers have been consulted. But a seer in contact with true God-Spirit is a rare jewel in a multitude of "channelers." Some visionaries are in contact with the divine voice, but many are dubious practitioners.

Often those who frequent psychic readers or mediums are confused by unreliable advice. This chaos arises from a lack of clarity within the reader and lack of clarity within the client. As a client you give your authority to that adviser, hoping to receive understanding you feel incapable of receiving on your own. Unfortunately, many self-interested mediums perpetuate the cycle of client dependency rather than help you learn to receive inner guidance yourself. For instance:

J. Z. Knight (channeler of "Ramtha") at first brought an inspiring, life-affirming message. Later, however, her teachings shifted to fear, secrecy, blind obedience, and doomsday prophecies. A mental health professional from Olympia, Washington, became a student of Ramtha, seeking more spiritual meaning in her life. She claimed to be emotionally stable when she joined the group. After only nine months she became suicidal. She described it as "the most devastating experience of my life. It took me three years to heal . . . I was full of self-loathing. Basically, I fell apart."[1]

What is the difference between channeling and receiving true intuitive revelation from Spirit? This depends entirely on how the word "channeling" is defined. Often people use the word "channeling" to describe the process of listening to any inner voice. However, I never use the word in this context.

Channeling, as it has been popularized today, is synonymous with psychic mediumship, in which a person opens his or her mind to invisible entities, often indiscriminately. During this process the medium becomes unconscious and allows an outside agency to take over his or her body and mind.

During this practice these mediums often get enmeshed in the psychic or subconscious realm, the "astral world." This realm includes the subconscious minds of human beings, the collective beliefs of the human race, and spirit entities.

When channels or mediums contact the astral plane, they receive advice or messages for clients. But this advice may come from any voice in the astral world and could be erroneous or misleading.

Beware of contacting inner voices indiscriminately. If a stranger arrived at your door, would you invite him into your home? Opening your mind to astral entities without discretion is like opening your door to a stranger.

When a medium opens to an entity or spirit, the spirit is happy to find a home, because that spirit has been without a body to inhabit. Some of these entities can be helpful, but some may not be so helpful. They would be as helpful as they were in embodiment. As Ernest Holmes, the founder of the Church of Religious Science, wrote in *The Science of Mind* regarding communicating with spirits: "What would we hope to gain? People out of the flesh know no more than they did when in the body."[2]

Concerning mediumship, one thing is certain—mediums inhabited by these spirits are weakened by their influence. Often channels go into trance and vacate their bodies while spirits take over. This is known as "trance mediumship." The coordination between the medium's mind and body is broken and the medium may become ill.

One author who teaches channeling, Kathryn Ridall, describes her experience of contact with her "guide" as a feeling of tiredness, heaviness, and weight in her body. After her session she reports feeling exhausted. She describes the feeling of tiredness as "an excellent sign" that one is "really channeling."

Psychic mediums who are genuine, who are channeling real entities, are often physically weakened by the entities and age more rapidly than other people. Investigative research has uncovered that mediums frequently experience degeneracy of mental powers, atrophy of brain tissue, and sometimes insanity or early death.[3]

There are other pitfalls to mediumship. Gullible individuals may place blind faith in channeled material, thinking it comes from a so-called "high" being. For example:

A woman from the Far East received messages through automatic writing that her former lover, a married man, was now a widower in England. She was told that she must search for him there. After selling everything and traveling to London, she consulted various mediums to locate him, but to no avail. Reduced to poverty, she was repatriated by the consul in London and returned home to find her ex-lover still in the Far East and still married![4]

Misguided people believe that mediums are somehow special, with gifts ordinary people do not possess. These "anointed" few may believe themselves to be the only ones capable of contacting "high" beings, calling themselves the "accredited" messengers, or similar drivel. These glorified gurus become undisputed leaders of cults. They demean human dignity by creating a world controlled by manipulative entities.

A famous channeler and cult leader with a large following gathered in Montana claims to be *the one and only* accredited messenger for the ascended master Saint Germain. Her followers are never taught to receive messages or to be channels for themselves.

Allowing anyone or anything to control you, whether it be an entity or the leader of a cult, is dangerous to mental health and a crime against self-respect.

On the other hand becoming a channel for your divine Spirit is a spiritual program for developing God consciousness. Nothing could be more of a contrast to channeling astral entities than true contact with Spirit. Spiritual revelation is received from a deeper level of consciousness, the divine realm. Those who are true channels for God-Spirit have an abundance of divine energy and tend to be more lively and youthful with time.

Only in one situation would I recommend contact with a deceased spirit. That would be in the case of a bereaved family member who seeks comfort from a departed loved one. The loving words spoken-through from beloved ones on the other side can provide profound healing.

A husband wished to contact his departed wife, whom he still loved very deeply. He had been unable to love another woman since her death. Her loving words helped him to find solace. In another case a daughter whose mother had committed suicide desired to know why her mother had left so abruptly. Her mother's words helped the daughter to heal the intense grief that she felt upon her loss.

In such instances the divine teachers guided these sessions and gave specific instructions to contact these departed ones. No mediumship was involved, since the dead never "took over" my body. My higher self simply contacted these loved ones and then I spoke words of comfort that were fed to me from divine Spirit.

In chapter 13 you will learn how to tell the difference between channeling entities and receiving clear, intuitive revelation from Spirit.

Forewarned Is Forearmed

Some people who attempt to contact an inner voice without guidance or safeguards have gotten themselves into trouble. Consider the following example: A woman from Washington, D.C., used to get readings from a trance medium who became unconscious during the readings while the entities took over. The information in these readings was always positive and often beneficial. After getting several readings from this medium, she began to spontaneously receive messages from the entities herself. Occasionally she did readings for others, not in trance but remaining conscious. But she noticed something strange. While she was receiving communications from the entities, the experience was pleasant. But once the reading was over, she felt hollow and empty inside, a depressing letdown. She felt drained and weakened as a result.

It is possible to take a class on psychic phenomena and open your mind to occult knowledge. Through drugs you can have flashy experiences. But be forewarned that dabbling in the occult can lead to great danger.

A man from California wrote to parapsychological author Martin Ebon that he experimented with psychic phenomena, mixing it with drugs, and found himself plagued by constant telepathic communication with his girlfriend and dominated by nightmarish thoughts and images.[5]

Cigarette manufacturers place warnings from the surgeon general on their labels. But occult organizations and practices, which can also be injurious, do not. Before experimenting with the occult, read the warning label by testing the validity of any practice. Use the nine tests in chapter 13 of this book.

Overly sensitive people can become susceptible to influences of lower astral entities and to negative vibrations of the collective consciousness of the human race. However, astral influence and possession are not just reserved for those sensitive to subtle vibrations. Many people are unknowingly influenced by thought-forms and entities around them. Beware of false inner voices disguised in sheep's clothing!

Is it possible to contact a divine voice? Can you discriminate between your own mind and the true voice of Spirit? Is it possible to distinguish between the influences from your environment and the divine voice within your heart? These are questions that everyone who has attempted to develop intuition asks. Such questions come from a sincere desire to establish clear communication with a higher power.

At last there is a way to receive direct, clear communication with the divine voice and to distinguish between that voice and other voices you "hear" in your mind. The ancient knowledge of divine communication that has been revived in the Divine Revelation teaching is a blessing for truth-seekers everywhere. The nine tests of discernment, described in chapter 13, are the central kernel of this teaching. With these nine tests, your doubts about the source of your inner messages can be dispelled.

> "For God is not the author of confusion, but of peace."
> —I Corinthians 14:33 (Christian)

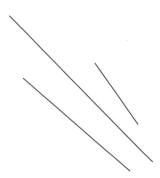

CHAPTER 13

Nine Tests to Prevent Psychic Deception

How can you distinguish the subconscious mind from the spiritual world? What is the difference between the ego-chatter of the surface mind and the true wisdom of the heart?

The subconscious mind can be insidious when you desire to receive true revelation from inner divinity. That is because it is ruled by the ego. It is filled with false beliefs about yourself, beliefs of your parents, teachers, society, and the human race. It is filled with error-thoughts. But you *can* learn to distinguish the difference by listening to the content of the message and, more important, by experiencing the feeling behind the words.

I have distilled nine basic tests to determine whether any message comes from a divine source or from the mental world. These nine tests are the result of thirty years of my research along with thirty-five years of pioneer research by Dr. Ann Meyer Makeever and Dr. Peter Meyer from San Diego.

These nine tests can be used to test inner messages that you or others receive. For example, while meditating, walking, or driving in your car, you could receive an inner revelation or inspiration. You might be using a psychokinetic method, such as muscle-testing, table-tipping, or dowsing with a pendulum or another object. You may be reading a book, hearing a tape, listening to a lecture, or visiting a counselor, and wish to test whether the lecturer speaks from the spiritual realm. You can test a healer or body-worker (such as a masseur, etc.) who is working on you. In fact you can use these tests in any situation in which you desire to ascertain your level of awareness or the level of awareness of those around you.

TEST 1: THE FEELING
This is the most important test. When you are in contact with Spirit, you will feel spiritually uplifted, loving, peaceful, joyful, fulfilled, whole, and unified.

TEST 2: THE INNER KNOWINGNESS
Your inner knowingness, a sense of knowing, without knowing how you know, is intuition. When you know that you know, then you are in contact with Spirit, without a shadow of doubt.

TEST 3: THE CHALLENGE
Test the voice by asking whether it is coming from God.

TEST 4: THE NAME
Test the voice by recognizing and validating its name.

TEST 5: THE SIGNAL
Test the voice by recognizing and validating the signal associated with each name.

TEST 6: THE AWARENESS
You are fully conscious, awake, and aware when in contact with the divine voice (unless you are receiving a message during a prophetic dream).

TEST 7: THE QUALITY OF THE VOICE
The voice spoken by Spirit is normal and natural, without theatrics.

TEST 8: THE QUALITY OF THE MESSAGE
The message given by a divine voice is wholly uplifting and positive.

TEST 9: THE RESULT
Test the the voice by the feeling you have after the message is over.

The remainder of this chapter is devoted to elaborating on these nine tests.

Test 1: The Feeling

Imagine that you are visiting a heavenly realm and have been ushered into a celestial room filled with golden light. Angels and other celestial beings surround you. All is bright, beautiful, and peaceful. How would you feel? Conceivably, you would feel unified, whole, integrated, fulfilled, loved, comforted, protected, happy, and free. You would probably also feel powerful, strong, balanced, serene, and relaxed. At the same time you would be uplifted and energized, perhaps even filled with light and bliss.

Of the nine tests, the most important test is *The Feeling*, and the most significant feelings are Unified, Whole, and Integrated. This is because divine consciousness is the only level on which a person can feel whole and unified. An astral entity cannot give you that feeling. The mental realm does not contain that feeling.

Now, understanding how you might feel while in contact with Spirit, it stands to reason that you would *not* be feeling angry, frustrated, agitated, worried, fearful, confused, scattered, or indecisive. You would *not* experience doubt, guilt, sadness, or pain. You would *not* feel imbalanced, restricted, intimidated, weak, or degraded.

When receiving a message, when reading a book, or when listening to a speaker, test for a positive, uplifted, spiritual feeling or a negative, imbalanced feeling.

Test 2: The Inner Knowingness

The second test is an *Inner Knowingness*, a feeling of certainty that what you are receiving is right. Inner Knowingness is beyond reason, beyond the intellect. It is intuitive—that is, you know simply because you *know*.

Dr. Gail Harriman of Greenwich, Connecticut, describes the first time she received a message from Spirit during her Divine Revelation breakthrough session: "I felt suffused with 'knowing'—with the feeling I always have when something is true for me. I could 'sense' more than I could talk. It was more than I expected or wanted—yet it is what I needed. I felt energized, questioning, yet at peace."

If you are not experiencing inner knowingness, then you are not on the spiritual plane. You are in the mental world. When you are in touch with Spirit, there is utterly no doubt.

All negative thoughts and emotions, including doubt and fear, are found on the subconscious mental level. If you are feeling doubtful, then you have slipped into the mental world. If you feel doubtful while you are experiencing inner knowingness, then you are jumping back and forth from the mental level (subconscious mind or ego) to the spiritual level.

BEWARE:

If your ego wants something very much, it can fool itself into a type of inner knowingness. This could be concerning anything from a relationship to a job, a social status, or a spiritual path. An example of such wishful thinking might be: "Oh, I just *know* that he's the right man for me!" How can you tell the difference? Sometimes, when your emotions are involved, it can be difficult. That is why there are nine tests. By using *all* nine, you can be assured that you are in contact with a true divine voice.

Test 3: The Challenge

The third test is called *The Challenge* because you indeed challenge the voice by asking if it comes from God. This test will help you determine "who" or "what" is the source of your inner messages.

If you were to undergo a period of extreme stress, would you accept psychiatric counseling from a stranger on the street? Or would you seek professional advice from a trained psychiatrist with credentials? Similarly, if you contact your in-house counselor, your inner voice, isn't it wise to identify what voice you are contacting? Isn't it prudent to ask for credentials from that voice? It is necessary to distinguish the true divine voice from subconscious mental voices.

I am continually amazed when people attending my lectures say, "I hear a voice inside of me. I don't know what it is, but I listen to it and follow it." Is this intelligent? No. Knowing how many false voices you could tap into, is this practice safe? No. "Safety First" is the motto of clear divine intuition.

In order to challenge an inner voice, simply ask the question, "Do you come in the name of God?" Or you may ask, "Do you come in the name of the Christ?"* Either of these questions will suffice. (It is not recommended to ask, "Do you come in the light?") If you receive a yes answer, this test has been passed. If you receive a no, then immediately do the Astral Entity Healing on page 142. If you receive no reply at all, you should also do the Astral Entity Healing immediately.

Now you may be wondering, "If this inner voice is a deceptor or a 'faker spirit,' then would it answer truthfully? Wouldn't it just lie? What if it says yes when it should say no?" I have not yet experienced a being who answered this question falsely, but should you encounter such a being, you have nine tests with which to verify. To be sure that your message is truly coming from a divine voice, *all* nine tests must be passed.

BEWARE:

It is stated in the Bible concerning testing spirits: "Beloved, believe not every spirit, but test the spirits whether they are of God: because many false prophets are gone out into the world. Hereby know ye the Spirit of God: Every spirit that confesseth that Jesus Christ is come in the flesh is of God: And every spirit that confesseth not that Jesus Christ is come in the flesh is not of God."[1]

Thus our advice is to ask, "Do you come in the name of the Christ?"

---

*If you feel an aversion to the word "Christ" because of your religious upbringing, recall the meaning of the word. "Christ" comes from a Greek word *christos*, meaning "anointed." Jesus the Christ was a title given to Jesus of Nazareth. "Christ" was not Jesus' surname. His full name was Jeshua ben Joseph (Jesus the son of Joseph). Every one of you has a Christ self within you, because you are an "anointed" divine being deep within yourself.

Test 4: The Name

Many people receive inner messages without inquiring who the messenger is. This practice of listening indiscriminately to inner voices is both risky and dangerous.

The fourth test is to ask for the calling card. Once you know that the voice comes in the name of God, ask for its name. Everything in creation that has a voice also has a vibratory quality. That vibratory quality is called a *Name*. If you are receiving a message, the messenger will have a name.

Now you may ask, "God doesn't need a name. Couldn't I just be getting messages from God?"

And the answer to that is: "Yes, you could be getting messages from God, and doesn't God have a name? Isn't God's name 'God'?"

Remember, there are two aspects of God, the personal and the impersonal. The *impersonal* aspect cannot speak to you or give you messages. It is beyond time, space, and causation. It is without qualities, nameless and formless. If you think that you are receiving messages from the impersonal absolute God, then you are deluding yourself. For this aspect of God does not and cannot speak.

The *personal* God is a personalization of the absolute, nameless, formless force permeating all of creation. The personal God is the one whom you can communicate with and receive messages from. Depending on your beliefs, you will experience the personal aspect of God in your own unique way.

For example, if a Moslem learns Divine Revelation, he or she might receive messages from Allah or Muhammad the Prophet. If a Jewish person learns, he or she may contact Yaweh, Father God, or Elijah. If a Christian learns, he or she may hear the voice of Jesus, Mary, or the Holy Spirit. Hindus might hear Krishna, Rama, or Shiva. A person who has no religious affiliation may receive messages from an aspect of God, the higher self, an angel, or ascended master. But don't be surprised if you receive messages from divine beings or deities associated with religions other than your own.

These personalized aspects of God are within you. You may believe the divine teachers and masters to be outside or inside yourself. It doesn't really matter. But you are a part of God and God is a part of you. All beings who come in the name of God are messengers of the divine voice. They speak as if with one voice, the voice of truth.

BEWARE:

Astral entities may identify themselves by a fancy name or pose as a "high" being. Names that sound "high" or "spiritual," such as a name from the Bible or other scripture, might be chosen. Or they may impersonate Jesus or Saint Germain or another master. Be sure that you challenge them first by asking if they come in the name of God (or the Christ) before you ask their name.

Test 5: The Signal

The fifth test is *The Signal*. A signal is a sign that you have arrived in the divine world.

Everyone has experienced a signal at some time. For example, do you ever remember being awestruck by a lecture, sermon, or concert, or by a thrilling scenic view or work of art? Perhaps you were having a deep conversation with a friend or were helping a person in need. Or you were touched by some inspiring music. At the peak point of this experience, you felt a physical sensation, either goose bumps, tingling, heat, a rush of energy, or a chill up your spine. Or perhaps you felt moved and tears of joy came to your eyes. Such experiences are called "signals."

The higher self within you recognizes truth and will alert you that you are in contact with beauty and truth by giving you a signal. This signal says, "Pay attention, because what you are experiencing now is of truth, of great importance."

Signals reveal themselves through the five senses: sight, sound, taste, smell, touch (or feeling), or through a movement in the body. You have probably experienced signals from time to time without realizing it. Signals often come during periods of meditation or silence or during emotional or inspiring times. For example:

Beethoven reported that at times of great inspiration his whole body shivered and his hair stood on end. He felt in harmony and oneness with the world and as though all of the forces of nature were his instruments.[2] The poet A. E. Housman described that when a line of poetry came to him, he experienced either a bristling of his skin, a shiver up his spine, constriction in his throat, watering of his eyes, or a sensation in the pit of his stomach.[3]

A signal is a vibrational signature, and each particular aspect of God or divine teacher that you contact has one that you can recognize. Each one of your inner divine names has an inner signal corresponding to it. In other words a name such as Jesus will have a particular signal, personal to you, identifying Jesus.

Here are a few examples of signals:

1. VISUAL SIGNALS.

You may see a light with your eyes closed, maybe a colored light in a particular place near the body or in a part of the body. In your inner vision you may see a symbol, the face of a saint, a divine teacher, or the face of a deity.

Nina Polaski, a store manager from Passaic, New Jersey, described her visual signal: "Streams of golden light came from the left and above my head. They poured down upon me. It made me feel as if I was being blessed by God."

2. AUDITORY SIGNALS.

You may hear the sound of rushing water, celestial music, an "OM" or humming sound, bells, or other pleasant sounds.

A legal secretary from Oakland, California, Pamela Montero, stated: "I heard music that was a kind of humming sound. It sounded very spiritual, like angels singing. It made me feel really happy. It sort of sounded like a stringed instrument. I thought that it was the electricity humming in the room, but then I realized that it went away when I opened my eyes."

3. OLFACTORY SIGNALS.

You may smell a sweet fragrance, like flowers, incense, or fruit, when there is no fragrance in the room.

Linda Whitney, a seamstress from Omaha, Nebraska, described her signal: "I saw a beautiful red rose and I smelled it, too. It was an extremely strong fragrance. I've had this smell before in my meditations, but it felt great to have this confirmation."

4. GUSTATORY SIGNALS.

You may taste a subtle, enjoyable sweet taste in your mouth or your throat even though there is no food in your mouth. This taste may or may not be familiar to you.

As Patricia Mackey, a photo stylist from New York City, described it: "My signal was an unusual, sweet taste in the back of my throat accompanied by a feeling of great inner happiness."

5. KINESTHETIC SIGNALS.

You may feel tingling, a rush of energy, heat or cold in a part of the body. Something may touch or press against you. You may sense the body expand or compress to a particular size or shape. You may feel spinning or spiraling or another kinetic sensation. Or you may feel something unique and indescribable that you recognize whenever you meditate or contact the divine.

A homemaker from Greenwich, Connecticut, Paula French, wrote: "I felt a strong energy in my heart area and recognized this energy moving in circular motion. The energy began to flow and expand."

6. PSYCHOKINETIC SIGNALS.

You may sense a movement in the body, such as the head going back, eyelashes fluttering, hands going up, shaking, quaking, rocking, or movement of fingers, toes, legs, hands.

Robin Corey, an aerobics instructor from Greenwich, Connecticut, experienced: "I felt at peace but still 'tingly.' I was very aware that my eyelids were fluttering, as if they were out of control."

These signals will be pleasant in some way and will always be the same and recognizable. Signals do not change except perhaps to become more subtle with time. Pay attention to the signals and always be sure you have a clear signal before proceeding to get any message. You should be receiving your signal the entire time you are getting a message. If the signal stops, it means the message has stopped or there is interference. If this happens, you should do a healing prayer.

Once you have a clear vibrational signal, you can use that signal to ask questions. You can ask your inner contact to give you a signal or make the signal stronger if the answer is yes. If the signal diminishes or disappears, then the answer is no.

Everyone has a unique, personal relationship with the divine, so everyone experiences unique signals. Also, signals often have particular meanings. For example, many people receive heat or energy in their hands—a sign of natural abilities as a hands-on healer or a creative artisan. One student from Toronto experienced a shaft of light running up her spine. The message from her divine teacher was that even though she was not feeling supported, she always has the support of almighty God.

I was attempting to define an inner signal for a woman from Staten Island, New York, during her breakthrough session. I asked her what she was experiencing. She said she was feeling "inner peace." I asked her to take deep breaths and go deeper. Then I asked her what she was experiencing. She said "peace." I asked her to take more deep breaths and go even deeper, and when she still said she was experiencing "peace," I asked her where this "peace" was located. She promptly said, "Oh, it's that feeling of the cloak around my shoulders." I said, "Oh, so you feel a cloak around your shoulders when you meditate?" She asked, "Doesn't everybody?" I explained that everyone has a very unique inner experience during meditation. Hers was the peaceful, protective sense of security of a cloak around her shoulders.

BEWARE:

An astral entity can give you a signal or mimic one of your divine signals. Psychic mediums have received "signals" from spirits for centuries. Just because you are receiving a signal does not mean that you are contacting a divine voice. Make sure that you ask the question "Do you come in the name of God?" before you receive your signal, and be sure to check all nine tests.

Test 6: The Awareness

Test six is *The Awareness* test. Simply stated, you are fully conscious when in contact with Spirit. It is not necessary to go into trance to allow Spirit in. You do not need to let anything else "take over" you. All the divine beings and deities, masters, angels, archangels, and messengers of God are already within you.

To test for awareness, simply notice whether you are awake, alert, fully conscious, and in complete control of your faculties, or whether you are in a "trance" or asleep and something has "come in" to take over your body.

The conscious experience of receiving a message from the divine is completely uplifting and joyful. You feel the thrill of inspiration going through your body as you receive divine ideas from Spirit.

The only time you would not be fully awake, aware, and conscious while receiving a message from Spirit is if you were asleep and receiving a prophetic dream.

BEWARE:

Ernest Holmes, the founder of the Church of Religious Science, wrote in *The Science of Mind*, regarding receiving impressions:

"To let go of the volitional and choosing faculties—which alone constitute individuality—and become immersed in subjectivity, is very dangerous. It is a crime against individuality to allow the conscious faculties to become submerged. We should control the subjective and not let it control us. . . . Never admit any mental impressions or images that you do not wish to receive or that you cannot receive consciously."[4]

Test 7: The Quality of the Voice

The seventh test is *The Quality of the Voice*. Many people overlook this as an obvious, striking sign that something is either very clear or very amiss. Can you imagine God speaking to you with a strange accent or a weird tone of voice? Any celestial being, angel, ascended being, or messenger of God will speak with great clarity, sometimes poetically, sometimes humorously, but always in a loving, natural tone of voice. God can speak to you in your own language and does not need to use a theatrical or unnatural voice.

The divine voice is often sweet, kind, compassionate, loving, calm, peaceful, intelligent, wise, and truthful. Astral voices might be domineering, coercive, intimidating, pretentious, melodramatic, frightening, abrasive, or hurtful. Entities from the astral world often speak with unusual accents or gestures. Such entities take over the body of the person channeling and use that body as a vehicle to speak through.

Many channels and mediums give melodramatic, theatrical performances. They often alter their voice, either consciously or unconsciously, to impress others or to create a greater mystique. Misguided, gullible followers are invariably impressed by unusual accents. I can't imagine why. Linguist Sarah Thomason of the University of Pittsburgh reported in *Psychology Today* (October 1989) that eleven famous channelers whom she studied all had fake accents. None of them spoke with dialects consistent with the time during which the entities supposedly lived.

In rare instances you may be in contact with a true spiritual being and still exhibit theatrics or strange voices. In such a case you may be blocking the true feeling and intent of the message, due to feeling incapable of contacting a divine being or Godly aspect of self, or due to a need to place power in an outside authority. Such fears create the need to invent a false persona in the form of an entity with an accent.

Inner revelation comes directly from Spirit within but is filtered by the subconscious mind before being cognized on the outer conscious level of the mind. Therefore, one receiving a divine message may unconsciously distort that message in any number of ways, including its intended method of delivery. As Babaji has stated, "Man adds fear to God's message." Be cautious and know that God can always speak in your own natural, loving voice.

BEWARE:

Without exception, if you or someone else is speaking in a strange accent while speaking an inner message, it is either an astral entity speaking-through or a false theatrical performance by a channel or medium (either consciously or unconsciously).

However, this test does not work in reverse. Just because a voice sounds natural does not necessarily mean that the message is clear or from a divine voice. Check all nine tests for clear discernment.

Test 8: The Quality of the Message

The eighth test is *The Quality of the Message*. Let us examine how voices from Spirit differ from other voices that might speak to you. Messages received from the divine voice are often peaceful, inspiring, comforting, helpful, and healing. Conversely, you are not in contact with the true voice of Spirit if your message is intimidating, controlling, or judg-mental.

This particular test requires more discernment and experience than the other nine tests, because you may not yet be familiar with messages from Spirit. There are many subtle as well as not-so-subtle differences between the divine voice and other voices, and it is important to learn the differences. In the following examples a negative quality is stated followed by an unclear, erroneous statement exemplifying that negative quality. Then, in contrast, an example of a positive, clear message from Spirit follows.

1. INTIMIDATING (GUILT- AND FEAR-INDUCING) MESSAGE

Negative, unclear, erroneous statement:

"If you do not read the Bible every day, you will go to hell."

Positive, clear message from Spirit:

"Do not be afraid. I am always with you. There is nothing to fear. I love you. Be at peace."

Spirit never intimidates. A religious organization, cult leader, or guru that controls its members by inflicting fear and guilt is not aligned with Spirit. God is not a punishing and guilt-imposing deity. "Hellfire and brimstone" is an erroneous message used to manipulate others. It is abuse of power.

2. CONTROLLING (COERCIVE, INTRUSIVE) MESSAGE

Negative, unclear, erroneous statement:

"This path is the only true path to enlightenment. If you leave this path, you will never be enlightened."

Positive, clear message from Spirit:

"You have the power within to open a direct pipeline to the divine. You need not be dependent on any person, thing, or organization to be your conduit for Spirit. You are the God self within and you have all that you need. Stand up and walk into the light!"

The divine voice never forces itself on anyone without an invitation. You must ask for the voice of God, otherwise it does not come. Spirit never brings an intrusive message. It encourages you to maintain your integrity and self-authority. On the other hand an entity from the astral world may attempt to dominate you or try to force communication. Messages may be coercive, against your will or better judgment.

A Pennsylvania housewife became obsessed by the Ouija board, which brought at first a benign and supportive "guide." Soon the messages became more intimate and eventually lecherous and obscene. She became uneasy and sexually unresponsive to her husband, thinking that her invisible guide was always watching her. Her guide became more coercive and possessive, seeking to break up her marriage and to "get rid of" her baby, so that their communications would not be interrupted. She was lucky enough to seek psychiatric care.[5]

"Shoulds," "should-nots," and "have-tos" are not from Spirit. You may ask Spirit what is highest wisdom for you. But this does not mean that you "must" do it. The idea of "have-to" assumes that you have no freedom to choose. Spirit is entirely permissive and never interferes with your free will.

3. JUDGMENTAL (CRITICAL) MESSAGE

Negative, unclear, erroneous statement:

"Past *karma* determines your destiny. Suffering in your present life is a result of evil deeds in past lives."

Positive, clear message from Spirit:

"You need not suffer in any way. There is no need to punish yourself with belief in retribution. You are free to choose happiness at every moment."

A judgmental message is not the true voice of Spirit. Judgment means condemning a person or group of people for their "good" or "bad" actions. Good or bad *karma* and reward or punishment for past deeds are erroneous ideas. Suffering or happiness is the result of your own free will to make positive or negative choices.

Spirit is never critical nor diminishes anyone or anything. It may point out what needs healing, but it never judges or makes you feel inferior. For example, you might receive a challenging message from Spirit about something you are unwilling to look at. But such a message ultimately has a healing effect.

A student of Divine Revelation from Iowa received an inner message that the pain in her neck and shoulders was because she felt burdened, carrying the weight of responsibility for her loved ones. Such a message was not "critical," however, because she was shown a truth about herself that helped her heal the pain.

4. BLAMING (VENGEFUL, VICTIMIZED, SELF-PITYING) MESSAGE

Negative, unclear, erroneous statement:

"You were victimized and abused and they should be punished. You are a poor, unfortunate victim. It is their fault. They deserve to suffer."

Positive, clear message from Spirit:

"Take responsibility for your actions and your thoughts and do not blame others for your problems. You are the creator of your destiny and can transform it in whatever way you desire. You have the power to make choices. Be not afraid to command your life and take control of the helm. Create a destiny of joy, good, and power."

A victim is someone who has not taken control or responsibility for self. Spirit encourages you to take responsibility and to have faith in yourself. A message from Spirit never contains blame, vengeance, self-pity, or persecution.

5. COMPLICATED (HIERARCHICAL) MESSAGE

Negative, unclear, erroneous statement:

"Behold the triumvirate host of Zimron bringing the extra-ray hand meridian coordinates activating the bipolar brain-induced Saturnian ray. The seventeenth hierarchy of the fifth ray of beings have come as messengers from the Rezacula galaxy of Extralondian. Jesus Christ was also a part of this hierarchy, just below the Alfracasus of Nibion."

Positive, clear message from Spirit:

"Be simple and be free. Be like a little child, and thou shalt enter the kingdom of God. God is with thee and thou art with Him. All Spirit is one Spirit. All God is one God. Be loved and loving and know the truth."

Complicated books or messages that contain complicated hierarchies and pyramid structures do not come from the divine voice. Spirit speaks simply, succinctly, and is easily understood. A hierarchical structure of beings who are better or less than others does not exist. Everyone is a being of divinity, for every living being has the divine spark within.

6. EGO-FLATTERING ("VANITY-FEEDING") MESSAGE

Negative, unclear, erroneous statement:

"You are the only true guru. Your teaching is the only true teaching. You are the chosen one, the reincarnation of Jesus Christ. Your disciples must pay homage to you."

Positive, clear message from Spirit:
"You are loved. You are the Christ. You have the power of God at your command. Never demean yourself or think yourself less than another, for all are equal in the eyes of God."

If a person claims to be "the only accredited channel" or "the only true messenger," then an entity from the astral world may be using that person as a pawn by "vanity-feeding." Entities gain control by winning trust through flattery, making you feel superior to others. They often say that you have passed "tests" and are "chosen by God" for a special task. These "faker spirits" may attempt to convince you to control and dominate your followers who are not as "evolved" as you. They isolate you, making you feel special and misunderstood. They increase this feeling of superiority by posing as "high" teachers and using "high"-sounding names that invoke greater trust.

A Methodist minister from Iowa received a letter from a man who said Jesus Christ had told him to establish a political party and become ruler of the world until the second coming of Christ. Another man wrote that he had been chosen by God to take an expedition to the center of the earth to locate the Ten Lost Tribes of Israel.[6]

The true divine voice, in contrast, may praise you and make you feel good about yourself, but everyone is considered equal in Spirit, and all are praised equally. Spirit would never place you above others or encourage you to control them. Beware of organizations in which a person is placed as a figurehead above others and is the only one allowed to receive divine messages.

Often people claim to be reincarnations of divine beings. For example:

At a flying saucer gathering in California two women came to blows, rolling in the dust and pulling hair, because they both claimed to be reincarnations of the Virgin Mary.[7] A man from Lincoln, Nebraska confessed that he is the one and only reincarnation of Jesus Christ.

Such common delusions are often the result of a faker spirit, but sometimes they spring from misunderstanding a clear divine message received from Spirit. The divine voice may say, "You are the Christ," "You are the incarnation of God," "You are a child of the living God," or similar messages. Such messages are never meant to be interpreted as singling you out as the *one* and *only* Christ. *Everyone* is a Christ and a child of God.

7. DETERMINISTIC MESSAGE (FORTUNE-TELLING, DOOM-AND-
GLOOM PREDICTIONS)

Negative, unclear, erroneous statement:

Example 1: "You will marry Ed by the end of the year."

Example 2: "Your business will fail this year and you will go bankrupt."

Positive, clear message from Spirit:

"You create your own destiny with your thoughts. Be careful what you believe and what you think, for the power of your thoughts and your speech is unfathomable. You have the power to change your destiny and to create your good. Think positively and you will reap the benefits of your optimism."

Fortune-telling comes from the mental realm and can be dangerous. If the prediction is positive, then it may create false security, expectations, or hopes. It could also create laziness, a feeling that there is nothing to "do" for the result to come. Such indifference could promote failure. If the prediction is negative, then it might have a demoralizing effect or create such fear that it produces the negative outcome.

How are predictions made? By reading your thought-forms, one can project these thoughts into the future to predict a possible result. You *could* receive an accurate predictive message, because the thought-seeds of the future are sown in the past. However, no one can predict precisely, because at any moment your thoughts can change and therefore your future can change. You have the power to change your future.

Beware that an entity from the astral world can make a prediction in order to control you or to make mischief. For example:

A husband reported that his wife had become addicted to the Ouija board, which warned her for months of her mother's death. She became increasingly agitated by these predictions. The Ouija finally forecasted the date of the demise, and the woman bought a plane ticket and packed a suitcase. When her mother did not die as expected, her husband broke the Ouija board to pieces.[8]

A message that warns of an unavoidable disaster is never from Spirit. Such a doom-and-gloom prediction, carved in stone, assumes no freedom of choice and accepts predetermination.

On the other hand it is possible to receive a clear message of warning from Spirit. This might be a gut feeling to avoid a certain voyage. Or you may get a sudden feeling to step back as you are crossing a street, unaware that a car is rushing toward you. You may feel uneasy about signing a particular contract or entering into a business deal. You may feel anxious about a particular person and want to avoid him or her. You may feel that a friend or relative is in danger. Such warnings may or may not be clear, but they can be tested by using these nine tests.

8. HARMFUL (LIFE-DAMAGING) MESSAGE

Negative, unclear, erroneous statement:

"In order to prove your faith, you must sleep only three hours a night."

Positive, clear message from Spirit:

"I am giving you my divine protection. I am filling and surrounding you with peace. There is nothing to fear at any time, and no harm can come to you. I am enfolding you in my arms of love. Be at peace."

Beware of any message that is harmful or life-damaging. An entity from the astral realm or your own subconscious mind may give a message to hurt yourself or to hurt another. Such messages never come from the divine voice.

Two teenagers claimed they contacted their "dead fathers" through automatic writing. They then communicated with a "friend" of one father, claiming to be a "guardian angel" of one of the girls. This entity told her to come to the other side and join them, since life did not hold much for her. She took the advice and threw herself under a bus, but she luckily survived.[9]

9. CONDITIONAL (DEMANDING) MESSAGE

Negative, unclear, erroneous statement:

"If you are a good, charitable, and kind person and you give generous donations to the church, then you will be healed."

Positive, clear message from Spirit:

"You are healed by the power of God, which is with you at all times. Call upon the divine Spirit for healing. There is nothing to fear. You can be healed by the power of your faith. Be calm and at peace."

The divine voice never strikes bargains. Spirit never judges your actions and then rewards or punishes you. God's love and benevolence are unconditional, with no strings attached. Conditional messages often come from the judging mind of the person receiving the message. Demanding messages often come from entities attempting to control humans. For example:

A man heard inner voices that correctly predicted shifts in the stock market. Then the voices said they were "testing" him, and if he would obey, they would give him an important job. Flattered and impressed, he complied with their angry, shouting demands to perform bizarre tasks. Soon he began blacking out and waking up in strange places. The voices then dominated his mind so much that he could not hear people talking to him. He was eventually hospitalized.[10]

10. ISOLATED MESSAGE (SEPARATE FROM GOD)

Negative, unclear, erroneous statement:

"God, you are so far away. I am insignificant. I am nothing and you are everything. You cannot hear my plea. I will do anything if you would only listen to me and help me."

Positive, clear message from Spirit:

"Dear one, I am one with you. I am the divine within you. I am with you always and always, until the end of the world. I love you. Be at peace."

There are several differences between the examples above. The first example is not a message from Spirit but a prayer of supplication, spoken by the voice of the ego. Conversely, the second example is a divine voice speaking through a person. In the first the voice speaks words of separation; that is, words that reinforce the idea of distance from the true nature of our being, our God self. The second brings a message of unity, not separation. I encourage you to pray for God's help or call upon God, but God is not separate from you. There is no need to beg or try to bargain with God, for God is already here.

BEWARE:

Astral entities can give you positive messages, healing messages, and truthful messages, but the feeling is not the same as the feeling from Spirit. Use all nine tests to verify.

"We must not trust every word of others or feeling within ourselves, but cautiously and patiently try the matter, whether it be of God."[11]

Test 9: The Result

The ninth test is called *The Result*. This is the last test—to be used once you have finished contacting your divine guidance. After you have received an inner message, whether during meditation or during the day, ask yourself "How do I feel now?" How do you think you would feel after you were truly in contact with Spirit rather than another voice? You might feel elated, fulfilled, refreshed, inspired, and filled with God's grace.

However, if you received your message from the psychic world, mental world, race-mind consciousness, astral plane, etc., you might feel empty, guilty, drained, let down, intimidated, or confused.

This test of The Result is very important, because it cannot be faked by an astral entity or by your own subconscious mind. Either you have a sense of inner peace, wholeness, and comfort, or you don't. In order for you to feel these positive feelings, Spirit must have been present. If any of the negative feelings are present, you know that your session was not entirely clear. It was tainted by the mental level or by astral entities, and you need to do healing prayers.

One medium reports feeling tiredness, heaviness, and weight in her body when she channels her "guide." Afterward she feels exhausted. Contrast this to the energetic and revitalized feelings after contact with the inner divine presence.

Methodology for Using the Nine Tests

Why is it important to use these nine tests? Receiving intuitive messages is tricky business. In the early days of television, there was often static in the reception. Similarly, for many students today, there is static on the line, distorting the reception of intuition from the spiritual realm. Often thought-forms and entities get in the way. In order to be certain that you are hearing a divine voice and not a delusion of your mind or an entity from the astral world, it is important to use these nine reliable tests.

When you wish to test an inner voice, ask the following questions:

QUESTION 1: "DO YOU COME IN THE NAME OF GOD?"

If you get a yes answer, then the test called "The Challenge" has been passed. If you don't get an answer, or the answer is unclear, or the answer is no, then immediately speak out the Astral Entity Healing on page 142. Remember, "Heal first and ask questions later." You can never do any harm by using the Astral Entity Healing. After you speak it take some deep breaths and go deeper. Then ask Question 1 again.

QUESTION 2: "WHAT IS YOUR NAME?"

If you get a familiar inner name that sounds and feels right, then the test called "The Name" has been passed. If you have any doubts whatsoever, then ask the voice if it comes in the name of God. If you get a no answer, or if the voice refuses to give you an answer or a name, then immediately speak the Astral Entity Healing on page 142. Take some deep breaths and go deeper, and then ask Question 1 and Question 2 again.

QUESTION 3: "PLEASE GIVE ME YOUR SIGNAL."

If you receive a strong, clear signal that you recognize as the signal corresponding with the name that you received in Question 2, then the test called "The Signal" has been passed. If you do not receive the proper signal, then "Heal all the way." That means do whatever healings are needed. The healings are listed and explained in chapter 10.

If the signal is not strong enough, then ask the voice, "Please make your signal stronger." If the signal is still not strong and clear, do healings. Then take some deep breaths and go deeper, and then ask Question 1, Question 2, and Question 3 again.

The signal will be present the entire time you are receiving a clear message from Spirit. If the signal stops in the middle of a message, then a healing is needed. If the signal stops when the message seems to be finished, then the message is over. It is quite common for a person to continue speaking after the signal has stopped, elaborating on the message. Pay attention to when the signal stops. It usually means the message is finished.

QUESTION 4: "DO I HAVE THE RIGHT FEELING?"

If you feel peaceful, loving, tranquil, unified, whole, integrated, balanced, then the test called "The Feeling" has been passed. If you do not feel good, or if something is "off," do whatever healings are needed.

Then take some deep breaths and go deeper. Start over with Question 1 and go through all the questions again.

QUESTION 5: "PLEASE GIVE ME YOUR MESSAGE."

Receive the message by either hearing a voice, seeing a vision, or getting a feeling. Then determine whether it feels right. If the inner knowingness is there, then the test called "The Inner Knowingness" has been passed. If it doesn't feel right, "Heal all the way" and then take deep breaths and go deeper. Begin again with Question 1 and go through the questions again.

QUESTION 6: "WHAT IS THE QUALITY OF THIS VOICE?"

Is the voice speaking in a weird accent or with strange gesturing? Or is the voice speaking normally and naturally? If the voice is natural and sounds like your own voice, then the test called "The Quality of the Voice" has been passed. If there is an accent or a different voice than your natural voice, then immediately speak out the Astral Entity Healing on page 142. Then take deep breaths and go deeper, and start at the beginning with Question 1 and ask all the questions again.

QUESTION 7: "WHAT IS THE QUALITY OF THIS MESSAGE?"

Ask yourself whether the message makes sense and whether it has an uplifting, inspiring, healing quality. If so, then the test called "The Quality of the Message" has been passed. If there is any judgment, coercion, or doom-and-gloom predictions, "Heal all the way." Then take deep breaths and go deeper, and start again with Question 1 and go through all the questions again.

QUESTION 8: "AM I CONSCIOUS OR UNCONSCIOUS?"

If you are fully aware and fully conscious while receiving the message, then the test called "The Awareness" has been passed. If you are receiving the message and you find that you are unconscious, asleep, or out of your body, then come out of that state and say out loud, "I am in control. I am the only authority in my life. I am divinely protected by the light of my being. I close off my aura and body of light to all but my own God self. Thank you, God, and so it is." Then start at the beginning and ask Question 1 and go through all the steps again.

QUESTION 9: "WHAT IS THE RESULT? HOW DO I FEEL NOW?"

Ask yourself how you feel after you have finished receiving the message. If you are feeling full, inspired, happy, motivated, and grounded, then the test called "The Result" has been passed. If you feel empty, let down, intimidated, or frightened, then you were not contacting the voice of Spirit. If this test is failed, then you need to do healing prayers and reconnect to a feeling of oneness with God. During your next attempt to receive revelation, make sure that you are clear and that the nine tests have been passed before you attempt to receive a message.

Example of Using the Nine Tests

Here is a hypothetical example of using the nine tests:

Student: "Do you come in the name of God?"

Inner Voice: "No."

Student: "Dear one, you are healed and forgiven, you are one with your own higher nature, your own divine self. You are filled and surrounded with God's love. You are filled and surrounded with God's light. You are free from fear, pain, and from the earth vibration. I ask the Holy Spirit to take you to your perfect place of expression. Go in peace. Is this healing complete?"

Inner Voice: "Yes."

Student: "Do you come in the name of God?"

Inner Voice: "Yes."

Student: "What is your name?"

Inner Voice: "The Holy Spirit."

Student: "Please give me your signal."

Inner Voice: (Feeding your signal to you and you receive it.)

Student: "Please make the signal stronger."

Inner Voice: (Feeding your signal stronger.)

Student: (Noticing whether your signal is clear and then noticing the feeling that you are getting.) "Please give me your message."

Inner Voice: "I welcome you in love. I am the Holy Spirit and I come in the name of the Christ. I am here today to give you love and light, to uplift you. Feel my holy presence filling and surrounding you now. I am the light of the world. I am the truth, the way, and the life. I AM that I AM."

Student: (Noticing quality of the voice, quality of the message, and the awareness. Coming out of meditation and noticing the feeling afterward.) All the tests have been passed. Now you know that the message was clear.

The most unique and supreme gift that the teaching of Divine Revelation has to offer, I believe, is the use of these nine tests. With these nine tests you have a sure path to the divine realm. The road is safe and secure. There are no roadblocks on the way and no unexpected turns in the road. You can travel safely and quickly to your goal without hesitation.

> *"Beware of false prophets, which come to you in sheep's clothing, but inwardly they are ravening wolves. Ye shall know them by their fruits."*
>
> —Matthew 7:15–16 (Christian)

CHAPTER 14

The Answers Are Within You

Yraou have learned to distinguish between the divine voice and "other voices" from the mental world. Now you are ready to master the art of asking inner questions and receiving clear divine messages. The following safeguards, developed by Dr. Peter Meyer after thirty-five years of teaching, are the keys to receiving clear, consistent divine messages from Spirit:

Safeguards for Receiving Clear Revelation[1]

1. Call upon an aspect of the divine by name and get a clear signal before proceeding. Call upon a divine contact, who comes in the name of God, before attempting to receive inner revelation. Be sure you know the name and signal you are contacting. Get a clear "calling card" before you receive any message.

2. Affirm protection while open or subjective. Close off your aura to all except your God self. Then, do not fear. Be sure to say, "I am in control, I am the only authority in my life, I close off my aura to all but my own God self," or do another prayer of protection. Do not fear anything, because fear takes you out of the spiritual realm into the subconscious level.

3. If you feel any question for any reason, do a healing. As Peter Meyer has stated, "Heal first and ask questions later." No healing prayer is ever wasted. If you ever feel anything wrong or sense a need for healing, then heal right away. (The healing prayers are in chapter 10.)

4. Avoid revelation when you are tired, ill, or experiencing strong or negative emotions. When you are tired, take a nap before receiving revelation. If you are ill, pray first before attempting to receive revelation. When under the influence of strong or negative emotions, do healing prayers first and be sure you are clear before proceeding.

5. Maintain an attitude of nonjudgmental objectivity while receiving revelation. If something sounds incredible, put it aside to examine later. As long as the nine tests are fulfilled, then you can assume the message is clear. The message may seem absurd or preposterous. But don't judge it until you have come out of meditation and are objective. If it still seems implausible, then put it aside until later. You may meditate on a particular problem many times before coming to a clear, unequivocal answer. If it involves an important decision, then confirm it several times. You may even want to consult a more experienced Divine Revelation practitioner to check its accuracy.

6. Avoid asking "fortune-telling" questions. The divine teachers honor and respect your choices and will support you in creating your destiny. Asking about the future is asking for trouble. The divine teachers will not answer fortune-telling questions, so you will be inviting "other voices" to answer your question. Dr. Peter Meyer states, "Truth is consistent. One truth does not invalidate another. There is no time element in truth."

7. Revelation is not a substitute for deep meditation or for prayer treatment. All three go together for balanced spiritual growth. Take time for deep meditation and take time to pray to fulfill your goals. It is not enough just to receive messages from Spirit. In order to have a balanced life, deep meditation is important. It provides rest to the body and spiritual renewal to the mind, resulting in subjective balance. Prayer treatment is important for objective balance. It helps you express your desires and then work to achieve them.

8. Avoid trespassing on another's evolution. This means avoid dominating others by telling them what to do. Encourage them to find answers within themselves. In this way you can help them to develop their intuition and make their own choices.

9. **In revelation, never pretend.** If you feel obligated to speak a spiritual message and yet you are not in contact with Spirit, then you may be tempted to fabricate a message. This message will not have the vibratory feeling of true revelation from Spirit. Yet you may receive adulation from those who are unable to discern. Pretending like this prevents you from receiving divine messages. Ask a Divine Revelation teacher for help if you are unable to receive clearly from Spirit. (See a list of teachers on page 271.)

10. **Beware of being misled by your own ego or subconscious mind.** Never trust vanity-feeding. It is not true spiritual revelation. Your ego may take you out of the realm of Spirit and into the mental realm. You may find yourself repeating worn-out platitudes to impress others, or you may speak messages that coerce or dominate others. An astral being or your ego may influence you to create a mystique of being "highly evolved" with "special" abilities others do not possess. This "vanity-feeding" makes you feel separate and superior to others. If you succumb to this trap, then a "faker spirit" can easily control you. Vanity-feeding is never true revelation from Spirit.

11. **You are always in control. Maintain individuality and free choice.** Be awake and in control while receiving from Spirit. If you are getting out of control at any time, then stop your revelation and say out loud, "I AM in control." Never allow an entity to "take over" your body or "use" you. The divine teachers never intrude in this way. There is no need to leave your body to receive true revelation from Spirit.

Now that you have learned the safeguards, it is important to learn more about "signals." Divine vibrational signals indicate which aspect of divinity (which name) you are contacting when receiving from Spirit. For instance, you may receive a signal from the Holy Spirit in the form of a beautiful pink light in your heart. To another person the Holy Spirit may come as a feeling of heat in the palms of the hands. Each of you has personal, unique vibrational signals that are signs of divine contact.

But it is necessary to master two other types of signals before you attempt to ask questions to your inner divine voice. The "yes and no" signals are for the purpose of answering simple questions that require a yes or no answer. The "healing" signals help you determine when a particular healing is needed before continuing.

"Yes and No" Signals

The first type of signals needed in order to get clear answers from Spirit are called the "yes and no" signals. These are confirmation signals indicating that an answer is yes or no. The "yes and no" signals come from divine Spirit, also known as your higher self. They come the same way other signals come to you, by asking your divine contact to give them to you.

These signals come as particular experiences, just like your divine vibrational signals. You may receive a visual signal—you may see a light, symbol, vision. You may get an auditory signal and hear a hum, musical sound, bells. You may receive a feeling signal, such as tingling, heat, cold. Or you may smell a fragrance or taste a particular taste. You may also experience a movement in the body—you may notice your head moving, hand moving, finger moving.

Here are examples of "yes and no" signals that some students have received:

1. The head moving to the right for a yes signal and to the left for a no signal.
2. A finger or hand moving once for no and three times for yes.
3. An inner vision of a green light for yes and a red light for no.
4. Seeing a minus sign for a no and a plus sign for a yes.
5. Hearing the word "yes" or the word "no."
6. Feeling warmth in the hands for yes and cold for no.

Of course, "yes and no" signals can be safely obtained in an advanced Divine Revelation course with a trained instructor. But you may also receive your "yes and no" signals by the following method:*

*Do not try this process unless you have a clear inner divine contact and a clear vibrational signal; you are emotionally stable, mentally clear, free from drugs; and you know how to use the healing prayers in chapter 10. Remember that when you are receiving any type of signal, astral entities can interfere and deceive you into believing you are receiving a clear signal from Spirit.

Step 1: Call upon a divine teacher with whom you are familiar.

Step 2: Ask your inner teacher, "Do you come in the name of God?"

Step 3: Get a clear inner name and signal with which you are already familiar.

Step 4: Check your inner feeling and inner knowingness.

Step 5: Complete the nine tests as described in chapter 13.

Step 6: Ask your inner teacher to feed you with a yes signal, and receive it clearly.

Step 7: Ask your inner teacher to feed you with his or her vibrational signal if your yes signal was received clearly.

Step 8: If you don't get a clear vibrational signal from your inner contact, then do healing prayers from chapter 10.

Step 9: Ask your inner teacher to feed you with a no signal, and receive it clearly.

Step 10: Ask your inner teacher to feed you with his or her vibrational signal if your no signal was received clearly.

Step 11: Do healing prayers from chapter 10 any time you need to during this process.

It is a good idea to check these "yes and no" signals with a qualified teacher if you have an opportunity to do so. Once you have a clear yes and clear no signal that you can rely on, then you are ready for the next step.

"Healing" Signals

Other important signals for helping to get clear answers from your divine voice are "healing" signals. Healing signals correspond to the healing prayers that you learned in chapter 10. The following are names of some healing signals that you might receive:

1. Thought-Form Healing signal
2. Psychic-Tie-Cut Healing signal
3. Astral Entity Healing signal
4. Façade-Body Healing signal

Any time you receive one of these signals, it is a sign to use the corresponding healing prayer. For instance, if you receive your Astral Entity Healing signal, it denotes the presence of astral entities. If you receive a

Psychic-Tie-Cut Healing signal, then you need to cut psychic ties with someone or something in your awareness or your environment. If you are talking or thinking about another person while receiving a healing signal, then that person needs healing. These healing signals are monitors of clarity in any situation.

A Divine Revelation student went to a bar after a movie. He began to feel a nauseous feeling in his stomach that he recognized as his Astral Entity Healing signal. He immediately spoke out the healing prayer quietly. His healing signal then disappeared, and it was replaced by an inner divine vibrational signal. He then knew that the entities had been healed.

You will receive unique healing signals. For example, one person may get pain in the chest as a sign that astral entities need healing. Another may get tightness in the forehead. Use the chart labeled "'Healing' and 'Yes/No' Signals" to record your individual "yes and no" signals and "healing signals."

"HEALING" AND "YES/NO" SIGNALS

TYPE OF SIGNAL	SIGNAL
Yes Signal	
No Signal	
Thought-Form Healing Signal	
Psychic-Tie-Cut Signal	
Astral Entity Signal	
Façade-Body Signal	
Past-Life-Mental-Body Signal	

Many of my students discovered that various chronic pains, aches, or uncomfortable feelings in their bodies were nothing other than healing signals.

A Russian woman experienced a dark feeling of discomfort in her heart for many years, which we discovered was her healing signal for astral entities. With repeated healing, her uneasiness lessened and eventually dissolved. A woman from Iowa found her chronic headaches were nothing but thought-form healing signals that disappeared when she spoke out the healing prayer. A man from Omaha found that the chronic pain in his heart was an indication that psychic ties needed to be cut between himself and his mother.

Here are a few examples of healing signals of students who took Divine Revelation courses. These will most likely be different from your own:

A Façade-Body Healing signal was a feeling of plate armor, a band around the head, a claustrophobic feeling, or a vision of a mask.

An Astral Entity Healing signal was a vision of a gray or black entity, a black dot, a feeling of nausea, a creepy feeling, or a pain in the shoulders.

A Thought-Form Healing signal was a pain in the forehead, a pain in the temples, a pain in the top of the head, or a constriction in the heart.

A Psychic-Tie-Cut healing signal was a vision of psychic ties or cords, a feeling of being pulled, a feeling of being attached by a cord, a tightness in the chest, a vision of an umbilical cord, or a pain in the temple.

You may receive your healing signals utilizing a similar method as for receiving "yes and no" signals:

Step 1: Call upon your divine teacher.

Step 2: Ask your divine teacher, "Do you come in the name of God?"

Step 3: Get your inner teacher's clear inner name and signal.

Step 4: Check your inner feeling and inner knowingness.

Step 5: Use the nine tests as described in chapter 13.

Step 6: Ask your divine teacher to give you a particular healing signal, such as the Astral Entity Healing signal, and receive it clearly.

Step 7: Ask your inner teacher to give you his or her vibrational signal if the healing signal was received clearly.

Step 8: Do healing prayers from chapter 10 when needed at any time during this process.

Once you have established clear inner vibrational names, inner vibrational signals, "yes and no" signals, and healing signals, and you have become skilled at using the nine tests and the safeguards, then and only then are you ready to receive clear, reliable answers from Spirit.

How to Receive Clear Answers

Here are steps that you would use to ask inner questions and receive clear answers. As you use these steps, be sure to check the nine tests.

Step 1: Call upon an inner divine teacher.

Step 2: Ask "Do you come in the name of God?" (or "Do you come in the name of the Christ?") and get a yes response with your yes signal. Otherwise, do an Astral Entity Healing prayer and then repeat Step 2 until you get a yes.

Step 3: Ask "What is your name?" and get a clear inner name, either through your inner ear or through psychokinetic revelation (for example, tapping out the letters of the alphabet with a body part, such as a finger, or with an object, such as a table or a planchette). Otherwise, go back to Step 2.

Step 4: Say "Please feed me your signal" and get a clear signal. If you don't get a clear signal, then say, "Please feed the signal stronger" until you get a clear signal. Otherwise, go back to Step 2.

Step 5: Ask "Is it clear?" and get a yes signal in response. Check to feel if you are getting any healing signals. If you are getting a healing signal, then do the healing prayer without hesitation and skip to Step 7.

Step 6: Ask "Are any healings needed?" If you get a no signal in response, then skip to Step 10. If you get a yes signal, then ask, "What healing is needed?" Wait to receive the healing signal and do the healing prayer indicated by the signal.

Step 7: Ask "Is that healing complete?" and get a yes signal in response. Otherwise speak out the healing prayer again and repeat Step 7 until you get a yes.

Step 8: Ask "Are any other healings needed?" and get a no signal in response. If you get a yes signal, then ask "What healing is needed?" Receive the healing signal and speak out whatever healings are needed. Then go back to Step 7.

Step 9: Ask "Is it clear now?" and get a yes signal in response. If you get a no signal, then go back to Step 8.

Step 10: Ask "Do you come in the name of God?" and get a yes signal in response. Otherwise, do an Astral Entity Healing prayer and go back to Step 7.

Step 11: Ask "Is this still [inner name]?" and get a yes signal in response. Otherwise, go back to Step 2.

Step 12: Check your vibrational signal corresponding to the name to make sure it is clear. Check all nine tests, especially the feeling. If your signal is not clear, go back to Step 4. If all tests have been passed, go to Step 13. If any test has not been passed, then do an Astral Entity Healing prayer and then go back to Step 1.

Step 13: Now you are ready to ask your question. Ask your question; you will get a yes or no signal in response or get a message from the divine voice in response, depending on the nature of your question.

Step 14: If you get a yes response, then ask, "Is this a true 'yes'?" If you get a no response, then ask, "Is this a true 'no'?" In either case, if you get a positive confirmation, then you know your answer was clear. If the answer is not confirmed, then go back to Step 6.

How to Word Your Questions

Your divine contact has such integrity that it will not answer certain questions posed to it. If you word your question inappropriately, you will either not receive any answer or you may draw a lower entity or your own subconscious mind to answer the question. Beware of how your questions are asked. Many entities and "faker spirits" are waiting to answer your predictive questions. They are ready to jump in any moment that you give them a chance. Here are some rules and examples to help you word your questions:

RULES FOR ASKING QUESTIONS

Rule 1: Avoid predictive questions.
Rule 2: Ask only questions that assume freedom of choice.
Rule 3: Ask for "highest wisdom" rather than "shoulds."
Rule 4: Ask for divine guidance.
Rule 5: Ask clear and simple questions.
Rule 6: Ask only one question at a time.

WHAT QUESTIONS ARE INAPPROPRIATE?

In this section are sample questions that one might hypothetically ask an inner voice. Every one of these questions is worded in such a way that it cannot be answered clearly by Spirit. That is because each of these questions violates one or more of the above rules. Each of the following questions is explained and then reworded in such a way that a clear answer from Spirit can then be received.

Sample Inappropriate Question: "How will my business do this next year?"

This is a predictive question. In other words you want to know about the future. The divine voice will not answer your question as it is worded now. You cannot receive an unequivocal answer to a predictive question, because predictions are dependent on current thought-forms, which are ever-changing. Which means the outcome is ever-changing. This week one may predict that you would do well with your business. Next week one may predict that you would do poorly.

Predicting the future is based on the assumption that your path is predetermined and that you have no freedom of choice. But you have free will and the freedom to determine your outcome through prayer and action. You may reword your question to say, "What is the best course for me to take to succeed in business this next year?" This reworded question assumes that you can take control of the situation and create success.

Sample Inappropriate Question: "What should I do about my daughter's drug addiction?"

The only problem with the wording of this question is the use of the word "should." Avoid this word in asking inner questions, because it assumes that you have no freedom of choice and there is only one path that you must take. If you use the words "what is highest wisdom?" in any situation, then you are asking for the best possible course, rather than placing yourself at the mercy of some force telling you what you must do. Therefore, you may reword this question as follows: "What is highest wisdom for me to follow regarding my daughter's drug addiction?"

Sample Inappropriate Question: "Should I go to Paris this year or should I stay in New York?"

This question has two questions in it. Also, it uses the word "should." Instead, word your first question as follows: "Is it wise for me to go to Paris this year?" The second question would be: "Is it wise for me to stay in New York this year?" Then you can receive yes or no signals in response to your questions.

Sample Inappropriate Question: "I don't know what to do about my relationship with Judy and I can't seem to find a job and I'm unhappy

202 // D I V I N E   R E V E L A T I O N

with my apartment. The people downstairs are driving me crazy. What should I do?"

This question is really many different questions jumbled together. Also, the word "should" has come up again. You could replace it with: Question 1: "Please give me guidance about my relationship with Judy at this time." Question 2: "What is the highest wisdom for me to follow about finding a job?" Question 3: "How can I best deal with the situation with my downstairs neighbors?"

Sample Inappropriate Question: "Will I marry Jean Whittler?"

This is a predictive question. Reword it in the following way: "Is it highest wisdom for me to marry Jean Whittler?"

Sample Inappropriate Question: "Will California have a big earthquake and will that earthquake hurt any people?"

This is two separate predictive questions. It could be reworded as follows: "Please give me wisdom concerning the geologists' predictions of major earthquakes in California" and "Please give me wisdom concerning people living in those areas in California considered to be high-risk areas for earthquakes."

Sample Inappropriate Question: "What should I do about my car? Should I keep it or sell it? When should I sell it?"

Again, there are too many questions being asked at once and many "shoulds." You might reword it as follows: Question 1: "Would it be wise for me to sell my car at this time?" Question 2: "Would it be wise for me to keep my car?" You might also ask, "Is there any further wisdom about my car?" You can always ask if there is anything further to be known about a question.

Sample Inappropriate Question: "When will I sell my condominium?"

This is another predictive question. It could be reworded as follows: "Is it highest wisdom for me to sell my condominium now?" Or you may ask, "Is it wise for me to put my condominium on the market now?" You might ask, "Is it wise for me to take my condominium off the market now?" You may ask your question in many different ways to receive a clear answer from Spirit.

Sample Inappropriate Question: "I have a bad feeling about a plane trip that my mother is taking. Will she get into a plane crash on that trip?"

The question is predictive and assumes an unavoidable, irreversible doom-and-gloom situation. It can be reworded in two questions as follows: Question 1: "I have a bad feeling about a plane trip that my mother is taking. Would it be wise for her to take the trip?" Question 2: "Would it be wise for her to cancel the trip?"

ASKING YOUR OWN QUESTIONS

If you feel confident with at least one inner divine contact and vibrational signal, clear "yes and no" signals, clear healing signals, and using the nine tests, then you are ready to ask your higher self specific questions. It takes time and practice to become proficient in receiving clear, reliable answers from your divine voice, but that practice pays off.

For beginners it is easier to ask questions that do not require a yes or no answer. Yes and no answers require greater clarity and a deeper contact with Spirit. In order to get a clear yes or no, your inner signals and nine tests must be impeccable. Otherwise, any number of influences from your own subconscious mind, the psychic world, astral entities, or "other voices" could slip in to answer.

Over the years I have seen disastrous results from students' attempts to receive "yes and no" answers without the advantage of the nine tests. My experience has shown that such puerile trials at receiving intuition can be dangerous and addictive.

If you are just starting to ask inner questions, it is easier to ask questions that require an answer that is spoken-through rather than a yes or no answer. I spent the first few years of my Divine Revelation training without ever asking one yes or no question. I would recommend the same path to beginning students.

If you wish to become proficient with *yeses* and *nos*, then I would suggest you learn to use "psychokinesis," described on page 215. With this method, the yes and no answers are more accurate because of an inherent checks-and-balance system.

Every time you ask your inner contact a question, whether you are in a car, on the subway, or in your favorite chair, be sure to use the methods outlined in this chapter and verify your answers with the nine tests. By using these tests, safeguards, and rules, you can be sure that the answers to your questions are clear and coming from a divine source.

These methods are tickets to a grand adventure—the ability to follow your divine guidance with clarity. Divine Revelation has implications that transcend simply asking mundane questions and receiving advice. Indeed, heeding your inner voice is the pathway to fulfill your destiny!

> "A white bone much resembles ivory; most men fail to distinguish the one from the other."
>
> —Huai Nan Tzu (Taoist)

PART VII
Waking Up Your Inner Genius

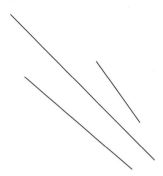

CHAPTER 15

Twelve Ways to Receive Inner Revelation

Your inner knower, the true Spirit within, communicates with you in many different ways. You will receive these revelations according to your own nature. Spirit first feeds messages into your emotional body, the deepest part of your subconscious. Your subconscious mind receives these messages as images, feelings, and ideas. Then your conscious mind perceives these subtle experiences as visions, sensations, and thoughts. Thus each message from Spirit is filtered through your subconscious mind into your conscious mind. The clarity of your subconscious filter determines the clarity of the message.

Each of these direct cognitions is received by you in the way that you can most easily receive and understand it. The three basic ways by which inner revelation comes to you are:

1. Receiving inner or outer visions (clairvoyance).
2. Receiving inner or outer sounds or messages in words (clair-audience).

3. Receiving feelings through inner sensing or bodily sensations (clairsentience).

These three are the universal methods for receiving messages from any invisible realm, mental or spiritual. Therefore, just because you are clairvoyant, clairaudient, or clairsentient does not mean your messages come from Spirit. You can receive visions, sounds, or feelings from astral beings, from your subconscious mind, or from the collective consciousness of the human race. Some psychics believe that just because they are capable of receiving inner impressions, their impressions are true or from a divine source. They may be mistaken.

Your inner revelation always comes to you in one of these three basic ways or in various combinations. There are many different ways that you can receive messages from Spirit. Twelve are explained here.

1. Clairvoyance

Clairvoyance means "clear-seeing"—the ability to see inner visual images or lights. If you are visually oriented, you will probably receive messages through seeing inner or outer visions. This form of revelation also includes seeing divine beings, lights, or auras.

You may receive visions that flash like a motion picture or a still photo in your mind's eye. These usually come during meditation or in a dream. You may also see clairvoyant visions with your eyes open. You may see a divine being or receive a message. Some clairvoyants see words flash before their eyes.

One example might be seeing a person in your mind's eye and then meeting that person the same day. Or you might receive an inner "motion picture" that depicts a story with a deep inner meaning. You might see an event taking place somewhere at a distance. Or a divine being, such as Jesus or Buddha, might appear to you, either in your inner vision or your environment. You may see how to proceed with a particular project or envision the project in its completion. You may see the fulfillment of a goal or the solution to a problem.

Albert Einstein attributed a vision that he had at age sixteen as his first inspiration for his theory of relativity. He saw himself pursuing a light beam with the same speed as light. He realized the light beam was an electromagnetic field simultaneously at rest and in motion with a wave arrangement completely independent of time.[1]

2. Clairaudience

Clairaudience means "clear-hearing"—hearing inner messages as thoughts or inner sounds. If you are an auditory type of person, you will hear divine messages through inner words or sounds.

You may hear an auditory message with your eyes open or closed. These are usually thoughts that come into your mind, just like ordinary thoughts. But thoughts coming from Spirit have a deeper content and meaning to them. They are thoughts of divine wisdom, usually "heard" inaudibly by your inner ear. You may also hear audible messages ("direct voice") with your outer ear.

For example, you may receive an inspirational message in the form of thoughts that arise in your mind. A divine voice may speak to you, either audibly or inaudibly. You may hear a message that seems to come from an object, such as a tree, a bird, or a person. Your name may be called when you are alone. You may hear a sudden warning about a hazard in your environment. You might hear celestial music, divine choirs, or a musical composition. A loved one's voice may speak comforting words to you.

Joan of Arc (1412–1431) began to hear the voices of saints Michael, Margaret, and Catherine at age thirteen. By following these voices she took up arms against the English and secured the crown of France for the dauphin, who later became Charles VII. She astonished Charles in 1429 by reciting his daily personal prayer to him. She accurately predicted her raising of the English siege of Orleans, the crowning of Charles, her wounds in battle, and victory over the English within seven years.[2]

3. Clairsentience

Clairsentience means "clear-feeling"—sensing intuitive messages through feelings. If you are a kinesthetic type of person, then you will experience your revelations as physical or emotional sensations. Clairsentience includes all subtle perceptions of smell, taste, touch, emotions, or physical sensations.

You may receive a message through feelings, sensations, or vibrations. You may feel led in a certain direction or feel the inclination to move your body in a certain way. You may feel vibrations or sensations that are somehow meaningful to you. Or you may feel something external, such as the vibrations in your environment nearby or far away. You may sense the presence of a divine being.

For instance, you may get a feeling about a person whom you first meet. You might get a hunch about the merits or dangers of a business deal. You may sense the best time to buy or sell a stock or commodity. You may feel subtle vibrations or ominous premonitions. Perhaps, while you are driving on a highway, an unseen hand pulls you over to the next exit. You might be crossing a street when suddenly you are pulled back by an inexplicable force, saving you from injury. You may feel ecstatic body sensations while listening to spiritual music or seeing a beautiful sight.

Richard Lawson, daytime television actor on *All My Children,* survived the USAir flight from La Guardia on March 22, 1992, which crashed into the freezing waters of Flushing Bay with twenty-seven fatalities. After taking his seat Richard heard the plane being deiced and got a dreaded sensation in his gut. He sensed that something was wrong. When the pilot announced seven planes were ahead of them, Richard panicked. His instinct was to demand to get off the plane or else inform the pilot that the plane hadn't been deiced properly. The plane took off without enough speed and crashed. In his shock he was angry with himself for not trusting his feelings. Richard ended up trapped upside down underwater, struggling to get free. Then an inner voice said, "Stop struggling." He relaxed. Another voice then said, "Take your seat belt off and get out." Oxygen-deficient, he moved things away hurriedly and suddenly found himself above water, gasping for air.[3]

4. Direct Cognition

Direct cognition means spontaneously receiving intuition through inner realization rather than receiving a message. The truth is simply *known* without knowing how you know. It is a flash of insight.

For example, you may suddenly receive the solution to a problem that you have been pondering for weeks. You may experience an inner knowing about the outcome of a certain event. You may receive unexpected insight into your field of study. Suddenly you may feel that you know God or how the universe was created. Or you might realize who you really are or what your true purpose is.

The NASA astronaut Edgar Mitchell, while on the Apollo 14 mission in 1971, looked back onto earth from his space capsule and suddenly realized that there was an intelligence at work in the universe. After this "aha" experience he left the space program and founded the Institute of Noetic Sciences to study the link between the physical universe and the human mind.[4]

5. Omenology

Omenology is a method of reading various signs or omens from the environment. It is often used by both East Indians and Native Americans. Those skilled in this practice may assign spiritual meanings to happenings in the natural world, such as the song of a bird or animal, an eclipse of the sun or moon, a meteor, or another natural event.

Here is a personal anecdote about omens:

After I wrote this book my literary agent suggested that I ask some famous authors for endorsements for my book cover. I wrote letters to several total strangers, asking whether they would look at my book. At that point I didn't even have a publisher! When I pulled up to the post office to mail these letters, I saw a man with only one leg walking on crutches toward the building. I felt this must be a bad omen. My inner voice said, "You don't even have a leg to stand on." It was true. I didn't know these authors personally. When I left the post office, I noticed the same one-legged man get into his car and drive off. My inner voice said, "You may not have a leg to stand on, but you will be successful anyway, just as this man is capable of driving, even with his handicap." I then realized the sight of this one-legged man was a good omen. The response to my letters was overwhelming. I received more endorsements than would fit on the book cover!

6. Visitations from Divine Beings

Visitations occur when spiritual beings take on an etheric or physical form to appear to a person and give a message or a teaching.

For example, a divine being may suddenly appear to you on the street.

You may be helped by a stranger who comes out of nowhere. Your life may be saved by a person who happens to appear at just the right time. When your car is broken down in the middle of nowhere, someone may suddenly arrive to fix it.

Three men suddenly appeared to the prophet Abraham in the desert on the plains of Mamre, where he sat in the tent door in the heat of the day. Abraham ran to meet them and bowed before them. He then washed their feet and gave them food and drink. One of them prophesied to Abraham that his wife Sarah would have a son. Since Sarah was beyond the age of conception, she laughed, thinking it was impossible. But later she did indeed have another son, Isaac.[5]

7. Seeing the Light

"I arrived at Truth, not by systematic reasoning and accumulation of proofs, but by a flash of light which God sent into my soul."[6]

Seeing the light means receiving a direct message from Spirit through an intense light on the inner or outer level. "I saw the light" is a very common phrase to mean "I received a great revelation of truth." You may receive such a light in your inner or outer vision.

Saul of Tarsus, while traveling on the road to Damascus on his way to arrest Christians, saw a dazzling light and, as he fell to the ground, heard a voice ask, "Saul, Saul, why persecutest thou me?"[7] Saul was blinded for three days. When his sight was restored by Ananias in Damascus, he converted to Christianity, called himself one of the apostles, and changed his name to Paul.

8. Foretelling Future Events

Glimpses of the future can come in four basic ways or in various permutations thereof:

Prophecy is a divinely inspired message foretelling events affecting the life of the people. Most prophecies have an element of importance to a large number of individuals, entire nations, or the world as a whole. Prophecies may occur in dreams, visions, or messages.

Michel de Nostredame, or Nostradamus (1503–1566), French healer and visionary, accurately prophesied many major events that would take place in European history, describing in detail, for example, the death of

Henry II, the fire of London in 1666, the French Revolution, the death of Marie Antoinette, and Adolf Hitler's reign of terror. He believed his inner visions and voices to be from the "Divine Presence."[8]

Premonition is a vague feeling about a future event or an event taking place at a distance. It is characterized by a state of uneasiness and a gut-level anxiety without any discernible reason. Premonitions usually take place during waking consciousness. Often premonitions prompt people to make unconscious decisions, saving themselves or others from impending disasters, such as choosing to avoid a particular plane, train, ship, or automobile trip.

More than nineteen documented cases of premonition about the ship *Titanic* in the two weeks prior to its launching, April 10, 1912, were reported by the psychiatrist Ian Stevenson. Several people canceled their passage abruptly, including J. Pierpont Morgan. Others canceled after dreaming that the ship was doomed or after having a dreaded feeling. Some survivors reported that they had had an uneasy feeling about sailing on the ship but went anyway. The ship sailed away with only 58 percent of its passenger load.[9]

Precognition is the most common ESP (extrasensory perception) experience. Precognitions usually occur in dreams but may also take place in other subliminal states of consciousness, such as daydreams or meditation. They are precise, realistic visions of future events, usually occurring within two days of the event, often giving a warning to avoid disastrous events. Precognitions are so vivid that you may think the event is actually taking place. For example, in Norway, *vardogr* is a phenomenon of hearing the sound of footsteps, a phone ring, a door slam, or a person's voice just before the event is to take place.[10]

Mark Twain, American author of the nineteenth century, had a lifelike dream of his brother's corpse in a metal coffin, balanced on two chairs in his sister's sitting room. When he awoke, he assumed his brother had died. However, he decided to take a walk before visiting the coffin. It wasn't until he had walked half a block away from his sister's house, where he was staying at the time, that he realized he had been asleep. A few weeks later his precognition came true, precisely as he had envisioned, down to the last detail, even the white carnations and one red rose that were placed on the coffin.[11]

Prediction is more deliberate and cultured through the development of intuitive abilities, such as clairvoyance, clairaudience, or clairsentience. Predictions may also be the result of divinatory methods, such as astrology, numerology, palmistry, tea-leaf reading, scrying, card-reading, runes, I Ching, psychometry, etc.

In 1925 Louis Hamon, the palmist known as Cheiro, predicted that Edward, prince of Wales, might become involved in a devastating love affair and give up everything, including the throne, rather than lose the woman he loved. In 1936 the prince was crowned King Edward VIII. Eleven months after his coronation, he abdicated his throne, choosing to marry a twice-divorced commoner. Cheiro also warned the journalist William T. Stead to be cautious not to travel by water in April 1912. Mr. Stead unfortunately ignored Cheiro's advice and drowned on April 14 with the Titanic.[12]

9. Synchronicity

Sometimes we have such amazingly coincidental experiences that we sense a higher power directly at work in the intimate, daily affairs of our lives. These synchronous events generate a state of awe at the workings of the mysterious universe. You may have experienced days in which people just appear at the right moment and every event naturally falls into place. At such times you feel in harmony with God and with all the laws of nature.

A stunning example of synchronicity are the parallel lives of John F. Kennedy, elected president in 1960, and Abraham Lincoln, elected one hundred years earlier in 1860:

Both Lincoln and Kennedy were involved in civil rights for blacks. Their wives had each lost a son while in the White House. Both presidents were succeeded by vice presidents who had been southern Democrats and senators—Andrew Johnson, born in 1808, and Lyndon Johnson, born in 1908. Lincoln's private secretary's name was John, and Kennedy's was Lincoln. The first public proposal endorsing Lincoln as the Republican candidate for president also endorsed a man named John Kennedy (formerly secretary of the navy) for vice president.

Lincoln was killed in Ford's Theater, and Kennedy was riding in a Lincoln, manufactured by the Ford Motor Company. Both were assassinated on Friday, with their wives present, by a bullet that entered the head from behind. John Wilkes Booth and Lee Harvey Oswald, southerners with extremist views, were both murdered before their trial. Booth shot

Lincoln in a theater and hid in a barn. Oswald shot Kennedy from a warehouse and hid in a theater. Lincoln's and Kennedy's name each has seven letters. Andrew Johnson and Lyndon Johnson each has thirteen letters. John Wilkes Booth and Lee Harvey Oswald each has fifteen letters.[13]

10. Prophetic Dreams

During prophetic dreams Spirit gives you messages while you sleep. Once you have awakened from the dream, Spirit may reveal its meaning to you.

Elias Howe, inventor of the sewing machine, dreamt he had been taken prisoner by a primitive tribe. The leader of the tribe threatened to kill him unless he immediately finished his invention. All the members of the tribe were pointing strange spears at him, with eye-shaped holes in their sharp tips. Mr. Howe had been attempting to use a regular sewing needle in his invention, with the hole in the dull end rather than the sharp end. He jumped out of bed and immediately finished his invention.[14]

11. Déjà Vu

Another example is the phenomenon known as "déjà vu." Déjà vu is a French expression literally meaning "already seen." It is an eerie sensation of suddenly feeling you have "been here before." It is a fairly common experience, and feels as if a scenario has somehow been re-created, right down to the last detail.

There are many theories about what déjà vu is. In actuality, it is a remembrance, the memory of experiencing an event previously, but this event did not take place in your waking life. It happened in a dream! In a prophetic dream you dreamt you would be a certain place and would experience certain events. Thus, you saw it before and are now remembering it. Therefore, your subjective experience is, indeed, that it happened before.

12. Psychokinesis

Psychokinesis is the movement of physical objects by mental energy without using physical force. "Psycho" means mind and "kinetic" means movement. Through psychokinesis you can receive yes and no answers, get confirmation signals, and spell words. However, psychokinesis can be very dangerous unless you have a clear contact with Spirit, and it is not recommended for beginners. The reason is that this method can attract lower vibrations if no safeguards are used, simply because discarnate entities, by nature, seem to enjoy moving physical objects.

Spiritual psychokinesis means uniting with divine Spirit and inviting your God self to move an object. When your energy is combined with a higher being or aspect of God, a physical object may move by spiritual energy and become a conduit for divine messages.

USING PSYCHOKINESIS SAFELY

PSYCHOKINETIC BODY SIGNALS

Body parts, such as a finger, hand, arm, or head, can be used to receive divine messages through autonomic movements. I recommend body signals as an aid to communicating with Spirit, but I caution you to verify these signals through proper instruction from a qualified teacher.

MOVEMENT OF PHYSICAL OBJECTS

Any object, such as a pendulum, table, chair, dowsing rod, or board with a planchette, can be used to receive messages from a divine being. One accurate way to receive spiritual revelation is by two or more well-trained practitioners using a small table. In this method aspects of God-Spirit transmit energy through the hands to elevate the table. The table tips up and down, balancing on two legs, according to a preestablished code for "yes and no" answers and for spelling words. This method is safe and reliable because two or more people create a circuit of balanced energy, a unification of the group, and a checks-and-balance system. As it has been said: "Where two or three are gathered together in my name, there I AM in the midst of them."[15]

This method of psychokinetic revelation, when used properly, can be a profound experience for the participants. In such a session they can receive divine wisdom, answers to questions, counseling, and healing. Students can break through to higher states of consciousness by contacting aspects of God within. A sublime spiritual presence fills the session with God's light, love, and peace.

The following factors are important when practicing spiritual psychokinesis:

1. Objective-Subjective Balance

Receiving clearly from Spirit requires an attitude of allowing and permissiveness. You are inviting Spirit to feed you messages, answers, and information of the highest truth, putting aside mental limitations and allowing your consciousness to lift to the highest level. You are not imposing your human will upon the divine will.

However, the biggest mistake of novices is their tendency to be *too* passive and not take charge of the session. A specific format and system exists for receiving clearly from Spirit, outlined in chapters 13 and 14. There is nothing like psychokinesis for training you to use this system precisely and accurately. But if you do not take control and ask the proper questions, then you are inviting big trouble. Oversubjectivity and overopenness mean allowing energies that are not from Spirit (astral entities) to control you.

When using psychokinetic energy, it is essential to be neutral and balanced, both subjectively and objectively. Not overly subjective, not overly objective, "Wise as serpents, and harmless as doves."[16] It is important to maintain control and permissiveness at the same time.

2. Spiritual Power

The use of spiritual power, rather than willpower or psychic power, is essential to receive divine intuition through psychokinesis. This power of love, not available in negative mental or emotional states, flows through a channel with a pure heart and clear mind who is alert, awake, and one with God. It comes from daily practice of deep meditation, proper rest, and nutrition without intoxicants. Most importantly, divine power comes from inner happiness. When you are truly happy, you have all the power you need to successfully use psychokinesis.

3. Alertness and Concentration

When using psychokinesis, it is essential to be alert and focused. Lapses in concentration can cause lower energies or thought-forms to influence the table, the pendulum, etc. When your mind wanders, you are no longer with Spirit, but in the mental realm. This is not the way to receive clear revelation.

For instance, if you are using psychokinesis to spell a word or name, it is important to stay alert and concentrate on each letter. Otherwise the intended letter may be passed by without stopping. Interruptions, idle conversation, fatigue, or other interferences break the continuity and create confusion in the session.

4. Clear Divine Contact

It is essential to use all the tests and safeguards described in chapters 13 and 14 when working with psychokinetic energy. It is important to call upon the divine name, to know that it comes in the name of God, to have clear signals, to do all the healings needed, and to have divine feelings. This must be done before attempting to move any object through psychokinesis. A divine teacher who comes in the name of the Christ or in the name of God is the leader of a clear psychokinetic session. Never invite other beings to lead a psychokinetic session unless you desire to attract lower energies. By giving over to God you can have divine ecstatic experiences and clear revelation from Spirit.

5. Unification

Unification of the group in love and divine consciousness is necessary for clear, unencumbered reception of Divine Revelation during your session. When you are in union with God, nothing can go wrong. When members of a group become disunified and scattered, or disharmonious feelings are present, then it is wise for the leader to reunify the group with a prayer of unification.

6. Highest Intention

Because "It is done unto you as you believe,"[17] your intention for your session will guide the outcome. An intention of love, healing, compassion, and the highest divine contact produces the most fruitful psychokinetic experience. Starting with a prayer is a step in the right direction. Asking questions according to the rules in chapter 14 helps you receive answers from Spirit rather than from the psychic realm.

A session done for the phenomenon of moving an object or for fortune-telling can produce lower vibrations. A session done for receiving spiritual power and energy and for healing the participants can be miraculous and awe-inspiring. It is a matter of the right intention and the use of safeguards.

7. Precise Training

An entire book would be required to give complete knowledge of accurate, clear, consistent psychokinetic revelation. It is an advanced science requiring a clear divine contact and hands-on experience. Receiving clear "yes and no" answers and spelling words—you might think this would be a simple practice. But it requires greater training than can be undertaken in this text. You can receive hands-on training in advanced Divine Revelation classes. On page 271 is a list of teachers you can contact.

After studying the healing prayers, nine tests, and safeguards in chapters 10, 13, and 14, you may experiment with psychokinesis by using "How to Receive Clear Answers" on page 199. But you may not have perfect results unless you have a clear inner contact, a clear inner signal, and your mind is clear. Remember, "Heal all the way." Any time you feel a lack of clarity in any method of intuition, "Heal first and ask questions later." You can never go wrong by using the healing prayers in chapter 10.

A Warning About the Methods in This Chapter:

Just because you use the twelve methods detailed in this chapter does not mean your messages come from Spirit. A medium in contact with an entity can use these methods, but would not offer the same uplifting vibrational content. That is why the nine tests of discernment and the safeguards in chapters 13 and 14 are essential to study.

How Spirit Teaches You

Your true inner revelations are entirely led by God and are in divine timing. Therefore, you receive exactly what is wisdom for you at any given moment. You may not be ready to receive every piece of knowledge that you are curious about at this instant. This is especially true in the case of questions about your past incarnations or traumatic memories from childhood.

Similarly, while you may desire to know your divine purpose, you may not be ready to accept it fully at a particular time. You may be discomfited to suddenly learn your deepest spiritual desires if you have built your life around false ego-desires that you had previously thought were true. So, in a sense, Spirit may spoon-feed you what you can handle when you can handle it. Your growth is step-by-step as you move toward fulfilling your life purpose.

You may receive messages that seem too great to believe. These prophesies or inspirations may be your divine teacher's way of encouraging or inspiring you to greatness. However, if the message seems preposterous, even though all the nine tests of discernment have been passed, it is a good idea to "place it on a shelf" until you can analyze it later.

Beware of messages that are simply "wishful thinking" on your part. Your subconscious mind may block the clear message from Spirit and create interference. You may receive what you think is a message from your divine voice, but it is actually a thought from your subconscious mind. Be sure to verify every message you receive by using the nine tests in chapter 13.

Conversely, if you receive divine wisdom and guidance that is clear and has been verified by the nine tests, then by all means trust it, and let go of all doubts. One of the biggest problems for students of intuition is a lack of faith in the clear messages that they receive.

For instance, Curt De Groat, a psychic from New York City, says: "I am tuning in intuitively to people all the time, yet I have a really deep problem with trusting. When I get these impressions, I don't know, but I really just have to go with what I receive, and I have to let it out, and just take that leap of faith, that bit of trust. Divine Revelation has helped me and enabled me to trust more. And that's a *big* case for all of us, that we've been taught to not trust our feelings, not trust what we get. First of all, we can't tell where it's coming from. We might feel right about it, but even then we may think, 'Well, I'd like this to happen. Is this my personal issue?'"

How many times have you regretted not trusting that intuitive inner voice that prompted you to take a leap of faith, to take that job, to make that investment, to get involved in that relationship? How many of your spiritual experiences have you denied or disbelieved? Have you been afraid to tell others about your experiences?

Sara Day, a beautician from Iowa, describes how Divine Revelation has helped her: "One of the values I gained almost immediately was understanding a lot of the experiences I've had since a child. I've had so many intuitive flashes that I never really trusted. I never really understood where they came from, and that doubt, and that lack of support from the environment, in many cases, counteracted them for me. Once I started Divine Revelation, I became aware of the truth of those and how in the past they had always been there for me. And the times I'd followed them, and the times I hadn't, I could see what had happened."

On the other hand it is wise to be discerning about the guidance that you receive and to never rush blindly into anything that makes you feel uncomfortable. Your inner guidance is just that—inner guidance, not coercion or force. You have complete freedom to make your own choices. You are not forced to do anything that your inner teacher suggests. Your will and free choice is a God-given gift. Divine Spirit never demands, "it stands at the door and knocks,"[18] and never comes in unless invited. Once you invite it to come, it gives inspiration, wisdom, and guidance, but it does not intrude in any way.

As you become more attuned to Spirit, your desires will align more with your true soul-desires and you will make better choices. You will learn as you go, making choices and enjoying, or else suffering as a result. In this way you will discover how best to use your free will and your self-authority and to allow the divine to guide you.

> "I will pour out my spirit upon all flesh; and your sons and your daughters shall prophesy, your old men shall dream dreams, your young men shall see visions."
>
> —Joel 2:28 (Judeo-Christian)

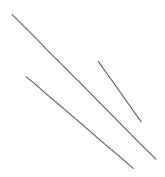

CHAPTER 16

Nine Ecstatic Expressions
of God

There are several ways to receive inner revelation and many ways to express the wonderful inspirations that you receive. The methods of expressing your spiritual revelations have been dubbed by the inner teachers the "ecstatic expressions of God." These expressions are called "ecstatic" because they bring with them an experience of inner bliss.

After meditating for twenty years, I discovered that the deep silence attained during meditation can remain dormant if it is not brought to the surface and expressed. Divine Revelation changed my life because it taught me to *express* the wonderful inner world I had been exploring.

Through Divine Revelation I learned to activate the inner silence by using specific creative expressions, such as "speaking-through," "dancing-through," "writing-through," and "singing-through." These are some of the ecstatic expressions of God explored in this teaching.

I have had profound experiences and tremendous inner growth with these ecstatic expressions, more pronounced than with silent meditation alone. They are sublime expressions of God, methods for expressing God consciousness. They fill your heart with joy and create joy in the environment as well.

Attaining God Consciousness

It is important to learn how to remain in contact with God while active in the world. The ecstatic expressions are ways to practice being one with God while at the same time being active. Some metaphysicians call this "practicing the presence of God." How do the ecstatic expressions help to develop God consciousness?

When you are in deep silence, with your eyes closed, far from the turmoil of the world, it is easy to be in a peaceful, loving state. But when you come out and begin to be active, you might feel adversely affected by the people, places, and vibrations around you. You may even become irritated, angry, and out of sorts. You may lose your state of serenity and became agitated and overly sensitive.

The "ecstatic expressions of God" are a methodology for remaining at peace and one with God while being active. These expressions illustrate how God's inspiration can flow through you during activity. The ecstatic expressions are the mark of true genius. Wherever there is greatness, it is born of divine inspiration. Those who made a long-lasting impact in their field of expertise have had one underlying theme in their lives: they felt their works came from a source or power greater than themselves; they were channels for higher inspiration to flow through them.

Your creative genius is easy to express when you contact inner divinity. Poetry, song, art, literature, drama, science, business, invention, philosophy, religion, spirituality, and other expressions are at your command. You can express your own unique gift for humanity, for your life has a meaning and a purpose, which is God's expression.

You have a singular destiny that conveys who you are, and who you are is unequaled. There is only one of you, and that one is one with the divine One inside. Through these ecstatic expressions, you can express your truth, the God within you, your unique divine nature.

Here are the nine ecstatic expressions and ways to express them.

1. Speaking-Through

The first ecstatic expression I recommend is "speaking-through"—speaking messages from the divine voice. Once this is mastered, you can move on to other expressions—"singing-through," "writing-through," and so forth. This way you can learn to remain in contact with God during activity, which can help develop God consciousness.

Speaking-through involves becoming a mouthpiece for the divine voice to speak messages through you. Your divine self uses your speech mechanism to communicate with you and with whoever is listening to you speak. In this case, you are not aware of what you will say until you open your mouth and begin to speak.

The prophet Jeremiah described the process in this way: "Then the Lord put forth his hand, and touched my mouth. And the Lord said unto me, Behold, I have put my words in thy mouth."[1]

Speaking-through is a direct link with Spirit without going through the filter of your mind. You are lifted to the divine level and become fully identified with Spirit. "I and my Father are one."[2]

This does not mean that you leave your body or go into a trance. You are in a fully conscious state of awareness during the process.

Often the words spoken are profound and enlightening. You may receive wonderful poetry, spiritual knowledge, answers to questions, or wisdom. Along with the words you may receive a surge of spiritual power and a realization of the truth of the ideas expressed, a direct cognition as well as a message. When you speak-through in a group, the audience listening to such a message is lifted to the level of Spirit.

Jesus had a profound ability to speak-through from Spirit. His words came directly from God and were spoken-through with clarity and perfection. When he referred to himself in his statements, he was not referring to his limited ego identity, but to the "I AM" self within him, his higher self.

For example, Jesus stated:

"I AM the way, the truth and the life: no man cometh unto the Father, but by ME."[3]

"I AM the light of the world: he that followeth ME shall not walk in darkness, but shall have the light of life."[4]

"I AM the resurrection, and the life: he that believeth in ME, though he were dead, yet shall he live."[5]

The use of "I AM" and "ME" in these phrases refers to the mighty "I AM" presence within every individual. Jesus was not alluding to his human embodiment or his ego identity when he said "I" or "ME." It is absurd to think that he was referring to his physical body when he stated, "Before Abraham was, I AM."[6] He was speaking of God within him. He was a mouthpiece for God to speak through him, and never claimed or desired to be deified.

Jesus said, "For I have not spoken of myself; but the Father which sent me, he gave me a commandment, what I should say, and what I should speak."[7]

"Believest thou not that I AM in the Father and the Father in me? the words that I speak unto you I speak not of myself: but the Father that dwelleth in me, he doeth the works."[8]

Because Jesus spoke from the level of his God presence, the "I AM" within, he was greatly misunderstood. Without the understanding that Jesus was speaking-through these statements, one might judge him to glorify his ego above others. He was therefore feared by priests and political leaders. A crown of thorns was placed on his head, and he was mocked as "King of the Jews."

2. Public Speaking-Through

Speaking-through a divinely inspired message for an audience is a completely impromptu, unrehearsed speech entirely guided by Spirit. Some orators and ministers have this ability to allow God to speak through them. The speaker's inner feelings often include rushes of divine energy and exaltation. The spellbound audience is emotionally moved and transported to delightful states of higher awareness.

Diane Matthew, minister of a Unity Church in suburban Toronto, Canada, stated, a few months after learning Divine Revelation: "Our co-founder, Charles Fillmore, referred to 'going to Headquarters' to receive one's guidance. This I found was exactly what your program is assisting one to do. It ensures that we move beyond the psychic realm to that place of Oneness with Spirit. I am personally grateful, Susan, in that I feel there has been a significant shift in the freedom with which the Spirit within speaks through me now, during my Sunday message, which I attribute in large part to your Breakthrough program."

Moses was instructed by God:

"Who hath made man's mouth? . . . have not I the Lord? Now therefore go, and I will be with thy mouth, and teach thee what thou shalt say."[9]

Jesus told his disciples:

"Take no thought how or what ye shall speak; for it shall be given you in that same hour what ye shall speak. For it is not ye that speak, but the Spirit of your Father which speaketh in you."[10]

3. Feeding-Through

In the process of feeding-through, you receive divine intuition in the form of ideas or words that are fed to you by Spirit. Then you may or may not speak the message out loud. You might receive one word at a time or whole phrases or sentences. You may also receive visions or feelings and then speak out your interpretation. This is an experience of feeling unified with Spirit, happy, whole, and peaceful.

Jesus described this process:

"For I have not spoken of myself; but the Father which sent me, he gave me a commandment, what I should say, and what I should speak . . . whatsoever I speak therefore, even as the Father said unto me, so I speak."[11]

4. Writing-Through

Writing-through from Spirit means allowing the divine aspect of your being to write or type messages through you. This writing-through may be either completely automatic or may be fed into your mind and then written. The inner experience while this is taking place is joyful and fulfilling. Those who read your literary piece are elevated into the higher consciousness in which it was written.

Helen Schucman, professor of medical psychology at the Columbia University College of Physicians and Surgeons in New York City, described herself as a conservative psychologist, educator, and atheist. She was surprised when she began to hear an unidentified inner voice speaking to her as rapid inner dictation. Although she had no belief in the concepts she was transcribing into her shorthand notebook, she felt this writing to have been a "special assignment" that she had somehow agreed to complete. A *Course in Miracles*, which she published anonymously, is believed to be dictated by the Holy Spirit.[12]

5. Painting-, Sculpting-, or Drawing-Through

These artistic expressions allow the divine aspect of yourself to either move your hands to create a work of art or to feed an image into your mind that you can then paint, draw, or sculpt. The experience is one of exaltation and delight. When you view such a piece of art, your awareness automatically rises to the level of the artist who created it.

Michelangelo, the greatest sculptor in European history, stated that the forms that he sculpted were already present within the slabs of stone before he even touched them. He believed that he merely chipped away the unwanted material from the forms, which were trapped inside the marble, waiting to be set free.

6. Dancing-Through

Dancing-through allows your spiritual self to move your body in wonderful, unique expressions of God. The experience of dancing-through quickens the vibration of your body and enlivens and awakens your cells. Your body may begin to tingle all over or you may feel rushes of electrifying energy. Watching such a performance can fill you with a feeling similar to the dancer's.

Sufis who are trained to dance in the Spirit are known as whirling dervishes. These entrancing dances raise one's consciousness to higher levels of awareness. Children from Bali receive divine messages by allowing Spirit to move their bodies and hands into gestures with specific meanings. They believe that they create a direct spiritual link, speaking to the gods through these improvisational dances.[13]

7. Playing-Through or Writing-Through Music

In this ecstatic expression you are creating spontaneous melodies from Spirit with a musical instrument. This is improvisational music with the added element of contact with Spirit. Such enthralling music can captivate listeners and carry them to a higher level of awareness.

Any great masterpiece of music, interpreted by a spiritually attuned conductor and played by sensitive musicians, can move an audience to tears and awaken inspiration, elation, and vibrational lifting.

Indian *ragas* are improvisational pieces performed with the express purpose of raising the level of consciousness of the listeners and transporting them to a divine state. In many cultures chanting or drumming is believed to create an altered level of awareness. The ancient Greeks thought music could promote healing, and it was used to treat various ailments, including indigestion and insomnia.[14]

8. Singing-Through

Singing-through means letting your higher self use your voice to create spontaneous sounds, melodies, or songs. By allowing these enchanting sounds to come forth, you can experience an inner state of wholeness and bliss. Singing-through can stimulate tingling sensations all over the body. It also elevates the vibrational level of the listener.

Native Americans sing-through spontaneous melodies from Spirit in their sweat lodge ceremonies, producing healing vibrations. American gospel music is elevating and inspiring, creating a heightened state of joy and lifting in mind and body. Hymns sung by church choirs can bring about rapturous spiritual states in listeners that can be accompanied by thrills and rushes of energy.

9. Healing-Through

During the process of healing-through, you allow Spirit to come through your hands or your divine energy to heal others. With this direct method of spiritual healing, an inexhaustible supply of energy can be tapped to receive healing power. Therefore, there is no draining effect while you are performing the healing. In fact the healer may feel great inner power, vitality, and divine love.

Jesus performed multitudes of miraculous healings, stating, "The Father that dwelleth in me, he doeth the works."[15] He laid no personal claim on his healing powers, but instead gave all credit to God. He was a perfect channel for God to heal through him.

Ambrose Worrall (1899–1972) and Olga Worrall (1906–1985) were hands-on healers who performed spectacular instantaneous cures, including shrinking tumors to nothing with just a touch. Olga reported her healing powers came from a higher power, not from herself. She believed that gifted healers take in God's high-voltage energy and then channel it through their subtle bodies to heal others. She said the process of healing is aided by love, compassion, and prayer and guided by spiritual beings. Ambrose felt a power building within him, which he believed to be the universal life force, which then flowed through his hands into the patient. Often he and his patient experienced tingling sensations.[16]

A NOTE OF WARNING:

These ecstatic expressions are ecstatic only if they come from the true level of Spirit. These nine activities can be performed from any level of consciousness: from the mental level, astral realm, or entity world. These nine expressions could be done by a psychic medium in contact with an entity or spirit. But they will not have the same uplifting vibrational content as the ecstatic expressions from the level of Spirit.

Use the ecstatic expressions of God along with the tests and safeguards in chapters 13 and 14. In this way you can develop your ability to be a clear channel for Spirit and a vehicle for God to uplift you and those around you. Through opening to divine inspiration, you can express the true genius that you came on this planet to express.

"The prophecy came not in old time by the will of man: but holy men of God spake as they were moved by the Holy Ghost."
—2 Peter 1:21 (Christian)

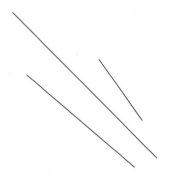

CHAPTER 17

Little Miracles in Everyday Life

After I first learned the meditation technique that I later named "Divine Revelation," I was motivated to practice it daily, since my experiences were so profound. At first my theme for each meditation was "deepening my inner contact." In this way I established many inner names and signals that I could work with. I focused on spiritual experiences, healing, and prayer, rather than on asking questions or receiving guidance.

After about a year, I began asking questions of my inner voice—but rarely. The inner teachers tell us that we can call upon them anytime, but I often forgot to ask.

I started a meditation group and then studied with Dr. Peter Meyer for several years, but I was still not using the teaching as much as I could have been.

How I Learned to Be Led by Spirit

A significant transformation took place for me one night while I was taking a long walk on a college campus. I heard my inner divine voice and felt the urge to speak-through aloud while walking. As I did this my consciousness lifted until I felt as if I were walking on air—expanded, blissful, and radiant. This profound experience taught me that I could contact my divine voice anytime, no matter what I was doing.

Soon I became involved in teaching Divine Revelation full-time and began traveling all over North America, lecturing and giving break-through sessions. However, I was still not using the teaching to its full capacity.

A great shift took place in my consciousness when Peter Meyer asked me to teach a teacher training course in New York City on very short notice. Since the course was not planned in advance, I had no other alternative than to ask my inner voice to advise me on how to conduct each part of the course as it went along.

When I came to the class each morning, I asked Spirit for guidance about the day's activity. Then I received a cryptic answer of one or two words, which gave me a direction. I followed that direction and incredible miracles and healing took place during the day. This course was an amazing experience for me and for my students.

I realized that if I had enough faith, I could be led by Spirit every day. If miracles could take place in one week, I was willing to let miracles happen all the time. This was quite a realization! I resolved to receive inner guidance daily. The only trick was keeping my divine contact clear. When I was unclear the inner teachers helped me recognize what needed healing so I could move through it. At first I didn't always remember to ask for guidance. But with time I began to ask more frequently.

As I started this I found my life took on new depth and meaning and became an exciting adventure, since I never knew what I would be guided to do next. I gained faith as I was led to do things that I ordinarily would never have had the nerve to do. It was not easy to do this. I encountered tremendous internal struggle and confronted many fears and limitations. It took enormous courage, especially when I was guided to do things contrary to my previously cherished beliefs or contrary to the opinions of people around me.

As my faith grew, experiences that were quite astonishing, even miraculous, became a frequent part of my life. Years of restriction crumbled as I broke through habits and patterns that had bound me to the past. I have had many amazing experiences since making the decision to be led by my inner divine voice, and my life has been greatly enhanced by following my inner guidance.

Many other students of Divine Revelation have had wonderful experiences by listening to their inner voice also. The remainder of this chapter relates a few of their personal anecdotes.

A Midnight Adventure in Faith
Michelle Kurtz: Belmont, California

One summer night I filled up my car with gas on the way home from work because I noticed the tank was low. I had had a hard day, so when I came home exhausted, I went right to sleep.

Suddenly the piercing ring of the telephone woke me up. A voice said, "I want you to get in your car and drive to Petaluma." In my half-conscious state I murmured, "It's twelve-thirty at night. I'm tired. I don't even know where Petaluma is." I didn't recognize this voice, so I hung up.

The phone kept ringing, and for some reason, I kept answering. Each time this mysterious voice urged me to drive to Petaluma, becoming more and more insistent. Thinking this might be some kind of sign—and knowing I wasn't going to get any sleep anyway—I figured *I might as well go!*

I started my car, incredulous that I was doing this. As I began driving, I thought, This is crazy. You have no address, but you are driving to Petaluma.

When I saw the sign for Petaluma, it was as though an invisible hand gripped the steering wheel and drove through town and out into the woods. Then the car died, and the gas gauge registered Empty. The trip should not have taken a full tank of gas!

I started to laugh and cry all at once. I thought, Now I've done it. Why didn't I stay in bed? Then I noticed a light in a house about twenty feet off the road. I ran toward it, hoping to find a phone so I could call for road service.

I knocked on the door. A voice replied in German, "Go away." I thought, Isn't that odd? I speak German. I answered in German, "My name is Michelle and I ran out of gas."

The door opened and there stood an old lady, about five feet tall, with gray hair tied back in a bun and tears streaming down her cheeks. She cried, in German, "My son is dead, my son is dead." Her son had brought her from Germany for an extended visit. He had died two days before. She couldn't speak English and didn't know how to use the phone or how to get anywhere.

Spirit had sent me to rescue her.

In the morning I called the German consulate and a local Lutheran church. A woman from the church who spoke German arrived to help her.

Then I called road service. They came out, but when I stuck my key in the ignition, the car started right away. The fuel tank was three-quarters full!

My Inner Voice Guided Me to My Husband
Tova Prager: San Diego, California

I was volunteering at the bookstore of a Unity Church conference in New Orleans. Just before leaving home one day, I received a message from my inner teachers: "Don't take your usual route, take another route, and don't leave on time. It's okay to be late." Usually I was a fanatic about being on time, but I trusted my inner voice and left fifteen minutes late.

As soon as I arrived at the bookstore, a man came in. It was love at first sight, instant attraction. He was a minister—good-looking, financially comfortable, and he loved children. He asked me out immediately, and that night he asked me to marry him. A month later I moved to San Diego. We married four months later.

I later learned that there was a very bad accident and a fatality on my usual route to work that morning. If I had been delayed, I would have missed meeting the love of my life.

Dreams Can Come True

Anne Rustin: Half Moon Bay, California

For several months my inner voice had given me repeated messages to move, but after looking for weeks on end, I became discouraged. One night I cried to God for help.

The next morning I woke from a dream in which I was doing Tai Chi inside a cave on a beach south of Half Moon Bay. From the mouth of the cave, I watched the ocean waves rolling onto the beach. I received an inner message to find this cave. Immediately I packed the car and started down Highway 1.

I drove south for miles, passing several beaches, but they didn't look like the beach I had seen in my dream. I thought, Maybe this beach doesn't exist. If I don't find it before I reach the next highway, I'll just call it a day and head home.

Then suddenly I started craving strawberries.

After a few miles I saw a sign: "Strawberry Ranch." Not more than fifteen feet away was a sign for San Gregorio Beach. I pulled over and the fog suddenly lifted. It was gorgeous, sunny, and warm. As I walked down to the beach, my inner voice said, "Go right."

A hundred yards down the beach I saw a cave on the side of the mountain. I went inside. It was pitch-black. I was shocked to see the mouth of the cave and the waves rolling up on the deserted beach—*exactly* what I had seen in my dream!

I realized that Half Moon Bay was the town for me. One day while I was driving around, answering newspaper ads, I said, "God, just show me where to live right now. Guide me where to go." My inner voice told me to turn onto a dirt road that led to a bluff with multimillion-dollar homes overlooking the ocean.

Three days after this experience I met a woman who was renting an apartment in Half Moon Bay. It had everything I had been praying for— a southern exposure, a balcony, and a gorgeous ocean view.

I'm now living in an apartment in one of the multimillion-dollar homes on the same bluff that Spirit had guided me to!

My Inner Voice Gave Me the Winning Bid
John Gilson: Indianapolis, Indiana

I noticed an empty forty-foot travel trailer parked next to mine at a trailer park. The park manager told me it was being foreclosed by the bank. When I meditated, I got a message from Babaji that I could buy it. I found out that the bank was having a silent bid auction on it. The trailer was worth about four thousand dollars, and it had a new roof and all the original wood. I asked Babaji how much to bid—"One thousand?" I got "No." I asked, "Eleven hundred?" "No." "Twelve hundred?" "No." I asked, "Under thirteen hundred?" "Yes." Then I asked, "Twelve hundred and five?" And I got a "Yes."

I knew I was going to win the auction. I sent in the bid, and within two weeks a woman from the bank called, saying, "You have been selected to buy the trailer. But I want to tell you something. We've never had an auction that was so close. The bid next to yours was twelve hundred dollars. Yours was only five dollars more!"

A Beautiful Angelic Healer
Robbie McKee: San Diego, California

My granddaughter was born with spina bifida, a spinal birth defect. I was visiting her in the hospital at Fort Bliss, near where my son was stationed. She was the only one in the ward, so alone and tiny in her bed.

One night I couldn't bring myself to leave her, so I stayed all night. In the middle of the night, I was startled by the presence of a nurse, who was bending over her crib, stroking her. The nurse was beautiful—a black woman, six feet tall, statuesque, with her long hair braided in cornrows. It was dark in the room, but a golden light shone on them.

The nurse turned and looked at me. She had the most beautiful golden-brown eyes I had ever seen. She sat down next to me, took my hand, looked me in the eyes, and said, "I want you to know your granddaughter is going to be all right. She will be very bright. You know in your heart that she's here for a reason, and you are right. She has an important mission. She chose you and your son because you would love her unconditionally and accept her as she is. Don't worry about her. The road ahead is going to be rough, but she will be all right." Then she patted my hand, pulled me to my feet, and gave me a hug.

I felt so relieved. All my questions had been answered. I thought, What a healer! The next morning I went to the nurse's station to thank her. After asking all the nurses I could find, I discovered that no such person existed. No black nurse even worked on that floor! Also, she had been wearing a white uniform, and they wore only blue.

Three days later the hospital pediatrician was examining the baby. I thought I would ask him. "I encountered an incredible healer here the other night. She was tall, black, beautiful, and wonderful," I said. He turned red. I asked, "Do you know her?" He said, "No, but I've heard of her." I asked, "From whom?" He replied, "She is seen around here from time to time." That's all he would say. But in my heart I knew she was an angelic presence. She was solid, earthy, and warm, and I could feel the energy pouring through her. When I looked into her eyes, she seemed so wise, ancient, and powerful.

My granddaughter is now entering the first grade. She's very bright, precocious, and loving. And when I look into her eyes, I see the eyes of that wonderful woman.

Devotion Was the Healer
Ruth Oswald: Kansas City, Missouri

A patient in her seventies was having violent convulsions four times a day. I was attempting to help her control them through acupressure. She had tried many different treatments, including acupuncture and medication. Nothing was working.

One day when I went to her home to give her a treatment, she said, "I'm afraid I'm going to have another convulsion." When I started an energy flow, she was about to go into her usual convulsion, but instead she relaxed in my arms. I received an inner message that she wouldn't have any more convulsions if she went into a place of total trust and surrender.

As I was working on her, her divine teacher suddenly appeared in a light form body. She and I both saw him. The message we both heard was "Relax and come to me. I am here for you. I am here to be with you." She melted and I completed the flow. She didn't have a convulsion then and hasn't had one since.

Why Didn't I Trust Myself?
Barbara Carey: Dallas, Texas

While I was going through a painful divorce, I started dating the brother of the minister at my church. It was a whirlwind courtship. He was very charming, and he was pressuring me to marry him, but my inner voice kept saying, "Don't get involved. Walk away."

Because of the tremendous stress I was under, I went to the minister of my church for guidance about the relationship. She said, "Go for it." But she was my boyfriend's sister, so I felt there was a major conflict of interest. When I questioned her, however, she assured me she was genuinely concerned about my well-being.

I ended up marrying this man, but I kept getting inner guidance to "Get out." Every time I wanted to get out, I went for counseling and the minister convinced me to stay.

On our first wedding anniversary my husband strangled and beat me practically to death. I had to have eight root canals as a result. He also stole all my money and destroyed my credit. Five years after our divorce he was still stalking me. I moved twelve times so he couldn't trace me through the electric or phone companies. Ten years later I still have not recovered from the emotional damage or gotten back on my feet financially.

When you are involved with an abusive man, counseling is supposed to be a healthy option. Yet this minister took no responsibility whatsoever. She did not tell me that her brother had a restraining order against him from a previous relationship. No matter how much we trust a counselor, we cannot put his or her advice ahead of the intuitive voice of God within us.

How I Gave Birth with God's Help
Rebecca Mahon: Champaign, Illinois

I had been in labor for sixteen hours trying to deliver my first son, and still I wasn't dilating. My doctor told me that I would need a Caesarean, but I said, "Could you please at least wait a little while?" I had been practicing yoga exercises and yoga breathing, so I was expecting an easy childbirth and a vaginal delivery.

I began meditating and focusing all of my energy on my breathing. I heard my internal voice say, "Everything will be fine. You will be giving birth normally." Within minutes I started dilating very quickly. The child was in the normal head-down position. In a very short time I had a normal delivery and a healthy, beautiful baby.

Spirit Gave Me the Words to Speak
Rian Leichter: San Mateo, California

My consulting business had landed a two-million-dollar contract that involved developing and manufacturing five thousand video game units very quickly. When we put the design and production prototype together, we found a flaw in the client's original design. Still, we were able to solve this difficult problem and meet the client's tight production schedule.

We expended a lot of extra time and energy, but hadn't stopped to renegotiate the contract. After the emergency work was done, we succeeded in getting the device into production. Then I went back to the company to bill fifty thousand dollars for the extra time. Absorbing this cost would have wiped out most of my profit.

The company wrote back, saying they wouldn't pay for any of it. This sent me into a tailspin. I procrastinated for three months, even though I knew the longer I waited, the less chance I would have to recover the money. Finally I arranged to meet the three vice presidents involved in the project. They had a reputation for being really hardball, high-powered guys. I thought, They're going to chew me up and spit me out!

The day of our meeting came. An hour before the meeting I was still clueless about what to do or say to them. At the end of my rope, I gave over to Spirit and asked for divine guidance. In an instant flash I *knew* exactly what to say to them—it just came to me. Then I meditated and got connected with my inner divinity, my "I AM," and said, "Guide me through this."

I was so centered in that meeting. I explained the situation calmly, allowing Spirit to speak through me with the clarity of perfect reasoning. Then they went into conference and returned with their decision—they accepted total responsibility.

My partner was astonished. I recovered forty-five thousand out of the fifty thousand dollars I thought I had lost.

Inspiration About My Ministry
Akasha Noelle: Saratoga, California

I was getting messages from my divine voice that one day I would take over a church organization. I didn't pay much attention because I didn't know if it was my ego talking.

Then one day in meditation I pierced the veils of illusion and went into a deep inner space. I saw two beings beside me—Babaji and Jesus. They were walking me down to a valley with a lake. They came to help me deliver a teaching to the people waiting there. That vision was so vivid that it has never left me.

Right after that I started teaching. I opened a center under the auspices of our church organization. Then my inner voice said, "This church is only half built. You're going to take over the other half of this church organization."

Five years went by. I went about my life and waited patiently, but I didn't know if it would happen. It seemed so far-fetched. Much to my surprise, eventually the day came when our center broke away from the main church, and we were given charge over another church organization. My vision was fulfilled.

Our House Was Built on Faith
Kitty Mrache: Aptos, California

My husband and I had gotten a building permit for a small, affordable house we had designed. But, during my meditation, Saint Germain said, "Build a large house that will become a spiritual center. Base your design upon the hexagon. The hexagon contains the six-pointed star, the symbol for the Christ consciousness."

Even though we had no way to finance it, we followed divine inspiration and designed this very unusual house. During the plans we kept asking, "How will we afford to build this?" Spirit said, "Don't worry. You won't have to borrow from a bank to build it." It was both challenging and fulfilling to follow this inner guidance. We sold our house and took all the equity to build the foundation for the new house. Then we had no money left. My husband's faith began to wane, and he applied for a loan, but we couldn't qualify.

Jesus assured us not to worry. In the meantime my parents built a house next door, and they owned it clear. They took out a mortgage and lent us the money. So we began building our house, but we ran out of money again before it was anywhere near ready. Once again my husband began to doubt our inner guidance.

We said, "Okay, Jesus. What now?" Jesus said, "Don't worry, the money will come."

We were really sweating it out. Then, by coincidence, a patient came into my husband's chiropractic office and said, "Do you know anyone who needs to borrow money?" His employer happened to be looking for an investment opportunity. He ended up loaning us just enough money to finish the house.

We have an amazing house with an incredible hexagonal room that we've been using for workshops and meditation classes. In the center is a skylight with a six-pointed star pattern in it. The vibration in that room is very conducive to spiritual experiences.

Spiritual Inspiration Guided My Career
Laura Lee: Seattle, Washington

A few years after I took the Divine Revelation course, Susan called to say she was coming to Seattle. She wanted to know if I would mind arranging a few interviews for her. I felt a strong inclination to do so, and went about calling the local TV and radio stations.

A week prior to her arrival, I called to confirm her appointment at a small radio station in Tacoma, and the owner of the station answered. He told me the show I had booked for Susan had been cancelled. Then he complimented me on my voice, asked if I had ever done any radio work, and suggested I come by for an interview. I did, and after we chatted for a few minutes, he offered me a job hosting a talk show!

My father is in the radio industry, so I wanted to run the idea by him first. While he thought a talk show would be good for me, he suggested that I talk to Brian Jennings, the program director at a big Seattle station, instead of taking the job at the smaller station, which was over an hour away. I met with Brian, knowing somehow that I would work with him, and with no experience! As I explained my concept for a talk show to Brian, I had an intuitive vision of how it would develop, what its purpose was, and how it was an important part of my own personal journey. The show has been a success from the beginning, and is now syndicated.

It Took Me Four Years to Take Their Advice

George Fitzgerald: New York, New York

When I was engaged to be married, I bought a condo at the penulti-mate peak of the real estate market. Like most real estate, it lost value precipitously.

My marriage only lasted two years. In my divorce agreement I took re-sponsibility for the condo along with all other debts. I rented it out, but I was still losing six hundred dollars a month on it. I was very concerned because I bought the condo with a balloon mortgage that was coming due.

In several Divine Revelation meditation sessions, I asked what would be wise for me to do about my condo. The messages I received were crys-tal clear: "Stop paying the mortgage and give it back to the bank." I didn't listen to my inner guidance. I was afraid. I kept paying the bills until the mortgage expired.

I tried to renew the loan. A bank officer told me I would have to get a new mortgage and pay the shortfall between the current appraised value and the total owed. I would need to come up with sixty thousand dollars to protect my credit. I offered to keep paying the mortgage if they would just roll over the loan. He denied my request. I said, "You are forcing me into bankruptcy." He said, "That's right." He advised me to pay the last installments on the balloon mortgage and then allow the condo to go into default.

The end result is exactly the same as what would have happened if, four years earlier, I had taken the advice of the divine teachers.

How I Met My Soul Mate

Evelyn Daniels: Boulder, Colorado

I had a burning desire to meet my soul mate. When I asked Spirit for guidance, I was told that my soul mate did not live in the area, but that I would meet him at the right time. I saw visions of him working with me in classes. He had dark hair.

Two years later I met Michael at a seminar. We tried to ignore it, but we felt tremendous love when we were together. After the seminar I couldn't get him out of my mind. When he called me a few days later, we were both overwhelmed by so much love that we couldn't even speak.

We began to ask Spirit about our relationship in meditation. We both received the information that we were soul mates and belonged together.

After we met at a second seminar, Michael decided to quit his job and move across the country to be with me. Meanwhile, he had a vision of Babaji, wearing a loincloth, holding a baby, standing next to me on the deck of my house. I was wearing a blue-green bathrobe. We were both waiting for Michael. (Michael didn't know it, but I have a blue-green bathrobe that I only wore after I had babies.)

Once we were actually together, we experienced Mother Mary coming through three times, asking us to get married and have a child. We felt this would be the outward fulfillment of something already set in motion inwardly, spiritually.

My divorce came through on Friday, we got married on Sunday, and I found out I was pregnant on Monday. Only then did I remember that Jesus had come to me shortly before I met Michael and said, "The winds of change are coming with gale force."

My Inner Teacher Was My Business Consultant
Bob Broska: San Diego, California

I really wanted to work for myself in order to have time for my spiritual practices, so I decided to start a house painting business. The first job I bid on was the trim on a duplex. I went into meditation with my friends and asked my inner teacher Babaji for an estimate. We received, "Two hundred twenty-five dollars." I wrote up a bid and gave it to the property manager. His reaction was "You see that next building? And the one after that? See as far as you can see? Well, you've got the estimate on all one hundred duplexes!"

A week later a house painter was selling his equipment. It was worth about five thousand dollars, but we were guided in meditation to offer six hundred. I knew he would take my offer, because I was receiving my inner vibrational signals to confirm. Finally he realized I was just starting to learn to paint commercially, so he accepted six hundred.

After two months we were painting a house every hour and a half with six guys working. Then we started bidding on other houses. We won 90 percent of our bids, because we used inner guidance to confirm whether to bid or not, and how much to bid. Most other painters got only about 30 percent of their bids.

Within six months we were painting hotels and condominiums. We always followed our inner guidance about what to do, and our guidance was always on target. This resulted in my having an incredibly successful house painting business with plenty of free time to do my spiritual practices.

Living on the Edge with Faith
Curt De Groat: New York, New York

During my trip to Maui I lived entirely on faith and on inner guidance, allowing the universe to support me—traveling with no money and no place to stay, not knowing anyone.

On my first day there I was repeating the prayer, "Lord Jesus Christ, have mercy on me," in order to assuage my fears about being homeless and penniless. As I walked into a park, suddenly a slim, attractive blond in her forties approached me and said, "You need to have more faith in Jesus." I answered, "You're absolutely right!" She said, "Do you need food?" I answered, "No, I had breakfast. I'm not hungry now." She replied, "Oh, you need a place to stay. You can come stay with me."

As I walked with her, she continued, "My best friend just died. He was the only one I could talk to about God. A few minutes ago I was praying for a spiritual companion to connect with. Jesus told me, 'Go to the park. There's someone waiting for you.'"

This theme of amazing coincidences continued throughout my stay in Maui. At every turn, even though my faith often gave way to fear, people appeared out of nowhere to support me in the most extraordinary ways.

When I was about to leave Hawaii, I tried to find work in order to raise money for a plane ticket back to the mainland, but to no avail. At the very last minute a man named Andy drove me to the ticket office. I had absolutely no money in my pocket. I was desperate, but couldn't bring myself to ask Andy for money. I told God I would do anything He wanted, even beg in the street. Just as I got out of the car, Andy handed me a sealed envelope, saying, "This is for you." He drove away. The envelope contained a hundred dollar bill, which turned out to be the exact amount of money I needed for the plane fare!

Divine Creativity Inspires Me Daily
Janice Coppola: Portland, Oregon

I feel that at night when I sleep I travel and meet my inner teachers. That's where I get my inspiration. In the morning, the moment I gain consciousness, I realize a whole conversation is going on in my head, and I quickly write down the instructions for the day. I often wake with very clear, detailed ideas in mind. It's as though my teachers are my muses, providing me with innovative, creative ideas.

I feel very lucky to receive such direct guidance. And through it I've learned that if I can just put my doubt aside, the process unfolds before me.

Be Who You Really Are

As these examples show, there are many ways to receive Divine Revelation and be connected with Spirit in your life. If you open yourself to the possibility, you may experience something totally new, exhilarating, and miraculous. But you must allow yourself to go inside and receive the gifts that Spirit has for you.

Divine Revelation is not only a technique for developing your intuition. Its purpose is much greater and far-reaching. That is because intuition itself is not just a sixth sense or extrasensory perception. It is my belief that it is a direct line to the divine. The voice of God speaks to you through your inner voice. This has implications that are immediately awe-inspiring and ultimately life-transforming.

Imagine being able to contact God directly to guide your path in each moment of your daily life. Such a possibility may have seemed far-fetched, but now, after you have read this book, it is more attainable than you could have ever imagined. It is within your grasp. You can develop a relationship with that presence that governs the universe and tap into that power for use in daily life. You have that power within you. It *is* you. Make use of it. Heal yourself, heal others, and heal the planet. You *can* make a difference. You have within yourself all that you need, all that you desire, all that you can attain. Realize who you are and live the life worth living, the life divine.

A Message from Spirit

You are not this body. You are not this mind. You are not this ego. You are the Christ consciousness, the God within. You are not limited by your habits, your past, or your environment. You are a God-conscious divine being. Radiate the truth of your being and live the light of life. Wake up to who you really are.

You are the creator of your destiny. Use your power wisely for the good of yourself and humankind. I am with you at all times. I shall never leave you. I am loving and guiding you forever, world without end. AMEN.

—*Mahavatar Babaji*

Glossary

Absolute pure consciousness. See "Consciousness, absolute pure."

Affirmation. A statement of ultimate truth that has a transforming and healing effect when uttered.

Akashic records. Sanskrit: *Akasha* ("Ether"). A body of knowledge, believed to be stored in the ether, containing the history of the human race.

Ascended master. A divine being who attained immortality during earthly incarnation and then made a choice to serve humanity. Ascended masters can appear anywhere at will, travel at the speed of thought, materialize objects, etc.

Ascension. The attainment of enlightenment and immortality while an individual is still in bodily form.

Ashram. Sanskrit. A secluded residential school or community for students to learn meditation and spiritual teachings in simplicity.

Astral beings. The collection of all beings who dwell in the astral world.

Astral body. A subtle form that contains thoughts, feelings, and emotions; also known as the "mental body."

Astral cloud, astral dust. A dense cloud of negative, pessimistic, erroneous thoughts and feelings that envelops the earth.

Astral entity. See "Entity, astral."

Astral Entity Healing. See "Healing, Astral Entity."

Astral oppression. Being influenced by an astral entity while remaining in control of one's faculties and identity.

Astral plane. The world of the individual and collective subconscious mind.

Astral possession. Being so controlled by an astral entity and so out of control of one's faculties that one forgets one's identity.

Astral projection. See "Projection, astral."

Astral world. See "Astral plane."

Astrology. A science of interpreting the position of the stars at the time of one's birth in order to predict one's life path. The stars are not the cause of the events, however. Their position at the time of birth is simply a reflection of the desires and beliefs of the individual born at that particular time. One chooses the time of one's birth to reflect one's beliefs.

Atman. The "I AM" self, the divine presence within, the aspect of individuality that is one with God.

Attributeless. Without any characteristics whatsoever, without fluctuations.

AUM or OM. A sacred syllable (*mantra*) in the Hindu religion. Equated with the universal "I AM," it is believed to be the eternal primordial vibration out of which the entire universe is created.

Aura. The subtle energy field that encompasses an individual's physical body.

Automatism (also **Automatic** or **Autonomic**). An involuntary body movement that is caused either by one's own subconscious mind, by an astral entity, or by a divine being.

Avatar. Sanskrit: "He crosses over." An incarnation of God. God embodied in human form.

Babaji, Mahavatar. The "Yogi-Christ" of India, who, it is said, lives in the Himalayas and is an immortal ascended master. He was celebrated by Paramahansa Yogananda in his book *Autobiography of a Yogi*. "Babaji," a respectful name for "father" in India, is often used as a name for one's spiritual preceptor.

Be-attitudes. Attitudes of being in which one lives in God's grace. These are true spiritual qualities, such as unconditional love, compassion, kindness, etc.

Beliefs: Attitudes accepted as truth by your subconscious mind.

Black witchcraft. Specific techniques used to manipulate, coerce, or dominate someone or something in one's environment.

Brahman. Sanskrit: "Worship, prayer." The ultimate reality, the supreme, eternal Spirit of the universe, the impersonal God, the attributeless absolute wholeness, "one without a second."

Brahman consciousness. See "Consciousness, Brahman."

Breakthrough experience. Breaking down the wall to experiencing the God-presence at the center of one's being. Opening one's awareness to direct contact with God-Spirit and experiencing one's true self.

Breakthrough intensive. An experiential guided meditation session in which students receive direct contact with aspects of God within. During this, vibrational liftings, healings, and inner messages come from Spirit.

Buddha. Sanskrit: "The enlightened one." One who embodies divine wisdom and virtue.

Buddhahood. A state of enlightened consciousness in which one has attained *nirvana*, the cessation of all desire and absorption of the individual by universal Spirit.

Buddhism. A religion founded by Siddhartha Gautama in India in the sixth century. It teaches that life is suffering and that the way out is through the cessation of desire and the escape from the wheel of birth and death by attaining *nirvana*.

Causal body. A subtle form containing the storehouse of all past actions, memories, experiences, and impressions of an individual.

Chakra. Sanskrit. A subtle energy center in the body, of which there are traditionally seven in number, corresponding to the endocrine glands. These centers are believed to be sources of spiritual power.

Channel for God. An individual who allows God to express through his or her body and mind, by speaking-through, dancing-through, healing-through, etc.

Channeling. Psychic mediumship. Allowing an invisible entity from the astral world to take over one's body and mind in order to give a lecture or a psychic reading or to answer a client's questions. The medium often becomes unconscious during this process.

Christ. Greek: "The anointed." (1) A state of higher consciousness. (2) Title conferred on one in contact with God. Jesus of Nazareth originally received the title "Jesus the Christ." Later "Christ" became part of his name (see "Self, Christ").

Christ self. See "Self, Christ."

Clairaudience. French: "Clear hearing." The ability to hear subtle sounds through sensing with the inner ear. Auditory acuity beyond the range of normal hearing with the ears. Hearing through extrasensory perception.

Clairsentience. French: "Clear feeling." The ability to feel, sense, taste, or smell through inner sensing. Kinesthetic acuity beyond the range of normal bodily feeling. Feeling through extrasensory perception.

Clairvoyance. French: "Clear seeing." The ability to see visions through perceiving with the inner eye. Visual acuity beyond the range of normal eyesight. Seeing with the "third eye," the eye of wisdom, through extrasensory perception.

Co-dependency. An addictive, destructive relationship with someone or something in one's environment.

Collective beliefs. Doctrines, morals, or convictions shared by groups of individuals.

Conditioning, false. Habits and beliefs that an individual has learned by continual repetition and has accepted as truth, but whose premise is entirely without basis in reality.

Conscious mind: That aspect of the mind known as the "attention," by which one is aware of one's experiences.

Consciousness. The higher identity, that intangible aspect of the individual that makes one conscious or aware. The aspect of self that is changeless, the silent witness of all thought and experience.

Consciousness, absolute pure. The impersonal aspect of God, beyond the senses and all forms and phenomena of creation, also known as *satchitananda.* The ultimate principle of life, the basis of all creation, which upholds the universe by its very being.

Consciousness, Brahman. Sanskrit: Brahman ("Worship, prayer"). The highest level of awareness a human being can attain, in which one realizes the supreme truth, that he or she is one with the supreme eternal Spirit of the universe, Brahman, and that everyone and everything else in the universe is also one with that Spirit.

Consciousness, cosmic. A state of awareness in which one is in continual contact with the impersonal God; transcendental awareness within, whether asleep, dreaming, or awake.

Consciousness, God. A state of awareness in which one experiences both the impersonal and personal aspects of God and realizes them within oneself.

Consciousness, higher. An altered state of awareness, beyond the waking, dream, and deep sleep states, in which one is in contact with Spirit.

Consciousness, pure. The absolute, transcendental state of awareness without thought or any fluctuations of the mind.

Consciousness, transcendental. An altered state of awareness beyond ordinary waking consciousness, in which one contacts the absolute God-Spirit in its impersonal form. In this state one's mind is completely quiet, calm, tranquil, and silent, without thought.

Consciousness, unity. A state of awareness in which an individual realizes him- or herself to be one with the impersonal God, Brahman.

Contact, inner vibrational. A personal aspect of God within, from whom one receives direct messages, teaching, healing, guidance, inspiration, love, spiritual awakening, etc. Inner contacts are identified by inner vibrational names and signals.

Cosmic self. See "Self, cosmic."

Cult. A group of individuals involved in an organization with a charismatic leader who indoctrinates them into beliefs that are considered indisputable, often using coercive brainwashing techniques. The leader is elevated to a position of worship and never questioned. Followers are often recruited by intimidation.

Dancing-through. Allowing Spirit to move one's body in dance movements.

Darshan. Sanskrit: "Sight." An audience with a saint, a guru, or an enlightened master, believed to bestow a blessing.

Deceptor. A faker spirit or a false belief in the mind that overshadows the truth and deceives the individual.

Deep meditation. See "Meditation, deep."

Déjà vu. French: "Already seen." An eerie sensation of suddenly feeling one has "been here before." It is, in reality, a remembrance of a prophetic dream.

Destiny. A seemingly inevitable consequence or succession of events in the future. One's fate, which some believe is already written and cannot be changed.

Determinism. The belief that one's fate is predetermined and that one has no control over future events. The belief that one's choices and one's destiny are the result of a succession of predestined causes.

Dharma. Sanskrit: "Righteousness." One's true purpose, that which one has chosen to accomplish in this incarnation.

Direct cognition. Spontaneously receiving intuition through inner realization, a flash of insight, rather than by receiving a message.

Direct voice. An audible spiritual voice speaking to a person as if from the environment.

Discarnate entity. See "Entity, discarnate."

Divination. Specific occult methods of fortune-telling, such as card-reading, palmistry, scrying, tea-leaf reading, astrology, *I Ching*, runes, tarot, etc.

Divine purpose. See "Purpose, divine or true."

Divine Revelation. (1) A system of meditation, intuition, and prayer that helps individuals to contact Spirit, to evolve spiritually, and to realize God. (2) Intuition and inspiration received directly from God-Spirit.

Divine self. See "Self, divine."

Divine voice. See "Voice, divine."

Doom-and-gloom prediction. A warning of a predetermined unavoidable disaster, over which, it is believed, one has no control.

Dowsing. A method for locating objects underground. It is a technique of holding a forked rod, wire, or branch while exploring a particular site. The rod moves up and down upon reaching the location of the desired object.

Earthbound spirit. A human astral body that is attached to and bound by the material plane after death; that is, it wanders the earth, lost and confused, with no means of escape. It is lost to the spiritual plane, where it would continue its path of evolution.

Ecstatic expressions of God. Methods of expressing one's spiritual revelations and inspirations, one's inner genius.

Eddington, Sir Arthur S. (1882–1944) Renowned British astronomer and astrophysicist.

Ego identity. One's belief about who one is, based upon one's history and memory.

Empath. One who is susceptible to feelings of others, particularly feelings of suffering, distress, or illness.

Enlightenment. A higher state of consciousness, free from ignorance, judgment, and prejudice. Also known as *jivan mukti*, liberation of the soul, in which one is free from the need to reincarnate. Attainment of supreme knowledge, the most profound knowledge one can fathom on earth.

Entity, astral. A bundle of thought-forms and memories left over after a person has died, also known as a discarnate spirit.

Entity, discarnate. An astral entity or spirit that is not incarnated, that is, it is without a body.

Eternal bliss. Beyond joy and happiness, an everlasting perfect state of inner rapture and ecstasy.

Ether. One of the five elements, along with air, fire, water, and earth, it is the element of empty space, otherwise known as the vacuum.

Etheric projection. See "Projection, etheric."

Etheric self. See "Self, etheric."

Exorcism. A Catholic ceremony in which a priest expels a possessing astral entity.

Extrasensory perception. Experiences that are sensed through clairvoyance, clairaudience, or clairsentience. Inner sensing that is heard, seen, or felt within the mind, not dependent on sensory organs.

Façade barrier. An illusionary wall that seemingly separates matter and Spirit. A false barrier of error-thoughts dividing one's ego and mind from one's true spiritual nature. A veil of subconscious beliefs preventing one from experiencing deep meditation and God-Spirit.

Façade mind. The aspect of one's mind that contains one's ego identity, beliefs, habits, and conditions.

Façade-Body Healing. See "Healing, Façade-Body."

Faker spirit. An astral entity who poses as a "high" being, such as a saint or a deity, in order to gain confidence and take control over an individual and then use him or her as a pawn.

Fatalism. See "Determinism."

Feeding, love. Unconditional love, healing, and comfort, being poured into one's heart, mind, and body by the divine presence.

Feeding, power. Spiritual power, strength, and energy being poured into one's heart, mind, and body by the divine presence.

Feeding, vanity. The process of an astral entity flattering a person's ego and making him or her feel superior. The purpose of this is to take control over a person and use him or her as a pawn.

Feeding-through. Receiving divine intuition in the form of ideas, words, feelings, or visions. Then one may or may not speak the message out loud.

Feeling Mind. The aspect of one's mind that senses and feels emotions, moods, and desires.

Fight-or-Flight-Reaction Healing. See "Healing, Fight-or-Flight Reaction."

Fillmore, Charles and Myrtle. Co-founders of the Unity Church of Christianity.

Forgiveness Healing. See "Healing, Forgiveness."

Formless. Without shape, beyond space or time.

Fortune-telling. Predicting future events by reading the current mental state of a person or a group of people, either by divination or extrasensory perception, and then projecting this mental state into its outcome. Such a process may or may not be accurate, since one's free will can change one's destiny at any moment.

God. A personal concept of a higher power, according to one's own beliefs about who or what that power might be. It is not confined to any particular culture, religion, or denomination.

God consciousness. See "Consciousness, God."

God, impersonal. The one invisible Spirit that pervades and encompasses the entire universe, absolute, unchanging, imperishable, infinite, omnipresent, omnipotent, within everyone and everything.

God, personal. A deity of any religion or philosophy, usually of an anthropomorphic nature, with personalized attributes and qualities.

God self. See "Self, God."

Grace. A state of awareness in which one is in contact with God's presence. In this state miracles can happen and divine blessings can occur. With the law of grace, one can overcome the law of *karma*, the law of cause and effect, and annihilate the effect of past actions.

Guided meditation. See "Meditation, guided."

Guru. Sanskrit. *Gu*: "Darkness." *Ru*: "Light." One who destroys darkness and illusion and brings light and truth. One by whose light true knowledge arises. A spiritual guide or teacher, ultimately one's supreme self.

Habit pattern. A way of thinking and acting that is unconscious and recurrent.

Healing, Astral Entity. A healing prayer that helps clear someone or something of discarnate spirit possession or oppression by healing the discarnate spirit and sending it into the divine light.

Healing consciousness. A level of pure, crystalline awareness in which those coming near one's auric field are automatically healed and positively affected so that they cannot remain on a lower vibrational level.

Healing, Façade-Body. A healing prayer that helps one heal defensive masks consisting of negative habitual unconscious thought-forms and patterns, which cover up one's true self.

Healing, Fight-or-Flight Reaction. A healing prayer that helps one heal an inappropriate instinctive high-adrenaline physiological response to situations in which no real physical danger exists.

Healing, Forgiveness. A healing prayer that helps an individual forgive those who have seemingly wronged him or her.

Healing, Past-Life-Mental-Body. A healing prayer that helps one heal crystallized, encrusted past memories, either from this incarnation or a past incarnation.

Healing, Psychic-Tie-Cut. A healing prayer that helps one heal psychic bondage, psychic coercion, attachment, co-dependency, or addiction.

Healing, Self-Authority. An affirmation to help an individual maintain self-control and self-authority by closing off one's aura.

Healing signal. See "Signal, healing."

Healing, spiritual. Restoring mental, physical, or spiritual health and wholeness by speaking the word of truth through prayer, faith, and conviction or by channeling divine energy to a person. Reconnecting someone or something to Spirit.

Healing, Thought-Form. A healing prayer that helps one heal any physical, mental, or emotional problem for oneself or for anyone or anything else.

Healing-through. Allowing God-Spirit to use one's hands, body, or energy in order to heal others.

Higher consciousness. See "Consciousness, higher."

Higher self. See "Self, divine."

Hinduism. Sanskrit: "India, land of the Indus." A religious philosophy based upon the ancient Vedic texts and rituals. It teaches that one can attain union with God through meditation, devotion, and other disciplines. Psychological attributes and aspects of divine awareness are represented symbolically by various gods and goddesses.

History. The memory of the past contained in collective thought-forms.

Holmes, Ernest. (1887–1960) Founder of the Church of Religious Science and author of *The Science of Mind*, pioneer of New Thought teachings.

Holy breath. Spontaneously breathing in a quick, rhythmical pattern or other unusual pattern as a result of receiving vibrational lifting from Spirit.

Holy fire. The *kundalini* energy, which may manifest as intense heat, pleasure, or pain, in the spine or in one of the *chakras*.

"I AM" self. See "Self, 'I AM.'"

Immortality. Eternal life that is changeless, incorruptible, and imperishable, and which persists throughout all incarnations.

Impersonal God. See "God, impersonal."

Indivisible. Supreme absolute wholeness and oneness that cannot be split in two.

Inner guidance. Messages, received deep within the mind, which give the individual direction, advice, inspiration, information, etc. These messages are seen, felt, or heard through clairvoyant, clairsentient, or clairaudient sensing.

Inner identity. Spiritual aspects of self beyond the normal ego identity. Higher states of awareness beyond the waking state of consciousness and limitations of the ego.

Inner knowingness. Intuition, a sense of knowing without knowing how one knows.

Inner teachers. The inner divine presence, aspects of God or of the higher self, located within the heart. Messengers of God or guiding masters, saints, sages, or prophets of all religions. Some of these beings are ascended masters who have attained physical immortality during their earthly incarnation. Some are deities, angels, archangels, or celestial beings.

Inner vibrational contact. See "Contact, inner vibrational."

Inner vibrational name. See "Name, inner vibrational."

Inner vibrational signal. See "Signal, inner vibrational."
Inner voice. See "Voice, inner."
Intuition. Inner listening, seeing, or feeling. Direct inner perception or knowledge without the use of reasoning.
Intuitive abilities. Capacities for inner sensing and direct inner perception and knowledge.
Intuitive messages. Communications from Spirit seen, felt, or heard through inner sensing.
Jain. Sanskrit: "Saint." A Hindu sect based upon the teachings of Mahavira. Its tenets include reverence for all living things, vegetarianism, and a Buddhist philosophy.
Jivan mukta. Sanskrit: "Liberated soul." One who has attained spiritual enlightenment and liberation from the bondage of ignorance. One whose soul is free from the law of *karma* and, hence, need no longer incarnate into physical form.
Karma. Sanskrit: "Action." The law of cause and effect, also known as the law of action and reaction, stated "As you sow, so shall you reap." The true meaning of this law is "As thou hast believed, so be it done unto thee."
Karmic wheel. In Buddhist philosophy, life is believed to be like a wheel that cycles repeatedly in reincarnation. Also known as the "wheel of birth and death."
Kundalini. The energy in the body that accompanies the awakening of bliss consciousness and self-realization, traditionally believed to be coiled up like a serpent at the base of the spine until it is awakened, at which time it travels up the spine to the top of the head.
Lama. In Tibetan Buddhism an enlightened master or saint who remains conscious during his previous death and present birth, and therefore remembers his past life.
Light-bodies. Inner bodies or subtle bodies that are either inside, above, beside, or near one's physical body. They are not necessarily confined to the space occupied by one's gross material body.
Light meditation. See "Meditation, light."
Love feeding. See "Feeding, love."
Mahavatar Babaji. See "Babaji, Mahavatar."
Mantra. Sanskrit: "Thinker." A phrase or word with special powers, either chanted aloud as a prayer or thought silently during meditation.
Maya. Ignorance or illusion, living in and bound by the world of the senses. Believing in the appearance rather than the truth.
Meditation, deep. A practice of silencing the mind and simultaneously resting the body, resulting in a state of consciousness without mental or physical activity, yet fully awake.
Meditation, guided. A meditation practice during which one listens to the instructions of a teacher. This can be done in person or with an audio recording.
Meditation, light. A practice of contacting a deeper level of awareness than one normally experiences during one's waking state.
Mediumship, psychic. See "Channeling."
Memories. The history of every experience you have ever had, whether consciously remembered or not.
Mental body. See "Astral body."
Mental impressions. Receiving inner visions, thoughts, or feelings that give information about mental states of a person or group of people.
Meyer, Dr. Peter (b. 1912). A pioneer of the Divine Revelation teaching, who developed this teaching in the early 1960s under the guidance of the master and *avatar* Babaji, the "Yogi-Christ" of India, and other ascended masters. Founder of Teaching of Intuitional Metaphysics, Inc. and co-founder of Teaching of the Inner Christ, Inc. Lives in San Diego.
Meyer Makeever, Dr. Ann (b. 1916). Co-founder of Teaching of the Inner Christ, Inc. who developed this teaching in the early 1960s under the guidance of the master and *avatar* Babaji, the "Yogi-Christ" of India, and other ascended masters. Lives in San Diego.
Mind reading. See "Telepathy."

Name, inner vibrational. A sound vibration of an aspect of God that identifies an aspect of one's higher self or a divine teacher within. Inner names help one identify whom one is contacting and receiving messages from.

Nameless. Without attributes or qualities, beyond space or time.

Near-death experience. A phenomenon that sometimes occurs when a person has a severe accident or serious illness. The person may experience him- or herself leaving the body and floating above it. Then he or she may see a brilliant light, often at the end of a tunnel or road. Departed relatives or guiding angels usher the way to the light.

New Age. Pertaining to a current cultural movement, characterized by interest in and study of higher consciousness, holistic medicine, healthy lifestyle, supernatural phenomena, occult sciences, and Eastern spiritual philosophies.

New Thought. Non-sectarian metaphysical philosophy that teaches that mind is primary and causative, God is indwelling Spirit, and metaphysical remedies, such as prayer and affirmation, heal all difficulties. Churches: Unity Church of Christianity, Church of Religious Science, etc.

Nine tests of discernment. Nine tests to use in order to help one determine what level of awareness one is in contact with. These tests, which help one avoid psychic deception, can be used to determine whether any message comes from a divine source or from the mental world.

Nirvakalpa samadhi. Sanskrit. *Nirvakalpa:* "Changeless, permanent." *Samadhi:* "A state of perfect tranquillity of mind and body." A permanent state of spiritual awakening and enlightenment from which one never returns.

Nirvana. Sanskrit: "Blowing out." (1) A Buddhist concept, meaning the cessation of all desires, the extinction of the ego identity, and the absorption of the individual soul. (2) A Hindu concept, meaning blowing out the flame of life through supreme union with the absolute impersonal God.

Occult. Pertaining to psychic phenomena and sciences, such as divination, magic, alchemy, astrology, card-reading, palmistry, psychokinesis, mediumship, etc.

OM. See "AUM."

Omenology. A method of reading various signs or omens from the environment. Those skilled in this practice might assign spiritual meanings to happenings in the natural world.

"Other" voice. See "Voice, 'other.'"

Ouija board. A board game in which one uses psychokinetic energy to move a pointer that spells out words.

Painting- sculpting- or drawing-through. Allowing divine Spirit to use one's hands to paint, draw, or sculpt a work of art. Receiving a vision from Spirit and translating it into a work of art.

Paranormal. Psychic or mental phenomena beyond the average scope of experience. Sensory perception beyond the norm, such as clairvoyance, clairaudience, clairsentience, etc.

Parapsychology. A branch of psychology dealing with psychic phenomena, such as extrasensory perception, telepathy, apparitions, mediumship, etc.

Past-Life-Mental-Body Healing. See "Healing, Past-Life-Mental-Body."

Pendulum. An object attached to a string so that it can move and spin; used to receive messages by psychokinesis.

Perfection. The truth of being without error, undefiled by worldly contamination, without limitations or shadows of fallibility.

Personal God. See "God, personal."

Pillar of protection. A visualization of seeing a ray of light streaming down from God into the midline of one's body, then radiating out from one's center. This creates an aura of divine protection and love and closes off one's aura to all negative influences, maintaining balance, self-composure, and self-authority.

Planchette. A pointer supported by two casters, sometimes with a vertical pencil, which one uses to spell out messages by psychokinesis.

Playing-through or writing-through music. Creating spontaneous improvisational music while in contact with Spirit.

Power feeding. See "Feeding, power."

Prakriti. Sanskrit. Universal substance, represented by the feminine aspect of God, the mother of creation. Symbolized by Mother Divine in Hinduism and Yin in Taoism, it represents the force of nature that takes cosmic energy, gestates and nurtures it, and then brings the entire creation into birth.

Prayer. (1) Affirmation of the truth, spoken with conviction and faith. (2) A petition or request to God or a divine being to assist one in need. (3) A conversation with God or a divine being.

Prayer of protection. A well-known affirmation from the Unity School of Christianity that is used to call upon the presence of God for divine protection.

Prayer of unification. A prayer or affirmation to unify an individual or a group of individuals with each other and with God-Spirit. Such a prayer is recommended before any Divine Revelation meditation or session.

Prayer treatment. A specific technique of creating goals and fulfilling one's desires through the principles of manifestation. In this technique one "treats" or heals one's mind and therefore transforms one's belief system in order to change the outcome.

Precognition. A precise, realistic vision of a future event, usually occurring within two days of the event, often giving a warning to avoid disastrous events. Precognitions usually take place in dreams or meditation.

Predetermination. See "Determinism."

Prediction. Foretelling a future event by means of intuition, extrasensory perception, or through divinatory methods.

Premonition. A vague feeling about a future event or an event taking place at a distance. It is characterized by a state of uneasiness or gut-level anxiety without any discernible reason.

Projection, astral. The process of the astral or mental body leaving the physical body and traveling outside it.

Projection, etheric. Traveling to subtle realms or spiritual places by projecting one's soul-body or consciousness.

Prophecy. A divinely inspired message foretelling events affecting the life of designated people.

Prophetic dream. A message from Spirit occurring during sleep.

Psychic. One who is sensitive to invisible forces beyond the physical world.

Psychic abilities. Mental powers, such as telepathy, psychokinesis, extrasensory perception, fortune-telling, psychometry, mediumship, etc.

Psychic attack. A calculated effort to undermine the psychology, health, or well-being of someone or something in one's environment by using one's willpower.

Psychic awareness. The aspect of mind in which one can develop supernormal mental powers.

Psychic barrier. An illusionary separation between matter and Spirit. A false barrier of error-thoughts separating one from one's true nature, a veil of subconscious beliefs preventing one from experiencing God-Spirit at the center of one's being.

Psychic bondage. An experience of undue attachment to or repulsion from a person, group of people, place, thing, organization, situation, circumstance, experience, or memory. One may feel intimidated, dominated, or coerced, or one may experience an addiction, habit, or co-dependency.

Psychic delusion. Illusion of the mind because of the inability to discern the origin of one's extrasensory perceptions and supernatural experiences. Deception of the mind in which one believes one's inner experiences come from a divine source when they, in reality, come from the astral plane.

Psychic mediumship. See "Channeling."

Psychic reader. An individual who gives advice, counseling, or fortune-telling by reading the thought-forms of a client by extrasensory perception, telepathy, psychometry, etc., or by a method of divination, such as astrology, card-reading, palmistry, etc.

Psychic sponge. An empath who experiences physical ills or emotional disturbances as a result of proximity with those who have such problems. One who is negatively influenced by vibrations and thought-forms in the environment.

Psychic tie. See "Tie, psychic."

Psychic-Tie-Cut Healing. See "Healing, Psychic-Tie-Cut."

Psychokinesis. Movement of physical objects by means of mental power rather than physical force.

Psychokinesis, spiritual. Receiving knowledge or messages from Spirit through the movement of objects in the physical world.

Psychokinetic revelation. See "Psychokinesis, spiritual."

Psychometry. A psychic technique of receiving knowledge about a person by touching an object that is associated with that person.

Public speaking-through. Speaking-through a divinely inspired message for an audience.

Pure consciousness. See "Consciousness, pure."

Purpose, divine or true. One's heart's desires and true talents, one's true soul purpose. That unique contribution to the earth that one feels compelled to fulfill, which has impelled one to be incarnated in physical form.

Purusha. Sanskrit: "Person." The original Person, known in Judeo-Christian philosophy as Father God. *Purusha* is the universal "I AM," the Will of God, cosmic energy. Symbolized by Lord Shiva in Hinduism and Yang in Taoism, it represents the force of nature that provides the impetus for creation of all forms and phenomena in the universe.

Quickening. Vibrational lifting of the mind and body, often accompanied by rushes of energy, electrical currents, increased breathing or heart rate, ecstasy, or warmth in the body.

Race-mind consciousness. The collective thoughts and beliefs of all of humanity.

Race thought-forms. See "Race-mind consciousness."

Reincarnation. The transmigration of a soul from one body to another.

Revelation. Receiving messages from divine Spirit.

Rishi. Sanskrit: "Sage." (1) A seer, one who cognizes the truth. (2) One who receives the hymns of the Vedas through direct mystical revelation.

Samadhi. Sanskrit. A state of profound inner peace and happiness by achieving perfect equilibrium and suspension—mind in complete silence and body in complete relaxation, with imperceptible breathing and heartbeat.

Sanskaras. Sanskrit: "Seeds of karma." Impressions of past actions, stored in one's subconscious mind (*chitta*), which are the origin for the creation of future actions.

Satchitananda. Sanskrit: "Absolute bliss consciousness." A state of awareness in which one is in deepest silence, in pure divine consciousness, wholeness, oneness, and peace, without thought.

Satori. Japanese: "To understand the truth of." A term used in Zen Buddhism to describe spiritual enlightenment and illumination.

Seeing the light. Receiving a direct message from Spirit through an intense light on the inner or outer level.

Self, Christ. Greek. *Christos*: "The anointed." A level of consciousness in which one is in contact with specific qualities of God: qualities of love, compassion, healing, forgiveness, etc. It is not confined to the Christian religion. It is an aspect of one's higher self, no matter what one's religious beliefs may be (see "Christ").

Self, cosmic. The aspect of one's divine self that is as large and vast as the universe. It is galactic, unbounded, omniscient, omnipotent, and omnipresent.

Self, divine. The aspect of self that is in continual contact with God-Spirit. Most individuals are not consciously aware of this contact.

Self, etheric. One's immortal soul, the true expression of a person as an individual. Its purpose is to fulfill one's true heart's desires and soul purpose in any incarnation.

Self, God. The personal form of God at the center of one's being, in whatever form one believes, realized as one's higher self.

Self, higher. See "Self, divine."

Self, "I AM." The individualization of the universal, impersonal God. The individual divine consciousness, the most basic component of one's individuality, yet with no particular uniqueness. The most abstract aspect of self as an individual.

Self-authority. Relying and depending on oneself, rather than on others, for one's direction, stability, happiness, guidance, and security. Self-reliance, being in control of one's life and making one's own decisions without the need for outside approval. Taking responsibility for one's own actions, not blaming others for one's problems.

Self-Authority Healing. See "Healing, Self-Authority."

Self-realization. Knowing fully who and what one's real and true self is, beyond all ego identifications and false limitations.

Shakti. Sanskrit. The power of God. See "Prakriti."

Shaman. A medicine man or woman, healer, priest, and spiritual adviser for Native American tribes and for certain peoples of northeast Asia.

Shinto. Japanese: "Way of the Gods." A Japanese religion, originally a form of nature worship, now influenced by Confucianism and Buddhism.

Signal, healing. A subtle feeling, vision, sound, body movement, fragrance, or taste that signifies the need for healing thought-forms, psychic ties, astral entities, façade bodies, past life mental bodies, etc.

Signal, inner vibrational. A subtle feeling, vision, sound, body movement, fragrance, or taste, corresponding to each inner vibrational name of an aspect of one's higher being, aspect of God, or divine teacher within. Signals help one identify which inner name one is contacting.

Signal, "yes and no." A subtle feeling, vision, sound, body movement, fragrance, or taste that signifies that the answer to a question is yes or that the answer is no.

Sikhism. Hindu: "A Disciple." A Hindu sect whose tenets include the belief in one God, dismissal of idolatry, and rejection of the caste system.

Singing-through. Allowing Spirit to sing spontaneous melodies through one's voice.

Speaking-through. Speaking aloud while receiving thoughts, visions, and feelings coming from the inner divine voice. Becoming a mouthpiece for the divine voice to communicate through one's speech mechanism.

Spirit. A life energy or force that underlies and pervades the universe, a concept that is multicultural and interdenominational, not confined to any particular religious philosophy or lifestyle.

Spirit mediumship. See "Channeling."

Spiritual. Connected with divine Spirit, in touch with God, experiencing higher states of consciousness, and manifesting qualities of Spirit in daily life, such as unconditional love, compassion, nonjudgment, kindness, etc.

Spiritual discernment. The ability to distinguish the mental level from higher levels of consciousness. The ability to recognize the difference between messages coming from the subconscious mind and messages coming from divine Spirit. The ability to differentiate between experiences on the astral plane and experiences on the divine level.

Spiritual experiences. Occurrences in which the individual comes into contact with God.

Spiritual healing. See "Healing, spiritual."

Spiritual life. A way of life attuned to Spirit, to God's presence, in the midst of daily activity.

Spiritual love tie. See "Tie, true spiritual love."

Spiritual master. One who has attained a permanent higher level of consciousness by practicing spiritual disciplines. One who is attuned to Spirit twenty-four hours a day.

Spiritual path. A way of life in which one progresses toward attainment of higher consciousness and greater unification with Spirit and with God, in whatever form one believes God to be.

Spiritual psychokinesis. See "Psychokinesis, spiritual."

Subconscious mind. The aspect of one's mind responsible for the experience of oneself as an individualized entity and for one's moods and desires. It is also the storehouse of all past memories and impressions and all one's beliefs and judgments.

Subliminal state. A semiconscious, deeply relaxed state of awareness, either experienced between sleep and waking, experienced during light meditation, or induced by hypnosis.

Sufism. A form of Islamic mysticism.

Supernatural. (1) Beyond the normal sensory range of human experience and not fathomable through known laws of nature. (2) Pertaining to the occult, ghosts, spirits, etc.

Supernormal. Beyond the usual or average levels of awareness experienced in the waking state of consciousness. Possessing skills of sensory perception beyond the norm, such as clairvoyance, clairaudience, clairsentience, etc.

Table-tipping or table-rapping. The use of a small table that moves up and down on two legs to spell out messages by psychokinesis.

Tai Chi. Chinese. A form of physical and spiritual exercise, one of the martial arts.

Taoism. Chinese: "The Way." A Chinese religious philosophy based upon the teachings of Lao-tzu, emphasizing simplicity, truth, and wisdom.

Telepathy. Feeling or sensing thoughts or emotions of a person from a distance.

Thought-Form Healing. See "Healing, Thought-Form."

Thought-forms. Thoughts so dense that they have crystallized into subtle form.

Tie, psychic. A subtle negative bond between oneself and something or someone in one's environment.

Tie, true spiritual love. A subtle positive, true love bond between oneself and something or someone in one's environment, manifesting as a golden cord of light that can never be broken.

Trance mediumship. A practice of leaving one's body and allowing an entity to take over the body, speak-through it, etc., while one becomes unconscious, without memory of the experience.

Trance state. A state of consciousness in which one becomes unconscious and absent from the body.

Transcendental. Beyond the phenomenal relative world, not limited by boundaries of the physical universe, beyond causation.

Transcendental consciousness. See "Consciousness, transcendental."

Transition. A term for physical death, but rather than implying a finality, it indicates a transformation into another state.

True purpose. See "Purpose, divine or true."

Turiya. Sanskrit: "The fourth state." The transcendental state of consciousness, beyond the three states of waking, dreaming, or deep sleep, also known as *samadhi.*

Uncertainty Principle. A theory, formulated by Werner Heisenberg in 1926, that is the basis of quantum mechanics. It states that the accurate position and velocity of any particle can never be measured precisely and therefore its future position can never be predicted.

Unity consciousness. See "Consciousness, unity."

Upanishads. Vedic scriptures of India that describe deep, esoteric metaphysical truths based on the ultimate reality of human existence.

Vanity-feeding. See "Feeding, vanity."

Vedanta. Sanskrit: "End of the Veda." An ancient East Indian philosophy based upon the doctrine that there is only one ultimate principle, one absolute unified reality, one wholeness without any independent, separate parts. It is embodied in the phrase "One without a second."

Vedas. Ancient scriptures of India, received as direct cognitions and revelations by ancient *rishis.* They are more than just words on paper, however. Believed to be the primordial vibrations that underlie and give rise to the entire universe, they embody the knowledge and structure of all that is contained therein.

Vibrational levels of identity. Myriad aspects of oneself that vibrate on distinct levels of energy and intelligence, each with a separate name and form.

Vibrational lifting. Raising the vibratory level of the mind and body. Purification and transformation of one's mind and body in order to sustain higher levels of consciousness. The subjective experience of vibrational lifting is one of divine energy, love, and power being pumped into one's mind, body, and emotions.

Vibrations. Invisible energies or emotional qualities, emanating from a person or thing, which can be felt on a subtle level.

Visions. Experiences seen with inner sensing through the inner eye.

Visitation from a divine being. A spiritual being taking etheric or physical form to appear to a person and give a message or a teaching.

Voice, divine. The voice of God, which can be heard, seen, or felt in a quiet state of awareness. The "still small voice" of God within. Messages from Spirit, heard, seen, or felt with spiritual sensing.

Voice, inner. Any message within the mind heard, seen, or felt with inner sensing, whether on the mental, psychic, or spiritual level of awareness. Any thought or idea within the mind that gives advice or direction.

Voice, "other." Any message, heard within the mind, whose origin is a mental source rather than a spiritual or divine source.

Wheel of birth and death. See "Karmic wheel."

Writing-through. Allowing divine Spirit to write or type messages through an individual.

"Yes and no" signal. See "Signal, 'yes and no.'"

Yoga. Sanskrit: "Yoking." (1) A discipline that helps the practitioner to unify with supreme Spirit, often involving meditation (*dhyan*), postures (*asanas*), breathing (*pranayama*), etc. (2) A system of Indian philosophy authored by Patanjali, an ancient seer. Its goal is to achieve liberation by absorbing the individual soul into supreme Spirit.

Yogi. Sanskrit: "One who is yoked." One who has achieved liberation of the soul and union with the supreme Spirit through East Indian spiritual disciplines that promote direct union with God.

Zen Buddhism. Sanskrit. *Zen:* "Meditation." *Buddha:* "The enlightened one." A form of Buddhism, practiced primarily in Japan, Korea, and Vietnam, whose goal is to attain enlightenment through spiritual practices, especially meditation, intuition, and simplicity.

Notes

INTRODUCTION
1. Exodus 33:11.

CHAPTER 1. GETTING SPIRITUALLY CONNECTED
1. Luke 17:21.

CHAPTER 2. THE SOUND OF STILLNESS
1. Solomon, *Beethoven Essays*, 126–129.
2. Psalms 46:10.
3. Psalms 4:4.
4. Acts 17:28.
5. Matthew 7:7.
6. Revelation 3:20.

CHAPTER 3. GOD IS WITHIN YOU
1. Hermetica Hermes, Libellus V. 2, Perry, *A Treasury*, 748.
2. Das, *The Essential Unity*, 22.
3. Dhammapada 1:1, 2, Perry, *A Treasury*, 484.
4. Arabian maxim, Das, *The Essential Unity*, 104.
5. I Corinthians 3:16.
6. Luke 17:20–21.
7. Acts 17:27–28.
8. Psalms 139:8–10.
9. Qur'an, Das, *The Essential Unity*, 98.
10. Ibid., 117.
11. Sufi writings, Das, *The Essential Unity*, 103.
12. Mumonkan 30, Wilson, *World Scripture*, 74.
13. Mahaparinirvana Sutra 214, Wilson, *World Scripture*, 147.
14. Platform Scripture 30.
15. Shinto-Dinju, Das, *The Essential Unity*, 159.
16. Kwan-Yin-Tse, Das, *The Essential Unity*, 147.

17. Adi Granth, Dhanasari, M.9, Wilson, *World Scripture*, 73.
18. Amita-Gati, Samayika-patha, Das, *The Essential Unity*, 146.
19. Bhagavad Gita 10:20.
20. *"Aham Brahma, Tat tvam asi, Esha ma Atma antar-hrdaye, Hrdi ayam tasmad hrdayam,"* (Sanskrit) and *"An-al-Haq, Haq-tu-i, Qalab-ul-insan bait ur-Rahman"* (Arabic)—Upanishads (Hindu) and a well-known Arabic maxim (Sufi). Das, *The Essential Unity*, 107.
21. Genesis 1:27.
22. Matthew 8:13.
23. Matthew 19:26.
24. Keshavadas, *Sadguru Dattatreya*, 133.

CHAPTER 4. YOUR INNER TEACHER
1. *Shree Guru Gita*, verse 9 ("The Song of the Guru," ancient Hindu scripture), Keshavadas, *Sadguru Dattatreya*, 59.
2. John 16:7.
3. Scripture of the Lotus of the Good Law, 3:9:13 (Buddhist).
4. The Heart Sutra (Buddhist).
5. The Avadhuta Gita 1:52 (Hindu), Keshavadas, *Sadguru Dattatreya*, 141.
6. Chandogya Upanishad 8.3.2 (Hindu), Wilson, *World Scripture*, 147.
7. Wang-Yang-Ming (Confucian), Das, *The Essential Unity*, 105.
8. Srimad Bhagavatam Mahapurana 11:21 (Hindu), Perry, *A Treasury*, 919.
9. Hebrews 13:2.
10. Bhagavad Gita, chapter 2, verse 54.
11. Bhagavad Gita, chapter 2, verses 55–57.
12. Ebon, *The Satan Trap*, 63.

CHAPTER 5. DISCOVERING WHO YOU REALLY ARE
1. John 14:12.
2. A familiar maxim of Vedanta, an ancient East Indian nondualistic philosophy, Srimad Bhagavatam Mahapurana 11:20, Perry, *A Treasury*, 819.

CHAPTER 6. DEVELOPING HIGHER CONSCIOUSNESS
1. Bhagavad Gita 2:48. (Hindu).

CHAPTER 7. WAYS TO HAVE A SPIRITUAL BREAKTHROUGH
1. Jeremiah 29:13.
2. Matthew 7:7.
3. Meyer, *Being a Christ!*, 52.
4. Yogananda, *How You Can Talk with God*, 9–10.

CHAPTER 8. MEDITATING YOUR WAY TO THE SPIRIT
1. T. S. Eliot, "Coriolan."
2. Matthew 7:8.

CHAPTER 10. SEVEN BASIC METHODS OF SPIRITUAL HEALING
1. Ebon, *The Satan Trap*, xi.
2. Matthew 12:43–45.
3. Meyer, *Being a Christ!*, 191.

CHAPTER 12. VOICES OF SELF-SABOTAGE
1. Brown, "Ramtha's New Age Shrouded in Doom," 20.
2. Holmes, *The Science of Mind*, part 4, chapter 23.
3. Fisher, *Hungry Ghosts*, 277.
4. Ebon, *The Satan Trap*, 182.
5. Ibid., vii.

CHAPTER 13. NINE TESTS TO PREVENT PSYCHIC DECEPTION
1. 1 John 4:1–2.
2. Das, *The Essential Unity*, 231.
3. Ibid., 77–78.
4. Holmes, *The Science of Mind*, part 4, chapter 23.
5. Ebon, *The Satan Trap*, 171–172.
6. Ibid., 102.
7. Ibid., 73.
8. Ibid., ix–x.
9. Ibid., 178.
10. Ibid., 101–102.
11. *The Imitation of Christ*, attributed to Thomas à Kempis.

CHAPTER 14. THE ANSWERS ARE WITHIN YOU
1. These safeguards are also described in Meyer, *Being a Christ!*, 170–174.

CHAPTER 15. TWELVE WAYS TO RECEIVE INNER REVELATION
1. Schilpp, *Albert Einstein*, 49–51; Bucky, *The Private Albert Einstein*, 26.
2. Guiley, *Encyclopedia of Mystical and Paranormal Experience*, 296–298.
3. Burrelle's, "People with Special Powers."
4. Nadel, *Sixth Sense*, 211–212.
5. Genesis, chapters 18 and 21.
6. Al-Ghazali (Sufi); Watt, *The Faith and Practice*, 25.
7. Acts 9:4.
8. Guiley, *Encyclopedia of Mystical and Paranormal Experience*, 407–409.
9. Ibid., 466.
10. Marshall, *Mysteries of the Unexplained*, 12.
11. Ibid., 22.
12. Ibid., 27.
13. Ibid., 65–66.
14. Goldberg, *The Intuitive Edge*, 177.
15. Matthew 18:20.
16. Matthew 10:16.
17. Matthew 8:13.
18. Revelation 3:20.

CHAPTER 16. NINE ECSTATIC EXPRESSIONS OF GOD
1. Jeremiah 1:9.
2. John 10:30.
3. John 14:6, emphasis added.
4. John 8:12, emphasis added.
5. John 11:25, emphasis added.
6. John 8:58, emphasis added.
7. John 12:49.
8. John 14:10, emphasis added.
9. Exodus 4:11–12.
10. Matthew 10:19–20.
11. John 12:49–50.
12. *A Course in Miracles*, vii–viii.
13. Belo, *Trance in Bali*, 180–182.
14. Guiley, *Encyclopedia of Mystical and Paranormal Experience*, 379.
15. John 14:10.
16. Guiley, *Encyclopedia of Mystical and Paranormal Experience*, 650–653.

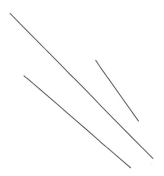

Bibliography

BOOKS

Belo, Jane. *Trance in Bali*. New York: Columbia University Press, 1960.

Bernard, Theos. *Hindu Philosophy*. New York: Philosophical Library, 1947.

Besant, Annie. *The Bhagavad-Gita*. Adyar, Madras, India: Theosophical Publishing House, 1973.

Bucky, Peter A. *The Private Albert Einstein*. Kansas City, Missouri: Andrews and McMeel, 1992.

Chan, Wing-Tsit. *A Source Book in Chinese Philosophy*. Princeton, New Jersey: Princeton University Press, 1963.

A Course in Miracles. Tiburon, California: Foundation for Inner Peace, 1975.

Das, Bhagavan. *The Essential Unity of All Religions*. Wheaton, Illinois: Quest Book, Theosophical Publishing House, 1969.

Ebon, Martin, ed. *The Satan Trap: Dangers of the Occult*. Garden City, New York: Doubleday and Co., 1976.

Elliot, T. S. *The Complete Poems and Plays*. New York: Harcourt, Brace, 1952.

Fisher, Joe. *Hungry Ghosts: An Investigation into Channeling and the Spirit World*. Toronto: Doubleday Canada Limited, 1990.

Goldberg, Philip. *The Intuitive Edge, Understanding Intuition and Applying It in Everyday Life*. Los Angeles: Jeremy P. Tarcher, 1983.

Gray, Dr. John. *What You Feel, You Can Heal*. Mill Valley, California: Heart Publishing, 1984.

Guiley, Rosemary Ellen. *Harper's Encyclopedia of Mystical and Paranormal Experience*. New York: HarperCollins Publishers, 1991.

Holmes, Ernest. *The Science of Mind*. New York: Putnam Publishing Group, 1989.

Holy Bible. Iowa Falls, Iowa: World Bible Publishers.

Karyalaya, Gobind Bhawan. *The Bhagavadgita*. Gorakhpur, U.P., India: Gita Press, 1984.

Kempis, Thomas à. *The Imitation of Christ*. New York: E. P. Dutton, 1910.

Keshavadas, Sadguru Sant. *Sadguru Dattatreya*. Oakland, California: Vishwa Dharma Publications, 1988.

King, Godfre Ray. *The "I AM" Discourses*. Schaumburg, Illinois: Saint Germain Press, 1940.

———. *The Magic Presence*. Schaumburg, Illinois: Saint Germain Press, 1982.

———. *Unveiled Mysteries* (original). Schaumburg, Illinois: Saint Germain Press, 1982.

Mahesh Yogi, Maharishi. *Bhagavad Gita, A New Translation and Commentary with Sanskrit Text*. International SRM Publications, 1967.

———. *Science of Being and Art of Living*. New York: Signet, 1968.

Makeever, Ann Meyer. *Self-Mastery in the Christ Consciousness*. Lemon Grove, California: Dawning Publications, 1989.

Marshall, Richard. *Mysteries of the Unexplained*. Pleasantville, New York: Reader's Digest Association, 1982.

Meyer, Ann P., and Peter V. Meyer. *Being a Christ!* Lemon Grove, California: Dawning Publications, 1988.

Nadel, Laurie, Judy Haims, and Robert Stempson. *Sixth Sense*. New York: Prentice Hall, 1990.

Neville. *Resurrection*. Marina del Rey, California: DeVorss & Company, 1966.

Perry, Whitall N., ed. *A Treasury of Traditional Wisdom*. Cambridge, UK: Quinta Essentia, 1991.

Prabhavananda, Swami, and Christopher Isherwood. *Shankara's Crest Jewel of Discrimination*. Hollywood, California: Vedanta Press, 1975.

Radhakrishnan, Sarvepalli, and Charles A. Moore. *A Source Book in Indian Philosophy*. Princeton, New Jersey: Princeton University Press, 1957.

Roman, Sanaya, and Duane Packer. *Opening to Channel*. Tiburon, California: HJ Kramer, 1987.

Schilpp, Paul Arthur, ed. *Albert Einstein Autobiographical Notes*. Chicago: Open Court Publishing Co.

Solomon, Maynard. *Beethoven Essays*. Cambridge, Massachusetts: Harvard University Press, 1988.

Spalding, Baird T. *Life and Teaching of the Masters of the Far East*. Marina del Rey, California: DeVorss & Co., 1924.

Vaughn, Frances E. *Awakening Intuition*. New York: Doubleday, 1979.

Vireswarananda, Swami, and Swami Adidevananda. *Brahma-Sutras*. Mayavati, Pithoragarh, Himalayas, India: Advaita Ashrama, 1986.

Watt, W. Montgomery. *The Faith and Practice of Al-Ghazali*. Cambridge, England: George Allen & Unwin, 1963.

Wilson, Andrew, ed. International Religious Foundation, *World Scripture*. New York: Paragon House, 1991.

Yogananda, Paramahansa. *Autobiography of a Yogi*. Los Angeles: Self-Realization Fellowship, 1981.

———. *How You Can Talk with God*. Los Angeles: Self-Realization Fellowship, 1987.

PERIODICALS AND TELEVISION

Brown, Leslie. "Ramtha's New Age Shrouded in Doom." *Morning News Tribune*, Tacoma, Washington (May 24, 1992): A1, 20.

Burrelle's Information Services, transcribers. "People with Special Powers." *The Oprah Winfrey Show* (September 24, 1992).

Clark, Nancy, and Nick Gallo. "Do You Believe in Magic?—New Light on the New Age." *Family Circle* (February 23, 1993):99–102.

Levine, A. "Mystics on Main Street." *US News & World Report* 102 (February 9, 1987): 67–69.

Lowry, Katharine. "Channelers." *Omni* 10 (October 1987): 46–48.

Roberts, Marjory. "A Linguistic 'Nay' to Channeling." *Psychology Today* (October 1989): 64–65.

Acknowledgments

I give gratitude to the divine teachers, ascended shining ones, effulgent with God's splendor, who are continually guiding me and feeding me peace, love, happiness, faith, inner strength, wisdom, and truth. Your direct inspiration brings this book to the world.

I am deeply grateful to Jeff Herman and Deborah Adams for getting this book into the right hands, for believing in me and not giving up. I thank Sheila Curry, without whom this book would not have been published. I am greatly indebted to Laureen Connelly Rowland for going far beyond the call of duty and for her love, energy, commitment, and brilliant editing. I extend tremendous gratitude to Emily Remes, whose patience, wisdom, and intelligence brought this book to press.

I thank those who have brought this teaching to me: Dr. Peter Meyer, Dr. Ann Meyer Makeever, Rich Bell, and Joanna Cherry. I am appreciative to those who have assisted in editing this book: Connie Fisher, Curt De Groat, George Fitzgerald, Alan Unger, Janet Di Giovanna, and Danny Rubenstein. I wish to thank the following people for their input in writing the prayers and affirmations in this book: Rich Bell for prayers on pages 115, 131, 138, 143, and 144 and Joanna Cherry for the prayer on page 149. I give special thanks to Maharishi Mahesh Yogi for his tutelage and inspiration.

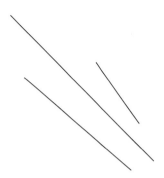

About the Author

Susan G. Shumsky has practiced meditation and self-development disciplines since 1967. For seven years she resided in remote areas of the Himalayas and the Alps on the personal staff of the famous enlightened master Maharishi Mahesh Yogi. During those years she spent many months in deep meditation and complete silence. She spent another fourteen years living and studying in her teacher's learning institutions. Since then she has studied with several other enlightened masters and teachers.

Susan was not born with any supernormal faculties but developed her expertise through thirty years of patient daily study and practice. Having walked the path herself, she can guide others along their path.

Since 1970 Susan has taught meditation, self-development, and intuition to thousands of students in the United States, Canada, and Europe. A skilled lecturer, teacher, healer, counselor, and prayer therapist, she has authored many seminars and classes.

She received a doctor of divinity degree from Teaching of Intuitional Metaphysics, founded by Dr. Peter V. Meyer of San Diego and affiliated with the International New Thought Alliance of Mesa, Arizona.

Susan is the founder of Divine Revelation®, a complete technology for contacting the divine presence and listening to the inner voice. Divine Revelation is not a theoretical practice, but a proven system that has worked for thousands of students.

All of Susan's years of research into consciousness and inner exploration have gone into this book, which can significantly reduce many pitfalls in a seeker's quest for inner truth and greatly shorten the time required for the inner pathway to God.

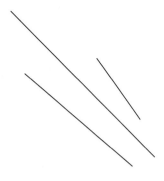

For More Information

You can receive more information about classes that teach the techniques described in this book by contacting any of the following* (arranged according to organization and zip code, for your convenience):

TEACHING OF INTUITIONAL METAPHYSICS, INC., DIVINE REVELATION
Rev. Susan G. Shumsky, D.D., One New York Plaza #315, New York, NY 10004-1901, 212-946-5132.
Husnu Onaran, 820 West End Ave. #11A, New York, NY 10025, 212-678-7933.
Curt De Groat, in care of 7819 Hampton Dr., Morrisville, PA 19067, 215-428-0317.
Linda Fuller, M.D., 12710 Teaberry Rd., Silver Springs, MD 20906, 301-933-2298.
Steven Ziebell, 2042 9th St. #76, Coralville, IA 52245, 319-338-0330.
Rev. Gaelia Babineau, 8509 Phoenix Ave. NE, Albuquerque, NM 87112, 505-294-1879.
Rev. Peter V. Meyer, D.D., (founder), 2333 Albatross St., San Diego, CA 92101.
Rev. Al Justice, P.O. Box 87581, San Diego, CA 92138, 619-560-8995.

*These organizations and individuals do not necessarily use or endorse all of the teachings in this book, but they are qualified to teach some or all of the techniques.

Rev. Sheva Edwards, 1121 Woodside Rd. #D, Redwood City, CA 94061.
Marsha Poulin, (prayer therapist), 7311 Shelter Creek Ln., San Bruno, CA 94066, 415-952-3339.
Rev. Rian Leichter, P.O. Box 25314, San Mateo, CA 94402.
Kitty and Michael Mrache, 3120 Trout Gulch Rd., Aptos, CA 95003, 408-662-3393.
Michael Keian Bohn, 6401 Bollinger Rd., Cupertino, CA 95015, 408-253-4161.
Rev. Akasha Noelle, D.D., and Rev. Deja Lui, P.O. Box 2533, Saratoga, CA 95070.
Rev. Thomas Coté, P.O. Box 599, Nevada City, CA 95959, 916-478-9355.
Rev. Joanne Allen, P.O. Box 1328, Hood River, OR 97031, 541-386-7471.

TEACHING OF THE INNER CHRIST, INC.
Rev. Mary C. Sewall, P.O. Box 162, Island Falls, ME 04747, 207-463-2277.
Rev. Peggi Garvey, 182 N. Sycamore Ave., Los Angeles, CA 90036, 213-939-3305.
Rev. Marilyn Glattly, 1775 Bellflower Blvd., Long Beach, CA 90815, 310-498-9211.
Rev. Norma Spry, D.D., 3057 S. Higuera #231, San Luis Obispo, CA 93401, 805-544-3127.
Rev. Michael Terranova, 1408 NE 65th St., Vancouver, WA 98665, 360-695-9885.

OTHER TEACHERS FULLY QUALIFIED TO TEACH THESE TECHNIQUES
Rev. Beatrice Paul Harris, 975 S. Clinton Ave., Rochester, NY 14620, 716-244-8250.
Kathleen Zmuda, (prayer therapist), 2005 Juneway Dr., Michigan City, IN 46360.
Rich Bell, 2030 9th St. #3, Coralville, IA 52241, 319-351-3295.
Rev. Maureen Jones, 1136 Woodlawn Ave., Dallas, TX 75208, 214-942-4454.
Linda Vandervort, 1750 30th St. #489, Boulder, CO 80301.
Rev. Carolyn Gilbert, Rising Dawn Study Group, 2615 Eldorado St., Boise, ID 83704, 208-376-5079.
Rev. John Beverleigh, D.D., and Rev. Lois Beverleigh, Society for the

Teaching of the Inner Christ, 275 S. 1100 East, Salt Lake City, UT 84102, 801-355-9210.

Rev. Sandra J. Parness, D.D., Inner Focus Seminars, 4390 Ridgecrest Dr., Las Vegas, NV 89121, 702-451-1395.

Rev. Bob Broska, Inner Awareness Counselling, 1433 E. 24th St., National City, CA 91950, 619-474-7630.

Rev. Jenifer Whisper, San Diego, CA 92105, 619-282-8614.

Asha Goldberg, 811 Arlington Ave., Oakland, CA 94608, 510-547-6355.

Nola Lewis, P.O. Box 674, Bolinas, CA 94924, 415-454-5175.

Rev. Shoshana Aurassia, 1413 Casa Buena Dr., Corte Madera, CA 94925, 415-927-3277.

Rev. Dale Cunningham, 1152 Sherwood Ave., San Jose, CA 95126, 408-249-8774.

Rev. Marie Sykora, Sacramento, CA, 916-391-9086.

Rev. Joanna Cherry, Ascension Mastery International, P.O. Box 1018, Mt. Shasta, CA 96067, 916-926-6650.

Carolyn Anderson, (prayer therapist), Seattle, WA, 206-368-0610.

Ruth Raziel, 546 W. 13th Ave. #5, Vancouver, B.C., Canada V5Z 1N7, 604-874-0451.

FOR A GUIDED MEDITATION TAPE

If you wish to purchase an audiotape to help you with your Divine Revelation meditation practice, please write a letter stating that you wish to purchase the Divine Revelation Guided Meditation Tape, and send $9.98 to Teaching of Intuitional Metaphysics, One New York Plaza, #315, New York, NY 10004-1901.

WRITE TO ME ABOUT YOUR EXPERIENCES

I want to hear about your experiences with Divine Revelation. Write to me at the following address and tell me your stories about following your divine guidance and the benefits that you have received: Susan G. Shumsky, One New York Plaza, #315, New York, NY 10004-1901.

INDEX